Introduction to
Social Marketing

Introduction to
Social Marketing

G.B. Mukherji

India Research Press
New Delhi

India Research Press
B-4/22, Safdarjung Enclave,
New Delhi – 110 029.
Ph.: 24694610; Fax : 24618637
bahrisons@vsnl.com
www.indiaresearchpress.com
contact@indiaresearchpress.com

ISBN : 81-88353-06-X

Cataloguing in Publication Data
G.B. Mukherji
Introduction to Social Marketing
by G.B. Mukherji

ISBN : 81-88353-06-X

Includes bibliographical references

1. Social Marketing 2. Development
I. Title II. Author

Printed in India at Focus Impressions, New Delhi – 110 003.

About the Book

This book is designed to introduce 'social marketing' as a discipline to social development planners and programme implementers. The book, in the form of a guide, suggests that the basic tenets of the marketing discipline as practiced in the commercial sector be followed in all development planning and execution, thereby reducing adhocism, but not individual initiatives. The book is not, by any stretch of imagination, a treatise on social marketing. Therefore, there would be many leads from which practical offshoots and refinements would be possible, indeed required.

Rather than academically introducing social marketing as a concept, an example of its application has been illustrated in the context of India's population stabilization programme. Side by side, the essentials of the social marketing discipline, as derived from the commercial marketing discipline, have been applied to the illustration. *The message sought to be conveyed is that social marketing can be applied to all programmes that aim to modify behaviour.*

This book is essentially meant for grass-root administrators, whatever their discipline is. Hopefully, they will find the steps suggested relevant and adjustable to their context. It is worth repeating that there has been no attempt to curtail creativity and initiative; indeed, it is hoped that such genius will find encouragement on the firm principles of 'producer–customer' familiarity and participation. It is also hoped that the state and central level planners will find the logic acceptable and will provide the support needed to the grass-root administrators. I will be elated if the book finds a place on the working-table of administrators, not only in India, but also in the developing countries.

This book is dedicated to my late father Capt. S.C. Mukherjee. He had made great sacrifices for my sake, and I wish he was here to see this book in print.

Getting leave during active service to study and write a book was, indeed a great favor. Hence, in the first instance, I would like to express my gratitude to Sardar Swarn Singh Boparai, K.C., Ex-Secretary to Government of India, Ministry of Coal for allowing me this privilege. Simultaneously, I would like to thank the Government of Orissa for concurring in this leave. I am also grateful to Mr. N.K. Sinha, Secretary Coal, and Mr. D.P. Bagchi, Chief Secretary, Government of Orissa for allowing me an extension beyond one year for completing the work.

A special thanks is due to Mrs. Firoza Mehrotra for going through my loosely tied first draft and for her comments and advice based on her wide experience of women and population related issues, including in the UNFPA.

I have also received valuable guidance from Dipankar Mukherjee, Associate Professor of Marketing, National Institute of Integrated Learning in Management, M.S. Swaminathan, Emeritus Professor and the recognized pioneer of the Green Revolution in India, Mr. Arvind Varma, Ex-Secretary Department of Personnel and Training, Government of India, Mr. T.N. Thakur, Chairman-cum-Managing Director of the Power Trading Corporation of India. His assurance that the concepts work in practice was a great moral booster. There are many others who have provided encouragement, and I hope they will forgive me for not specifically mentioning them individually.

Finally, I acknowledge the support that I received from my wife. Besides the endless cups of tea that she fortified me with, her tolerance of my prolonged presence at home and at my desk, was indeed wonderful.

I am also grateful to Anuj Bahri for finding my manuscript worthy of publication. But for this gesture there would have been little possibility of the guidelines reaching a wide readership, and indeed, the introduction of this new discipline to the social development field.

Contents

INTRODUCTION

A commercial organization exists as long as it can manufacture and sell its products. A product in turn will sell if the consumers are convinced of its relevance, need or desirability, and be motivated to purchase it over alternatives. The consumer is, therefore, the ultimate deciding factor in the survival of a business, and it is marketing that establishes a relationship of exchange – long term at that -between the producer and the prospective consumer. Very squarely, therefore, the success and indeed, the very existence of a business organization is dependent on the effectiveness of its marketing operations. Likewise, a social and/ or development organization can have a reason to exist as long as it can provide products and/ or services for the welfare of its beneficiaries. Its beneficiaries must also be convinced of the need for accepting what is on offer. Logically, therefore, for the performance of the aforesaid exchange, a social service organization, irrespective of whether it is of the government or the semi government, must also establish a relationship between itself and its beneficiaries. Social marketing aims to do just that.

A commercial organization does not manufacture and market its products and services unless and until it has studied its identified consumers. The products offered are the ones needed or when a direct indication of this is not available, the latent are encouraged. Except when undeveloped needs are created and satisfied, the starting and ending point is always the consumer. In the social sector, however, policy makers, planners and programme implementers have always taken upon themselves the responsibility of knowing what the people want and what is good for them. They have, accordingly, been devising programmes for the beneficiaries as per the perception of the 'seller'. In the process, social programmes across the board, from the national to the specific (like programmes to stabilize the nation's population to the tackling of sickle cell anaemia among a few tribal groups) have been churned out with the same perspective, and with scant regard to the characteristics, differing needs and desires of the beneficiaries. Marketing in the social sector has not been seen to be important in the same way that it has been accepted in the commercial sector.

A distinction has always been drawn between social programmes, (as being in the realm of ideas), and the marketing of tangibles (as professed by the manufacturing sector), concluding thereby that ideas cannot be marketed. The word 'motivation' is often used in the social context but rarely has it been practiced in the context of the theories of behavioural science or brought under the rigours and discipline of marketing. Even when service support for products, which is also an intangible, has found a prominent place in marketing, the marketing of social services has not. 'Administrators of nonprofit organizations' have continued to 'approach marketing with some skepticism because it has the image of being exclusively a tool for use in commercial business...' (Kotler, 1975). The 'growing evidence that managing toward customers is a successful way to do business, and customer information is a key to making this approach work' (Woodruff and Gardial, 1996) has not yet found favour with the policy makers, planners and implementers of social programmes.

A deeper analysis of marketing as practiced by the business sector will, however, show that behind what they actually market in the form of tangible and physical products is nothing but 'ideas'. The manufacturer of a lipstick in reality markets 'hope' and 'confidence' to the user. An automobile maker does not market the contraption of steel, chrome, rubber, leather and glass as such but its 'convenience', 'property value' and perhaps its 'social relevance'. What then is the difference between a commercial marketer and a social marketer? Indeed, none. The marketing manager of a business house and the administrator of a social programme both aim to provide a certain value or service in exchange for some other value or service, including change in life-style patterns. So, if marketing is essentially the marketing of ideas and encompasses all that is necessary to establish an enduring relationship between the goals of an organization and the needs of a specified group of beneficiaries in the form of a mutually relevant and desirable exchange function, there is strong reason to believe that the established techniques developed for it by the business sector since the 1950s will be equally relevant and applicable to the social sector. Unfortunately though, in the vocabulary of government, marketing still does not find a place; if at all, it is confused with selling.

There is a significant difference between a commercial organization and a bureaucratic, government organization. While the former exists only if it can market its products, the latter apparently, is independent of this. Theoretically, non-performing social and development sector organizations should wither and die. But in practice, one rarely sees this happening. Organizations providing social service carry on irrespective of their performance; new programmes are continually added regardless of past performance. As funds are budgeted and provided for on an annual basis, there is, therefore, no fear of organizational or programme survival. Consequently, such organizations do not feel the need for marketing their products or services. On the other hand, there is an assumption that everyone wants the service. What then is the incentive for an organization in the social sector to adopt marketing as an essential strategy?

Notwithstanding this conceptual and structural problem, there are policy makers, programme planners and administrators who, I believe, are motivated by desires and goals higher than bureaucratic impersonality, permanence and simple continuity. My belief is that marketing of social ideas and programmes is of relevance and importance to them, primarily because it shows them a way of achieving their principal objective: a better and healthy life-style for the people. For such persons, and I will henceforth call them social marketers, at stake may, indeed, be the rationale and reputation of the organization they have been entrusted to serve, besides their own satisfaction, conscience and reputation. I am confident that enlightened social marketers will welcome a well, and time tested set of tools that will enable them to perform better as opposed to functioning based almost entirely on hit-and-try methods. 'Strategies do not evolve and get implemented on their own. They require effective leadership' (Andreasen, 1995); and effective leadership requires skills. Marketing is a discipline that provides one with all of these.

There need also be no apprehension that marketing concepts developed for the 'market' do not apply to the 'public'. From the point of view of an organization, 'a market is a potential area for trading of resources.' A social sector organization offers certain services to the public, and in return, it expects certain norms of behavior (small, well nourished family) or even services (community cleanliness) or action (plantation, or voluntary sterilization). Actually, the service that a social sector organization offers to the public is, in the ultimate analysis, a value it receives in terms of better living and health conditions of the community, state and the nation. The trading of resource condition is thus adequately satisfied.

This study aims to identify the basic marketing techniques that have been developed over many years, and applied successfully in the private, commercial sector. The same techniques, appropriately modified to suit differing scenarios will be shown to be applicable to the social sector. The advice of Mr. David F. Webb that a "marketing practitioner must recognize that his justification lies in his ability to understand the consumer's most pressing needs and harness available resources to meet it" will be held up to apply equally to the administrators of social programmes. It will be proposed that the same administrator become like the professional marketer 'who is very good at understanding, planning and managing exchanges, who knows how to research and understand the needs of the other party, to design a valued offering to meet these needs, to communicate the offer effectively, and to present it in a good place and under timely circumstances' (Kotler, 1975). An attempt will be made to carry forward the urgings of another expert when he suggests: 'What is still largely untapped is the immense potential to massively improve the quality of people's lives that this approach (marketing) would have if it were put in the hands of government agencies and a wide variety of nongovernmental organizations and private voluntary organizations around the world' (Andreasen, 1995).

I would not like to create an impression that social marketing is the only formula for success and that it is an easy way forward. 'Most of the behaviour related changes to improved health, nutrition and family planning involves tremendous adjustments and costs in time, money and socio-cultural norms – not the mere purchase of a toothpaste' (Mckee). Yet such behavioural changes have to take place; so while social marketing 'is no template for others to copy' (Grifiths), it certainly shows a structured way to go about. If, indeed, the effort can be made to feel as easy as the purchase of a toothpaste – like the one time polio drop campaign (not foul tasting at that) – then all the better.

Just as an example, the national population stabilization programme is being offered for applying the marketing techniques. 'Because influencing behaviour is social marketing's fundamental objective, the discipline can be applied to a wide range of topics and audiences. For, example, the social marketing framework is not only valuable in changing the behaviour of ghetto teenagers in U.S. urban centers, farmers in rural areas, and mothers in Bangladesh, it can also be used to influence the behaviour of health workers, private physicians, government officials, even the staff of social marketing programmers themselves' (Andreasen, 1995). In the context of India's population stabilization programme, to the extent possible, analogies and links have been drawn across the two frames of commercial marketing and social marketing. The results after every action point have been highlighted in the form of prescriptions. To re-emphasize, no impression is being given that simply applying these prescriptions would stabilize the rate of growth of India's population. Indeed, nothing in life is so black and white. At the same time, I believe that marketing techniques are indeed important signposts, the notice of which will make the programme implementation process less randomized, and therefore more likely to satisfy the needs of the market/ beneficiaries.

I am firmly of the opinion that bright, knowledgeable officers are not lacking in the system. The main hurdle before coordinators of social programmes is the lack of time for pursuing one or two programme packages[1] or ideas *uninterruptedly*. Multiplicity of products makes customer recall and, therefore, 'movement' difficult. I have myself experienced and repeatedly heard from field level administrators that a plethora of schemes (products) makes any focused attention impossible. The assessment of the Planning Commission of India is similar. According to a report (Business Standard. New Delhi. 10th September 2001) it has recommended that 'the number of such schemes (Centrally Sponsored Rural Development) be brought down drastically to just about 20 to 40 ... from the "staggering 210"'! Multiplicity of schemes make it impossible for field administrators to organize and follow through any of the social development programmes effectively, leave alone conduct regular field visits for supervision and feedback. Good work, however, can only come out of uninterrupted time, advance planning, training, sincere implementation and feedback. This, in the present context implies and indeed, cries out for prioritization. The application of marketing techniques to such focused packages of programmes holds great promise if commercial and international social marketing experiences are anything to go by. Hopefully, the system will allow programme administrators a chance to go through the essential processes at least for the national priority programmes, and shall not find fault with them for *not* paying attention to the peripherals. Perhaps there is a case for someone to market this idea in the first place among planners and makers of government policy.

Finally, a word about the treatment of the topic in the various chapters. Chapter 2 is aimed at introducing the reader to the world of commercial marketing – not in detail, but just the main concepts. In reading Chapter 2 it would be seen that the marketer's understanding of consumer behaviour and the basic elements of the 'exchange function' are essential ingredients for programme success. Chapter 3 aims to understand the rudiments of buying behaviour, the essentials of behavioural change, and the ways of 'fostering sustainable behaviour'. Chapter 4 attempts to distill the way some social programmes have been promoted by the government and government-related organizations. The objective has been to identify the major techniques and tools applied, if at all, by them. The National Population Policy 2000 and the National Plans forming its background have been specifically studied for two reasons: first, to find similarities between its strategies vis-à-vis marketing, and second, to better understand the concept of social marketing that has been introduced in its context. Chapter 5 is meant for those who feel that commercial and social marketing do not mix. It shows where the main differences lie, yet concludes that the commercial marketing techniques are, indeed applicable to the social sector. Finally, in Chapter 6, in the process of applying the marketing techniques described in Chapter 2 to India's population stabilization programme, the discipline of social marketing is introduced and elaborated.

The conceptual and operational chapters of the book can now be studied with the encouragement that 'social marketing really works' (Andreasen, 1995).

CHAPTER 1.

ESSENTIALS OF MARKETING

The marketing concept was first formulated in the 1950s in the context of business firms. At that time, marketing was defined by the American Marketing Association as 'the performance of business activities that direct the flow of goods and services by producers to consumers'. Marketing was thus conceived only as a business activity within the overall economic functions of a state. At a subsequent stage, the concept was broadened to cover 'human activities directed at satisfying human needs and wants'. All that was 'required for marketing to occur (were) two persons able to communicate and deliver, each having something of value to exchange freely' (Lazniac et al., 1987). This broadened view, in effect, released 'marketing' from the bonds of just business to almost all areas of human activity. Through many 'expositions, refinements and extensions' and passing through a 'production orientation, a sales orientation, and more recently, a marketing orientation.' (Kotler, 1975), marketing is now a discipline that relates the development of a product or an idea (thereby catering to the objectives of any organization – business, social, political and so on) to satisfy the latent, or emerging or felt needs of a set of customers. In order to fulfill this broadened role, marketing undertakes surveys on consumer attributes and preferences, research to develop the best product at an affordable price, communicates the availability and features of the product and its relevance in meeting the customer's needs, and ensures efficient distribution at the most convenient point to the customer. The applicability of the marketing concept to all organizations is no longer in question.

The concept of marketing as followed in the business sector is a 'consumer-oriented' approach and rests on the three pillars of 'Need',

'Exchange of value' and 'Choice'. Since the customer is the center stage, these three pillars are influenced by the customer's socio-cultural-economic environment. Understanding these influences is the first stage in shaping a change in the consumer's attitude towards a product.

No worthwhile manufacturing or service providing company would come into being without first assuring itself that there is indeed, a felt need for a product, and that consumers will be willing to buy it at a *price* and with some degree of *service support*. If the product is already available, then the proposition offered to the consumer is *alternatives* from which he or she can make a choice and exchange one value for another. *If a product is not needed i.e., the demand is absent or latent, then creating a demand is also a part of marketing*. Further, marketing is not only an issue of creating and maintaining a demand. It is the *'task of regulating the level, timing and character of demand in one or more markets of the organization'* (Kotler, 1975). The levels range from a negative demand, which is the hardest to counter, through no demand, latent demand, faltering demand, irregular demand, full demand, overfull demand, to unwholesome demand (Kotler, 1975).

Marketing is different from selling. Marketing is a consumer centric doctrine that takes into account the socio-politic-economic-technological environment of a target population with which a producer or service provider has to relate in order to encourage a mutually beneficial exchange. Selling, on the other hand is a limited exercise by the seller of taking a product to any customer willing to pay a fixed price. 'A consumer orientation is probably the key element of all forms of marketing, distinguishing it from selling – and product – and export-driven approaches' (Kotler et al., 1996).

According to Peter Drucker, 'There will always, one can assume, be need for some selling. But the aim of marketing is to make selling superfluous. The aim of marketing is to know and understand the customer so well that the product or service fits him and sells itself'.

Marketing is also not just communication, 'advertisement, public relations and the slick packaging of communications material' (Young, 1988-89). Indeed, when marketing becomes selling, that is, dons a 'supply' orientation then aggressive advertisement and communication becomes a necessity. 'Such a decision may be founded on what is administratively convenient, the whims of a "top man" who considers it a "good idea"...' (Littler, 1985). The result in most of such cases is a failure even though, for a short while, there may be apparent success. This 'supply' oriented approach will be discussed Chapter 4, in the context of social marketing of contraceptives.

Selling is of two recognized types – the hardsell and the minimal. The *hardsell* type relies very heavily on advertisement, incentives, promotional drives and so on. Automobiles, consumer durables come under this category. The product in these cases has already been marketed, is established and is standardized. What remains is only to assign yearly sales quotas and hardsell that. There is no need to immediately change the design or the contents. 'Even family planning effort in certain developing nations is characterized by hardsell tactics including offers of transistor radios or pots and pans...' (Kotler, 1975). *Minimal* marketing relies heavily on the intrinsic value of the product - education for instance. Universities, till recently did not need to advertise. In the recent past, when the Universities in the UK, Australia and New Zealand found themselves competing for students with a capacity to pay, they began to shift from minimal to hardsell. In effect, Universities have had to sell themselves in order to survive. The present trend in both the manufacturing as well as in the social sector is a combination of both - produce quality products and hardsell the same. A University that has commenced new courses without ensuring infrastructure, especially teaching support, will not be able to draw quality students (ref: Delhi University course on information technology and science). Similarly, a family that has once suffered at the hands of a carelessly organized cataract operation camp will surely discourage its neighbour or acquaintance to go to the next one. If selling has become important, it follows that the marketing exercise, which comes before and goes beyond selling has become more so.

The marketing exercise can be shown in the form of a flow diagram:

THE MARKETING FRAMEWORK

Market Analysis

- Segmentation
  - Geographic
  - Demographic
  - Psychographic
  - Survey
  - Quantitative & Qualitative techniques
  - Market positioning

MARKETING PROGRAMME DEVELOPMENT

- Image and goodwill
  - Definition
  - Measurement techniques
    - Responsive
      - Unstructured interviews
      - Object sorting
      - Multi-dimensional
    - Judgemental
      - Image attribute listing
      - Semantic differential
- Product decisions
  - Idea generation
  - Concept development
  - Economic analysis
  - Product development
  - Test marketing
  - Product launching
- Price decisions
  - Profit maximization
  - Cost recovery
  - Incentive pricing
  - Disincentive pricing
- Distribution decisions
  - Storage
  - Intermediate agents
- Communication and promotion decisions
  - Advertisement
    - Media selection
    - Theme selection
    - Evaluation

- Publicity
- Personal contact
    - Selling
    - Servicing, and feedback
- Incentives
- Atmospherics

PROGRAMME ADMINISTRATION

- Organization
    - Levels/ hierarchy
    - Intermediaries/ distributors/ opinion makers/ focus groups
- Planning and control
    - Method
        - Top-down
        - Bottom-up
        - Combination
    - Objectives
        - Long, short and medium term
    - Strategy
        - Long, short and medium term
    - Action Plan
        - Long, short and medium term
    - Control functions
        - Budgeting

Each of these issues is being discussed in order to draw analogies to the social sector.

MARKET ANALYSIS

Though rarely stated in textbooks on marketing, a commercial organization initiates marketing activities only after it has formed a general idea – maybe after studying feasibility surveys and reports - about a product or a set of products that it hopes to produce and sell. Only then does it embark on market analysis, essentially for refinements - for unless the organization has an idea of the product in the first place, it cannot be focused in its survey. Textbooks on marketing tend to give an impression that all marketing activities start with market analysis, and based on the feedback, the shape of the product is decided.

Segmentation.

The market needs to be segmented for a *careful analysis of consumer behaviour and attitudes*. The idea is that all needs/demands may not be uniform over socio-economic situations, whereas behavioural trends are likely to be similar over similar groups. An essential component of successful targeting of programmes is, therefore, the use of 'lifestyle clusters'. 'The clustering concept is based on two underlying assumptions:

- Birds of a feather flock together. People living in the same neighbourhood are likely to have similar lifestyles... similar health behaviors.

- A neighborhood cluster will have the same lifestyle characteristics regardless of the cluster's geographical location...' (Taylor et al. 1999).

'Marketing means the selection of target markets rather than a quixotic attempt to win every market and be all things to all men' (Kotler, 1975).

An important aspect of marketing is the designing of appropriate communication aimed at achieving an exchange. Studies on mass communication by De Fleur (1970) show that the response to a media message varies according to demographic differences while 'members of a particular category ... select more or less the same communication content and ... respond to it in roughly equal ways'. This is a strong rationale for segmentation.

Market segmentation is not random, but made on the basis of a small survey on one or more of the following criteria:

Geographic
- Rural/ Urban
- Forest/ plains/ coastal/ etc.

<u>Demographic</u>
- Age
- Sex
- Family
- Income
- Occupation
- Education
- Religion
- Caste
- Literacy

Psychographic[1]
- Lifestyle
- Culture

(An additional item for social marketers will be the person's place in the social hierarchy)

1. ['Psychographic (or lifestyle) studies examine people's spending patterns, their major interests, their aspirations, beliefs and prejudices, and their perceptions or opinions concerning issues, institutions and themselves. Psychographics is an attempt to "get inside the consumer's head" and find out what he or she is thinking and why' (Mintz and Steele, 1992)]

Survey

A market survey determines the demand/ need for the product or the possibility of generating the demand. (A distinction is made between 'need', which is basic, and 'demand' which is a perceived need and can, therefore, be artificially created. Often, marketers, therefore, can also remove the mist hiding a basic need heightening the absence of that which will or may satisfy the need).

> Many marketing experts raise issues of 'ethics' in creating needs. This question is not being discussed here essentially because the danger of social marketers taking recourse to unethical marketing will be rare.

Indeed, *creating demand* is an essential part of progressive marketing for it brings home ideas and products that a customer may not be aware of. Akio Morita, explaining Sony's vision says, 'Our plan is to lead the public with new products rather than ask them what kinds of products they want. The public does not know what is possible, but we do'. But in order to create a demand, the marketer must be aware of the lifestyle of the market or segments of it. Only then can he or she dovetail the product with the best place for its germination. Also, a survey ascertains from the market what a customer denotes as *'value'* for a product or service, what *stage of behavioural change* the customer is at, the existence of special organizations and groups of persons wielding influence, and so on. Such information, ascertained on a segmented basis is essential for deciding the marketing strategy. Indeed, if not addressed at the beginning, the subsequent steps might be taken on wrong premises.

> Harvey (1999) has reported that the non-recognition of a prominent set of functionaries (rural medical practitioners) in Bangladesh and

their involvement in a programme to market contraceptives was responsible for a significant setback for the programme. A market survey helps determine the competition for the product in terms of alternatives, as well as activity barriers. Indeed, there often are barriers to the undertaking of a survey itself – unnecessary expenses, or shortage of time, or unavailability of trained surveyors and so on. But, no worthwhile marketing strategy can be designed without understanding the market needs, the strengths and the weaknesses.

The value that a customer attaches to a product or service has three hierarchical levels of relationship. According to Woodruff and Gardial (1996), at the basic level is the physical 'Attribute' of the product or service. In the social context, it would mean the looks and feeling of an Intra Uterine Devise (IUD). It would also include availability of options to 'return' or 'exchange'. 'Apart from good quality of care, an IUD must respect women's right to adopt or discard the Copper-T at will' ('The Ten Year Copper-T', 2000). 'Exchangeability also encourages impulsive purchase'. The next level is the consequence, or the 'Experience of Usage'. Again, in the example of IUD, it could mean differences ranging from an uncomfortable to a carefree life, as well as the insertion time and anonymity/ privacy. Finally, the most important level is 'Desired End State' or the user's 'core values, purposes and goals'. For the IUD user, this would mean a small and healthy family. This third level is very important in the social context because the identification of the core values of a product for an individual or a family, and therefore, for a community may often have to be 'facilitated' or pointed out by an organization promoting a particular cause. In the marketing context, it would mean planning for a market with 'no demand' for that product/ concept. It is also interesting to note that the present practice of assessing customer satisfaction, based on the 'value' hierarchy, in most cases touches only the 'attributes' and the 'experience' aspects and not the 'end use'.

Survey techniques.

The first step in market survey is to decide on the method to be followed in order to measure need/ demand. This is done through *quantitative (surveys) and/ or qualitative (in depth interview) methods.* While quantitative data collection is quick and economic, it is more rigid. The content has also to be limited in order to engage customer interest. In contrast, qualitative measures require 'more flexibility in the amount and type of customer information gathered than is typically represented by surveys. *Understanding customer values requires a "peeling back" process' like that of an onion'* (Woodruff and Gardial, 1996).

In undertaking a survey, the manager has also to decide on the *customer sample.* This is particularly important in the case of qualitative measures, as the sample has to be small in order to be interactive, yet representative. Only the inflexible, quantitative survey method allows samples that are large. 'In selecting participants for your convenience sample, you must first make sure that the strategically important customers or customer groups are represented, even if this means that they are disproportionately represented' (Woodruff and Gardial, 1996).

Though the assistance of *Opinion Leaders* (OLs) is generally not taken by the business sector for product promotion (they rely more on wholesale and retail distribution networks), the opinions and impressions of such persons are very often gathered at the time of market survey. This is because 'ideas often flow from radio and print to opinion leaders and from those to the less active sections of the population' (according to the 'two step flow' model of communication discovered by Lazarsfield, while analyzing voting behaviour during the 1940 US Presidential elections).

Studies show the following as the characteristics of opinion leaders (Mehta, 1973):

- They occupy strategic positions,
- They provide leadership over a number of products,
- They are more gregarious than others,
- They are comparatively more innovative,
- Their sphere of influence is limited to individuals who are lower in status,
- They are likely to belong to families having long residence in that community,
- They read more newspapers and magazines (watch more TV),
- They are effective in their own neighbourhood (mass OLs are rare),
- In some states like Gujarat, women OLs predominate over men. Men often have extra community interests, and
- Women OLs are more innovative and open to new concepts.

(These characteristics have been enumerated, as they will come in useful in formulating social marketing prescriptions in Chapter 6.)

Qualitative data gathering processes are of three types: observation, focus groups discussions and one-to-one in-depth interviews. Considerations of time, money and field practicability are likely to decide whether one or all three are taken up. In all three methods, it is about observing customer behaviour and/ or asking the right questions so that the marketer gets an idea as to the customers' needs, habits, inclinations as well as the type of product and service that may satisfy, if not delight them. The broad differences between the three methods are indicated in the table:

OBSERVATION	FOCUS-GROUP DISCUSSION	ONE-TO-ONE INTERVIEWS
By surveyors or video	Involving representatives of a community	Involving randomly selected individuals
Observing	Ascertaining	Ascertaining
• purchase behaviour • hesitations • promoter influence • male/female involvement	• product needs • product and supply conveniences • product attributes • price payable • competition	• decision makers • needs and aspirations • product attributes • service attributes • price payable • competition
Expensive Time consuming	Convenient Persuasive	Time consuming Highly persuasive
True picture	Likely to be influenced by the dominant member's ideas. Dependant on skill of facilitator	May be made-up by surveyor to save embarrassment, or bias or time. Dependant on skill of surveyor.

In advance countries, postal and telephone surveys have proved to be useful under certain conditions. While postal surveys tend to generate very little response, of the order of 20 to 40 per cent, the sincerity and quality of response is generally good. In addition, it works like a randomized result. Telephonic surveys tend to be irritants, though once again, the sincerity of those willing to respond is of a high order. Notwithstanding the following observation made on postal advertisements: 'One of the interesting findings of family planning campaigns in Asia has been that direct mail can be effective even among families unable to read. It is so unusual and exciting to receive a letter that the recipients make sure they find someone to read it to them' (Schramm, 1971). The afore-mentioned two methods are not being elaborated as they have limited applicability in developing countries, on account of high illiteracy and low telephone density.

In ascertaining need and value, two qualitative techniques applied by modern managers are the 'laddering' and the 'grand tour' (Woodruff and Gardial, 1996). In the laddering method, the interviewer first makes an attempt to get the customer *to identify all the specific attributes of a product or service (separately) as per the value hierarchy, either by itself or in comparative terms.* Thereafter, using the laddering technique for each attribute, the relationship between that attribute and the higher order consequence and desired end states can be obtained. For example, the participant might, in the course of discussions reveal that his ultimate desire is for a happy and healthy family rather than earning more money through more children. Indeed, the technique might as well show the contrary. Depending on the outcome, the communication message and the product can be designed for delivery or the competition can be squarely identified. A simplified example is indicated below:

I would like condoms to be readily available nearest my house (service attribute)	I do not know where condoms are available nearest my house (service attribute)
↓	↓
Condoms should be well packaged for easy hiding (product attribute)	No, I do not use anything during bedtime (need not felt – negative usage trait)
↓	↓

At the same time, I would like them at easy reach during bedtime (product attribute) ↓ Both my wife and I are afraid of accidental childbirth (negative consequence) ↓ My wife can work hard and look after my family better when she is not pregnant (negative consequence) ↓ I can provide food, clothing, shelter to just two children (negative consequence) ↓ I want my wife and children to be healthy (desired end result) ↓ I want my children to get a good education (desired end result) ↓ I love my family (desired end result)	Yes, I have three children already; two of them I have sent to Ahmedabad to work in a tea-shop, and the third I am planning to send to school. (positive consequence) ↓ After education, he will earn more for the house. (positive consequence) ↓ My wife looks weak and sometimes is not happy, but she can bear more children. We are nine brothers and sisters, and my mother lived till ninety. (attitude towards behaviour) ↓ More children means more food for us all. (desired end result)
STRATEGY – Develop communication on family care and welfare.	STRATEGY – Develop communication on economic benefits of a small family and push products that are woman friendly.

The second technique 'attempts to understand the value hierarchy indirectly by exploring in detail how the product or service is experienced by the customer in a particular context. To begin the *grand tour*, the interviewer asks the participant to imagine him or herself in a typical real-life situation. The interviewer then asks participant to describe, in as much detail as possible, what is going on in that situation.... As the participant talks through his or her grand tour, the interviewer is free to probe for additional details or meaning' (Woodruff and Gardial, 1996). For instance, the interviewer can discuss the experience of a housewife when she had gone to the health center for an IUD insertion.

> How did she know of the product and service? What arrangements did she make for the children at home? Did her husband know? Did he support? If not, what were his and her apprehensions? Still why did she go? What was her experience? How long did she have to wait? Did she experience any discomfort then and now?

These are some of the pertinent areas of *conversation*. From the collected data, it will be possible to understand the overall motivation, the competition, the product and service improvement items, and so on. As has been mentioned earlier, it may be possible to estimate customer satisfaction by concentrating more on the achievement of the desired result instead of the product and service attributes. Finally, all data analysis should be done on segment basis rather than for the entire market. This is most likely to bring in similarity in value judgment. (The details of these two techniques or the analysis of the collected data are not being discussed, but the reader can refer to the quoted literature on the subject. Joseph E Kivlin has authored a book that deals with rural survey in a simple manner, and may be worth referring to (Kivlin et al. 1971).

It bears repeating that surveys need to be simple (in order to minimize costs and for ease of analysis); 'focusing on interrelations rather than on isolated details and elements' (Kennedy and Schneider, 2000). *Surveys, unlike those undertaken by academic institutions must also be objective oriented* –'the costs must outweigh the benefits'. As one programme manager, promoting the use of contraceptives in Bangladesh said, 'we are here not mainly to study problems in order to solve them, but to study problems mainly to solve them'. (An objective- wise, simple survey sheet has been suggested in Annexure 2.1).

In order to best understand the mental framework of the market segment, based on which the output is being generated, *surveys need to be carried out by persons of the same locality* (could also be through institutions or bodies in the locality which have already established a relationship of trust with the people) who are trained enough to ensure that the interviewer's bias does not come in. The possibility of the surveyed offering wrong information 'because the young surveyors – college students from the city – seemed pleased with a positive response' (Ciszewski) should not be overlooked.

Positioning.

Market positioning is the exercise conducted, on the basis of market segmentation and the results of the survey, for deciding the product, the area of operation and most important, for the etching of the product in the minds of the targeted segment. 'Successful positioning involves affiliating a brand with some category that consumers can readily grasp and differentiating the brand from other products that belong to the same category' (*Business Standard*, 2001). In a society bombarded with various channels and forms of communication, positioning can be instrumental in getting a message noticed by the intended segment and hopefully, understood. Positioning enables the marketer 'to organize information so that other strategies (e.g., target selection and choice of creative platform) can be more effectively combined. Ultimately, the objective is to form a coordinated, integrated programme in which each strategic component fulfils its proper role in helping to position the message to the target segment selected' (Burnett, 1988).

Market positioning is a two way process. The marketer, on the basis of the broad product characteristics, homes on to that market segment he or she feels will have the greatest interest in. Thereafter, the marketer must analyze the characteristics and attitude of the segmented market in detail so that one or at the most two aspects of the product meet the bill can be better identified than those of the competition. The rest of the marketing strategy should highlight these 'unique selling points' so that it is etched in the minds of the target, and they are drawn towards the product like a magnet. In a simple diagrammatic form, the positioning strategy would look like the following:

RELATE BROAD PRODUCT
CHARACTERISTICS
TO

↓
↓

A MARKET SEGMENT →→→ ANALYZE CHARACTERISTICS
OF THIS SEGMENT

↑ ↓
↑ ↓
↑
↑ WHICH CHARACTERISTIC(S)
↑ OF PRODUCT THAT BEST
↑ MEETS THE TARGET'S NEEDS

↓
↓

DEVELOP MARKETING STRATEGY ←←←←
ON THIS BASIS

In deciding which of the product strengths a marketer must highlight in positioning a product, the behaviour characteristics of the buyer, as discussed in the next chapter, should be kept in mind. In a nutshell, the strengths should cover as many of the following as possible:

- Product characteristics like exceptional quality, durability, style, or ease in handling, the goodwill of the company that is offering the product, etc.
- Price – affordability with quality, i.e.,value for money.
- Service – promptness, longer warranty, trained staff, etc.
- Ease of delivery

Generally speaking, stressing on one quality that distinguishes a product over that of a rival is the best for retaining buyer interest. Sometimes, companies promote two just to be in tune with market inclinations; sometimes even three, But then the company risks its product being equated with the rest, thereby losing the interest of the targeted market. Dettol was once the only antiseptic liquid used in homes and hospitals. With the arrival of competition from Savlon it felt the need to diversify. So, it went into the bath soap market. When the demand for deodorants drove buyers to the deo-soaps, Dettol too launched a product with two 'USPs' – antiseptic and deodorant. Pepsodent's USP for some time was a 'three-in-one' toothpaste.

MARKETING PROGRAMME DEVELOPMENT

Image and goodwill.

'Once an organization has chosen its basic markets, analyzed their needs and preference, and considered the values it would exchange, it is ready to enter into a more tactical analysis of the problems of achieving the desired market response' (Kotler,

1975). At the outset, however, a commercial organization needs to know its reputation in the market, for if this is bad, then no amount of efficiency in product mix will result in sales. One recalls the pre-World War II days when Japanese goods, in spite of their low pricing, failed to sell as there was no goodwill. Today, even if some Japanese products are not known for its quality, the name 'Made in Japan' sells. 'Amul', the taste of India sells notwithstanding the presence of multinationals, not only because it is Indian and cheaper, but also because it has a reputation for quality. 'We have honoured our contract with consumers close to fifty years. Amul has provided quality, day after day, and value for money...' is how Dr V. Kurien puts it. A commercial organization also needs to know what impression it has on its competitors in order to plan strategies to catch up or stay ahead as the case may be. *If there is a variation between self-image and public image, corrective action has to be set in motion at the very beginning.*

Studies in the private sector show that consumer image is the 'end result of a person's experience, recollections and impressions. Most of these images are formed on the basis of symbols, rather than facts alone. People hardly ever react to reality alone; their subjective feeling or impressions is far more important to them' (Mehta, 1973). In other words, an organization wishing to improve its image in a market has not only to improve its factual performance, but also all false impressions that may have been created against it. An organization's origin, history, performance as well as its resource backing are the factors that make up its image in the long run and not what it advertises for itself. Of particular importance are the following pitfalls identified in losing image and corporate goodwill:

- Unfulfilled promises and exaggerated claims.
- Failure to inform about conditions of service.
- Frequent discontinuity of products.

Indeed, failure of one product to perform as promised affects not only the sale of that product, but also then entire range of other products, essentially because the corporate goodwill has been tarnished.

> *What is an image?* 'An image is the sum of beliefs, ideas, and impressions that a person has on an object' (Kotler, 1975). It is therefore, something more than a belief, and therefore dependant on the character of the object, and the extent and source of information that a person has received in forming the image. Consequently, images can be influenced by providing 'corrective' information and also by modifying the character or behaviour or dealing that a market can have with an object or organization. However, image changes cannot be brought about over-night. Studies show that individuals are selective absorbers of new information and tend to disregard information that is contrary to their beliefs. Only very sensational and earth shattering information can change old beliefs. *Organizations have to be very patient and should show quality improvements over a period of time and also ensure that the public is being given this information through a reliable and neutral source, repeatedly.* The bottom line, however, is that an organization should attempt to make an investment in developing the best image it can for the advantages this might bring' (Kotler, 1975).

An essential part of goodwill is *corporate honesty*. Even if the product on offer fails to reach expectation levels, a business organization will still have clients if the people are convinced that the seller has sincerely tried. A seller, in trying hard, can also appeal to nationalistic feelings – Wipro, for instance, offering world class products in competition with multinationals, successfully draws a large number of nationalistic customers.

Image is person specific, i.e., subjective, and images across individuals in a market need not be homogeneous. Surveys can bring out the variations through appropriate measurements. *Image measurement techniques* fall under the following classes (Kotler, 1975):

- Responsive
    - Unstructured interviews
    - Object sorting
    - Multi-dimensional scaling
- Judgemental
    - Image attribute listing
    - Semantic differential

Unstructured interview is a direct interaction with the subject regarding his or her opinion of the organization. It has three drawbacks. First, it is dependant on the subject's comprehension and awareness; second, it is interviewer dependant; and third, it is costly. Under the *object sorting* technique, the subject is asked to sort and classify a group of similar organizations in whatever manner or category he or she desires. It is up to the interviewer, thereafter, to form an opinion by analysis or by direct questioning as to the attributes of classification. *Multi-dimensional scaling* is a statistical technique based on a subject's impression on the similarities and dissimilarities of three organizations, and plotted on an 'x', '-x', y, '-y' axis. In this process, the relative impressions rather than the values are determined.

In *image attribute listing*, the subject is given a set of attributes (developed either in-house or after interviews with sample subjects) and asked to rate the organization. This method is popular as it is easy to administer and is inexpensive (Kotler, 1975). Finally, in the most popular *semantic differential* method, a respondent is given a range of attributes for an organization, covering two of the following three categories and asked to give his impression on a two dimensional, 'x', 'y' scale:

- Evaluation (good-bad qualities)
- Potency (strong-weak)
- Activity (active passive)

Commercial organizations spend a lot of time and resource on developing a *brand* or *logo* that carries the corporate culture, image and goodwill to its consumers and potential consumers. Field tests are carried out either for an original name or for a set of 'potentials'. Some experts believe that the meaning behind a name is not always important as long as it is not offending or denotes something against the corporate interest. The names Coco-cola and Pepsi are flagged to emphasize this approach point. What, according to them is important is the way that the organization builds up its reputation or the attribute of the product. Sometimes a brand changing exercise is done to draw attention; sometimes such an exercise fails. Air India undertook such an exercise recently, but is now going back to its 'Maharaja' image as the new logo, an orange

'Sun', did not create any positive impression. British Airways, on the other hand found that its psychedelic painting on aircraft tails helped in changing its image from that of a staid, traditional airline to something in tune with the times.

Once an organization has taken a decision regarding image development (new organization) or image enhancement, it can then plan the next steps for achieving a desired market response. In marketing jargon, this is done through an appropriate 'marketing mix'. *The most popular marketing mix covers the 'four Ps':*

- Product,
- Price,
- Place, and
- Promotion.

Refinements in marketing discipline have suggested that the aforesaid 'product oriented' mix should be the platform on which the 'customer oriented' superstructure should be built. *The four Ps should be substituted by the four Cs* (Kotler and Armstrong, 2001):

- Customer solution,
- Customer cost,
- Convenience, and
- Communication.

Product

The term product can be broadly defined 'to cover anything that can be offered to a market for attention, acquisition, or consumption: physical objects, services, persons, places, organizations, or ideas' (Kotler, 1975). In commercial marketing, the character of the product, the items in the product line, and the product life cycle are very important. In social marketing (dealing with ideas), the product is both the physical product as well as the idea that is being offered to the market. *The movement of the beneficiary from unawareness to awareness to a favourable attitude towards the product/ idea to overt action, and finally to continued practice is the ultimate aim of marketing.* (Influencing consumer bahaviour in favour of a product is worth a separate treatment because it plays a key role in the formulation of the entire marketing strategy, from product development to promotion and communication. Accordingly, this concept will be developed separately at the end of this chapter).

Having received a detailed feedback from the targeted consumers on the need/demand for a product or service, the organization has to apply itself in producing a product that meets the need at a price that the consumer will be willing to pay. 'In attempting to develop appropriate new products, it is useful to determine the attributes that the market would ideally like to see combined in the product. Thus Berelson has proposed that the ideal contraceptive is one that would be "logically easy, effective, simple, one-time, reversible, trouble-free, culture-free, doctor-free, coitus-free, and inexpensive." This is a tall order but at least the attributes suggest directions for the search of an improved product concept' (Kotler, 1975).

The question of competition for a product has also to be addressed. Marketing must ensure that the item(s) on offer provide better value to a customer than those of a competitor. Competition can also be considered an obstacle in the path of marketing. Such competition can very well come from the environment in which the market operates. For instance, when Kellogg, the breakfast cereals giant entered the Indian market, it had not only to compete with cheaper, local brands like Mohan's and Champion, but also with the Indian habit of having a substantial brunch of items normally consumed at lunch. Ultimately, the pricing issue has limited its consumption mainly to the upper class. Lifestyle factors are very relevant in the marketing of social ideas. Social attitudes and mores favouring sons and discriminatory attitudes towards women are examples of actually competition to the marketing of population stabilization programmes.

There are six steps in the development of a product:

1) *Idea*: Generation and crystallization of one or more ideas for further consideration;

2) *Concept*: Development and testing — 'calls for selecting a sample of potential target buyers and collecting their reactions to the concept' (Kotler, 1975);

3) *Resource analysis*, including the tying up of resources for manufacturing, distribution and after sales service;

4) *Product* development: Could be physical or intangible like staff training, depending on whether the product is tangible or a service;

5) *Test marketing*; and

6) *Product launching*.

The exercise does not end here, however. Frequent surveys are required in order to know whether the product continues to serve the needs of the market and how it fares in relation to its competition. Depending on the feedback, modification or even discontinuation of the product may be called for.

Organizations that offer service or consultancy are in the business of customizing products. In the process of product development, an intimate and effective inter-personal relationship develops between the seller and the buyer. That is the reason why buyers of consultancy products are always referred to as 'clients'. When the customized product satisfies the client's fullest expectations, the product becomes an 'experience'. In such situation, clients are *unlikely* to seek alternatives. *Social marketing has a lot to learn from this concept*.

A product and a brand are intimately related. 'A brand is a name, term, sign, symbol, or design, or a combination of these, that identifies the maker or seller of a product or service' (Kotler and Armstrong, 2001). So, in effect, a consumer buying a product or service (here service is distinguished as a product from an organization like security from 'Globe Detective Agency', or consultancy from Arthur Anderson, as opposed to service that is a support/ user-convenience to a product) is always relating his or her experience to his or her impression of a company. *Branding, as has been mentioned earlier, is thus an extension of an organization's goodwill through its product to a customer.*

The following are the advantages of branding:

- It helps a customer to easily identify and select a product, essentially because the customer does not have to undergo the comparative analysis that he or she had gone through when deciding on the product, among alternatives, for the first time.
- The customer knows that product characteristics and quality for the same brand will be uniform over time.
- It enables a manufacturer to develop different variations of a product, with different branding, for different segments. Mercedes 'D' class is for economy and thus a favourite taxi-cab; 'E' class is for executives; 'SL' class for sporty types, and so on.
- It provides legal protection against competition and copy.
- *It can be pushed in advertisements. Thereafter, it can push advertisements.*

Most marketing experts, including Philip Kotler, advise that brand selection be done carefully and after a lot of research. The name, they suggest, should reflect the special characteristic of the product (e.g., contraceptives 'Nirodh' implying preventive, 'Masti' or 'Kamasutra' implying pleasure) and/ or the manufacturer, be short and simple, and should not offend or have a negative connotation. Yet, though such an exercise may, indeed, produce a meaningful brand, this by itself does not ensure product success. Some marketing managers like Philip D. Harvey argue that once a brand name has been selected, its promotion depends on other aspects of marketing, not on the name. 'I don't mean to devalue the market research that addresses these issues. Market research is extremely important in deciding how to *position* a brand (for example, as a high quality import versus a low-cost, user-friendly, easily available local brand) as well as helping determine which product attributes ate the most important to focus on. But with the exception of the caveats above, the selection of the brand name seems to be pretty unimportant' (Harvey, 1999). The names Coca-Cola or Pepsi, as has been remarked earlier, mean nothing but are powerful international brands. According to one estimate, the brand equity [brand value] of Coca-Cola is $84 billion, Microsoft is $57 billion, and IBM is $44 billion (Kotler and Armstrong, 2001). Indeed, nearer home, the trusted popular brand 'Tata' is a popular synonym for 'bye-bye' but does not certainly convey this sense for its products.

'Till recently', according to Kanika Datta, 'brand managers had one challenge to face in the battle for market share: to agitate the market. And the weapons with which to do this were fairly standard: extensions, freebies, promos, point-of-purchase slogans, campaigns ... and so on. All this works fine as long as there is limited competition. When competitors crowd in armed with similar ammunition, the battle for the consumer's wallet not only gets harder but more expensive' (*Business Standard*, 2001). The smart companies focus their attention to service – as a relationship building and maintaining exercise; sometimes it extends to the selling of one product, then hopefully another from the same stables. On another front, companies that once offered products on the strength of quality at an affordable price or technology are also getting into service. Unilever plans to introduce cleaning services in Europe. The service will also include feedback on the cleaning products, which will form part of the company's constant market research efforts (Dutta, 2001).

The short point is, therefore, organizational goodwill, product image and brands are all interwoven in the mind of any consumer. The purchase action takes place only when the combined impetus is greater than the justification for the status quo.

Pricing

Pricing decisions taken by an organization generally fall under the following catergories:

- Profit maximization,
- Cost recovery,
- Incentive pricing, and
- Disincentive pricing.

Since price is the economic indictor of the manufacturing cost of a product and it reflects the seller's view-point, including his returns on investment, business organizations are attracted to the first, i.e., profit maximization while social service organizations adopt any one or more of the remaining three. In the context of family planning, the pricing of contraceptives may be just sufficient to cover production and distribution costs or may include subsidies to 'push' usage. The latter is an example of incentive pricing. Tobacco pricing, on the other hand, is a good example of disincentive pricing because government would not want manufacturers to run at a loss and at the same time cannot encourage people to smoke. While business organizations adopt sophisticated models for price determination, this is generally not the case for social programmes. Welfare budgeting makes up the shortfall in the latter case.

If seen from the customer's point of view, 'price should be a reflection of the value that is created by the product' (Woodruff and Gardial, 1996). In other words, it is the price a customer will be willing to pay in monetary and convenience terms. It is often the lost and alternate opportunity cost that dominates the purchase or usage decision. Organizations that recognize this in the first place are less likely to get into a sticky situation later on.

Place/ Distribution

The third component of a marketing mix is 'Place' or 'Distribution'. The issue under consideration is how an organization reaches its product to its customer and in what time. Ideally, it should manage the distribution at the right time and at the door of the customer, but for this there is a cost; cost of storage, supply and response to complaints. The organization has to decide whether the cost of ensuring this will make the product very costly or if there is an alternative. The alternative could be the use of intermediate agents who may have the infrastructure, the capital and the expertise to ensure a reasonably good network, thereby freeing some of the resource and investments of the manufacturer, in return for a commission. The savings can be deployed by the organization for promotion or advertisement, for instance. From the point of view of the consumer, a proper distribution arrangement means that the product and the service for the product are within reach. In pricing terms, the product that means less inconvenience scores over another similar product that is available at a greater effort. E-shopping is hoping to reduce consumer inconvenience to the minimum by making shopping possible from the comforts of home. Banking services have already become on-line in many cases. These are the major 'enablers' – a term to be dilated in the next chapter - to the commercial sector

Most business houses, especially those that deal with large volume consumer durables, engage a network of distributors. They engage these middlemen on the basis of well laid-out terms and conditions. Provision for periodic evaluation and training/ motivation sessions are built in. Successful dealers are rewarded; the present trend is of sending them and their families on vacations within the country or abroad.

Communication and promotion.

Having decided on a product and distribution network that best satisfies a consumer need, *a marketer has to undertake a logical series of steps that appropriately address their mental make up.* For the consumer who is not aware, he or she has to be informed; for the ones that are informed but have not decided on any action, the effort has to be to 'push' him or her into action; and for those who have already acted, the endeavour has to be to keep him or her unwavering. The paragraphs on behavioural change discusses these issues in detail, and hence, at this stage, it may be sufficient to lay down the following concepts that govern effective communication:

- Communication should not be global. It has to be specifically addressed to meet the need of a segmented market or challenge the competition.
- Communication must know the behavioural stage of the segmented market and then decide on the message.

There are five items that need to be addressed in order to develop an effective promotion mix for marketing. These are:

- Advertisement,
- Publicity,
- Personal contact,

- Incentives and
- 'Atmospherics'.

Advertisement is a subject by itself. In line with the concept that marketing begins and ends with the consumer, advertisement has to be *target specific* in order to be effective. To take an extreme example, it will, indeed be a waste of effort and resource if the message is designed for the literate while the target is illiterate. Secondly, advertisement must take into account the *state of awareness* of the target as well as their socio-economic conditions and beliefs. There is again no point in designing a message on basic awareness on the need for a small family when the target is well aware of it, and the problem of non-adoption lies elsewhere. Finally, it is essential to decide on the *timing* – whether to be concentrated at the time of an event, or to be spaced but continuous - *and frequency* of advertisement. Most often, the physical and financial resources will determine this aspect, including the reach. It is advisable to allocate the budget 'according to their expected marginal response' (Kotler, 1975). This point is discussed in details in the section under evaluation.

An important point to be noticed is that advertisement is carried out in the *framework of voluntarism* and not coercion. Though government programmes can include an element of coercion, there is no substitute for voluntarism for long-term acceptance. The Indian experience of coercive family control is well known, as well as the backlash that resulted in the suspension of the entire family welfare programme for a number of years.

Advertisement takes into account the findings of the original market survey. Appropriate motivational messages are then designed. While marketing managers 'must anticipate needs and wants,' advertisement managers 'must shape dreams and aspirations.' There are *three stages in the process of shaping dreams and aspirations*:

- Media selection,
- Theme selection, and
- Evaluation.

In the first instance, it is necessary to decide the *media mix* that is print, audio, visual, including outdoor visual that will be selected for communicating the message. The familiarity of the media to the target market and the costs of using the media are major inputs in taking such a decision. Thereafter, it is necessary to select, if possible, sub-categories within each for gaining the maximum effect. For instance, it is likely that *TV* stations beaming in vernacular may be more effective than the English *print* media even if the costs are substantially more.

There are three methods generally used for *selecting a theme* that supports the objective of advertisement. In method number one, homogeneous segments of the market are asked to discuss the issues involved and the designer obtains ideas from this interaction. There could be variations of this and in Chapter 6, it will be suggested that school and college students may be encouraged to draw, debate, or write essays on the subject in order to know how best to design a theme that is in harmony with the thinking level of the target. In method number two, the designer interacts with the programme personnel only and designs the theme. A third method is a combination of both. The actual process of selecting the best theme out of several calls for experience, innovativeness and imagination of the designer. A theme, according to Twedt 'must say something desirable or interesting about the offering; it must suggest a distinctiveness from other offerings; and it must be stated in a believable manner' (Kotler, 1975). It has also been suggested that a feedback be obtained from the selected market on a scale for each attribute.

The structure of the message should force a conclusion to be drawn, either explicitly or implicitly (depending on the awareness status of the target), through a direct approach or through comparison. Experiments in the West suggest that such messages are most effective. *The Indian experience, if the knowledge gained from agriculture extension is anything to go by, is likewise.* Most important, the message should not only encourage action or compliance, but *should show the way of doing it.*

It is always advisable to do a test run of a designed message, through a small sample of the market, before the actual advertisement. The techniques that can be used for *message evaluation* are:

- *Direct evaluation.* The users or customers are asked to rate the message out of a questionnaire, which can be simple or detailed, covering aspects of attractiveness, simplicity, recall factor, etc.
- *Test method* in which the message is given to a test group, taken away and then asked to recall and evaluate on the basis of the same, detailed questionnaire.

If the results are encouraging, then the advertisement exercise can commence. However, continuous feedback is desirable using recall tests. It has to be recognized, however, that these tests do not measure the attitudinal change. That can be known when the sale of the product increases or a behavioural change is brought about.

A simple model for the development of communication materials would look like this:

DISTILLATION OF MARKET CHARACTERISTICS, NEEDS AND DESIRES DECISION ON MEDIA MIX

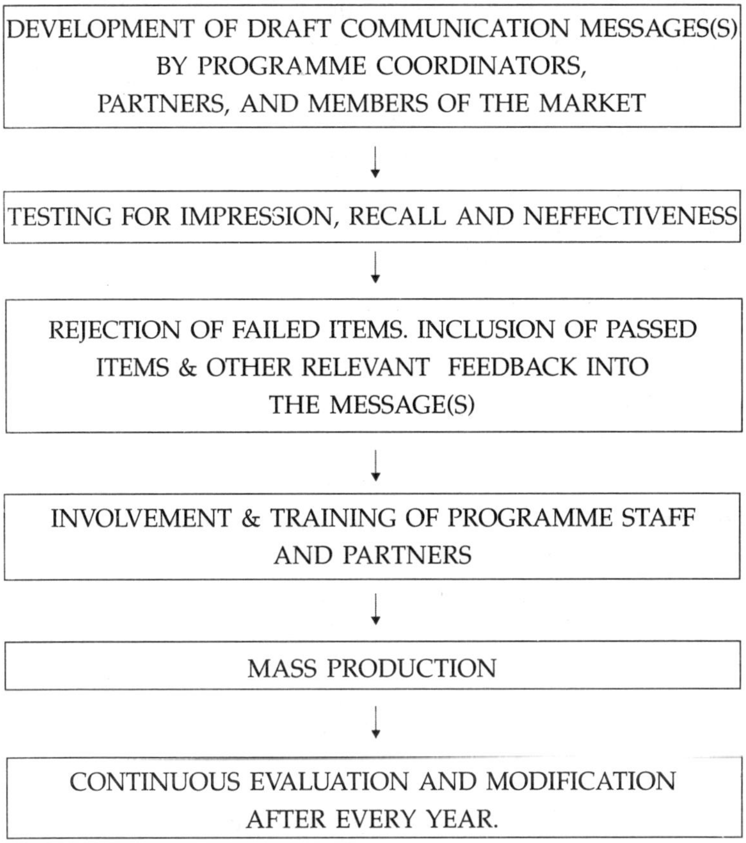

DEVELOPMENT OF DRAFT COMMUNICATION MESSAGES(S)
BY PROGRAMME COORDINATORS,
PARTNERS, AND MEMBERS OF THE MARKET

↓

TESTING FOR IMPRESSION, RECALL AND NEFFECTIVENESS

↓

REJECTION OF FAILED ITEMS. INCLUSION OF PASSED ITEMS & OTHER RELEVANT FEEDBACK INTO THE MESSAGE(S)

↓

INVOLVEMENT & TRAINING OF PROGRAMME STAFF AND PARTNERS

↓

MASS PRODUCTION

↓

CONTINUOUS EVALUATION AND MODIFICATION AFTER EVERY YEAR.

'Typical commercial advertising', according to Lazerfield and Merton (cited in Kotler, 1975) 'is effective because the task is not one of instilling basic new attitudes or creating significantly new behaviour patterns, but rather canalizing existing attitudes and behaviour in one direction or another.' *Effective social communication, on the other hand, is more complex as it generally attempts to change behavioural patterns or bring about new ones. Consequently, social communication that aims to bring about incremental changes is likely to be more effective.*

Publicity, sometimes termed as propaganda, is the planting or release of information as items of news to the media without paying for it. This is an instrument primarily used by government, though not exclusively. Commercial business houses are also known to organize press briefings so as to gain free advertisement for their activities, and indirectly thereby for their products; even though they have less control on the final news or message that goes across. Quite often, government agencies attempt to publicize achievements through press releases.

When the source promoting the publicity is evident, message neutrality is lost and the communication is likely to be taken as nothing but propaganda, and discarded. On the other hand, *because publicity has the potential of emanating as news from an independent third party, it can have higher credibility than advertisement*. The designing of the content has, therefore, to be substantively different from that of advertisement. In the first place, the involvement of the media has to be seen to be very unbiased; no hint of the organizer manipulating an event for publicity should be discernable. The most popular way of doing this is through invitation to special events or guided tours. *The publicity material has to be designed essentially by the marketers but in a form, including visuals that can be easily assimilated and carried by the media*. This aspect will be dilated in Chapter 6. In fact, innovativeness and publicity, according to many communication experts, go hand in hand.

Business houses, as well as government organizations consider *personal contacts* to be a very important part of their promotional programme. Indeed, most believe that personal contact is more focused and interactive and hence more attractive than advertisement. Personal contact can be of many forms, but broadly, these can be categorized as:

- selling and
- servicing.

Selling, as has been mentioned earlier is not marketing and the two terms should not be considered as synonymous. Companies spend large sums of money in training their sales force and for organizing demonstrations. While government or semi-government organizations use their own staff for establishing personal level contacts with the beneficiaries, except perhaps for organizations like the Life Insurance Corporation Of India, the stress on this aspect is routine and unimaginative. 'Even public administrators with good intentions often find it difficult to train their field employees in proper concepts of customer service because there are few incentives they can offer and recalcitrant employees are protected by civil service' (Kotler, 1975).

After-sale service is an important part of promotion through personal contact. Some consider it to be the best form of advertisement. With the assurance that he or she will not suffer or repent after taking the decision, customers are effectively encouraged to go in for a product. The quality of servicing has a direct impact on future sales as well as in generation of product and company goodwill. Consequently, service is a long-term approach and is based on periodic feedback. Its importance has been widely accepted in the private sector since *'retaining customers is much less expensive than replacing them'* (Woodruff and Gardial, 1996).

Marketing and advertisement, being integral functions of any organization, knows no stage of completion. Both these continue as long as the organization continues. The continuity takes into account the fact that 'consumer understanding will never be complete and a certain amount of trial and error will always be inevitable' (Mehta, 1973). Continuity also guards against the offering of superior value products by competitors. Product improvement is possible not only through concentrated research in laboratories, but also from the feedback from discerning users.

Housewives, for instance, are often 'very perceptive, discriminating, and economy conscious judge' of products as well as performance. Very often, in designing products, the housewife 'will show remarkable powers to detect subtle changes in molecular architecture which puzzle the laboratories - until they discover she has found something they have long overlooked' (Webb).

An *incentive* is a tool, often linked with personal contacts, for encouraging a desired behaviour within a market, especially for new products or sometimes for old products when other methods have been unable to make them attractive per se. In commercial marketing, incentives go under the term 'sales promotion'. The use of incentives are often resorted to when the acceptance of a product is considered possible only through trial and for this, potential customers have to be tempted with 'freebies'. Regular users are sometimes encouraged not to 'migrate' away to the competitor by including price or similar benefits with every continuing purchase. Commissions to distributors and retailers are also incentives. Incentives can also be used in a subtle way to generate goodwill for an organization. The stress on this aspect by cigarette manufacturers by sponsoring sport events, in spite of the recognized harmful character of tobacco, is a particularly telling example. Incentives have been widely used by the non-profit sector in many countries for promoting social programmes. Such incentives have been in cash or kind, and have been offered both to the beneficiary (individual or community) as well as the staff establishing personal contacts. Other participants like the doctors carrying out family planning operations in India have also been beneficiaries.

Atmospherics is the term used to describe the environment of the interface between an organization and its market or customers. The commercial sector has slowly come to realize its importance and have since been investing huge sums of money and effort in designing and constructing sales outlets, in dressing up sales and service staff, and in packaging of promotional material. In India,

Maruti automobiles for the first time introduced uniforms for its staff in order to highlight its Japanese parentage and distinctiveness. All major service providers or manufacturers - whether of equipment or food, like the Haldirams - have made 'buying is a pleasure' an integral part of marketing. In the non-profit sector, however, the idea that such investments are a waste of money still lingers. That atmospherics 'is not always a matter of extra cost [and] often it is simply a matter of thoughtfully designing the space for the group that will use it' (Kotler, 1975) has not come across.

Programme Administration

Programme administration is being discussed very superficially as it is an integral component of any organizational structure, falling within the ambit of management rather than marketing. It is presumed that all social marketers would be aware of and functioning within an established arrangement. Only certain inputs essential for the success of the marketing function are being pointed out. A more detailed exposition will be attempted with reference to social marketing in Chapter 6.

Organization

Commercial organizations, though with variations depending on size, objectives, resources etc., all have a distinctive, marketing hierarchy. This structure has essentially, three levels:

- The marketing head
- Functional and product heads and their assistants
- Territorial heads and the sales force

Of particular importance is the sales force. They are the ones actually responsible for participating in each and every aspect of the marketing programme. The degree to which they are able to do this determines the success of the organization. Indeed, the sales force 'represents a company publicly and is entrusted with its most important corporate asset: the customer' (Zoltner, 2001). It is necessary for the management to devote attention to the functioning of the sales force, allocating activity time, and monitoring the results. Successful sales force deployment has the following characteristics:

- They are deployed geographically or customer-wise, depending on the market segmentation and targeting options.
- They are continuously trained and motivated to convert prospects into customers.
- Their numbers are not increased or decreased routinely, but increased as far as possible in anticipation of additional demands, including new product lunches, and after carefully evaluating the expected returns on investments following the additional expenditure.

Planning & control

The main task of the marketing hierarchy is to prepare a marketing plan including objectives, strategies, action plans, budget and monitoring. The process of planning can be top down, bottom up or a combination of both, covering the long, and short-term scenario as well as product-wise specifics. Marketing is the set of techniques that are applied to achieve the organizational goals, through a structured set of strategies and plans. Finally, control functions are inserted at appropriate junctures in order to ensure that the stage-wise results are as per the plan. Such control systems have four attributes:

- Clear and preferably quantitative objectives,
- Measurable results,
- Identification of areas of slippage, and
- Corrective action.

Each and every member of the marketing organization is subject to this control, and as a part of the hierarchy, a controller too. The variables that need to be controlled (Kotler, 1975) include:

- Total market response,
- Market share,
- Cost per unit of market response, and
- Market attitude.

Progressive companies do not like to distinguish between the plans of the organization and that of their marketing wing. Indeed, the company's mission statement is always held up to be the guideline of the marketing department too. While in the past, mission statements like 'Cornering 50 % of the market share' or 'We will continue to make the best lipsticks' were considered appropriate, the present day thinking is more 'market and consumer related'. 'We provide the best service' or 'We care most for your feet' are the changes that have appeared in mission statements. Consequently, the linkage with the marketing wing has become more substantial.

> While it is possible for companies manufacturing and selling one or two products to have a product specific mission statement, it is not that easy for a social organization. Typically, such organizations have a multiplicity of programmes covering education, health, family welfare, nutrition and so on. A possible mission statement for such an organization may be: 'We will provide all opportunities for nurturing healthy and contented families'. Implicit in such a statement will be the offerings of the aforesaid programmes. The social marketing wing can thereafter, get on with respective strategy, goal and action plan development.

Information systems

Planning and control functions are possible only if an organization has well-established information and monitoring system. According to Kotler, a marketing information structure should gather information from the 'environment', and analyze and process this data for the user-manager. Diagrammatically, this process flow can be represented as:

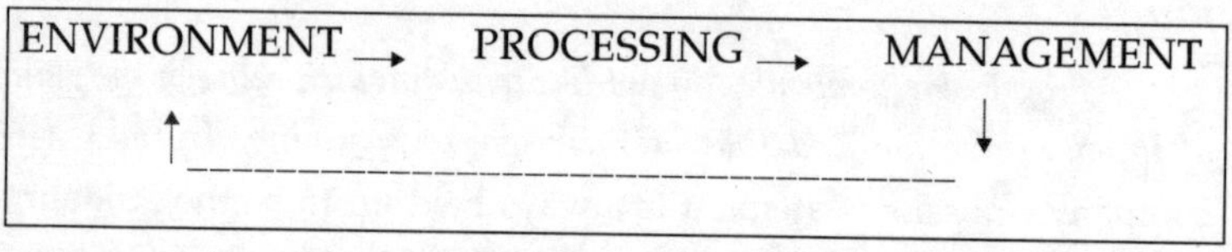

ENVIRONMENT → PROCESSING → MANAGEMENT
↑_________________________________↓

Under 'environment' is included:

1. Macroenvironment
   - Economy
   - Technology
   - Government & Law
   - Culture

2. Task environment
   - Buyers
   - Channels
   - Competition
   - Suppliers

The headings being self explanatory are not being expanded except to say that economic analysis is needed for undertaking the pricing, the selling (including export) and the servicing of a product. Technology determines the quality in order to keep ahead of the competition. Government regulations and fiscal policies impact on the entire manufacturing and selling scenario while cultural beliefs and trends decide the buyer's response. The needs, attitudes and inclinations of the buyers, the middlemen, the competitors and the suppliers are important inputs from the Task environment.

The processing/ analysis functions include:

1. Gathering
    - Internal records system
    - Market intelligence system
    - Random gathering by field staff
    - Structured gathering by field staff
    - Formal gathering by specialized staff or bodies
    - Market management science system (operational research)

2. Processing
    - Storage and retrieval
    - Dissemination
    - Evaluation

3. Utilizing
    - Describing
    - Alerting
    - Deciding

The flow ends with the manager exercising:

- Planning
- Execution and
- Control

The results return as usable information back to the 'environment'. An important feedback for any organization is the level of customer satisfaction. When marketing was just restricted to 'products', the increase in sales volume was a prominent indictor of satisfaction. In the present-day context, with a broadened view of marketing, sales per se are considered momentary and non-indicative of any future trend. Further, though "the complete fulfillment of a need or want", which is the dictionary definition of satisfaction is rarely achievable, a large number of business organizations do not take time to measure even partial fulfillment. Yet, such assessment is desirable and possible through:

- Unsolicited consumer response (suggestion boxes)
- Observational methods (directly observing reactions)
- Direct reports (questionnaire based survey)

Trends

As has been mentioned, marketing as a concept began in the 1950s. A period of hardsell followed. However, in the 1980s, the emphasis shifted to quality when it was realized that what the customer wants is value for money. A point was then reached 'where organizations had to deliver quality just to stay even with competitors (Woodruff and Gardial, 1996). New sources of competitive advantage, as predicted by Peter F Drucker, have come from 'creating, communicating and delivering superior value to carefully targeted customers'.

There has, however, been a change in the customer's attitude towards quality, especially in the realm of automobiles and electronics based consumer goods. With new and new models coming into the market ever so often, a discerning customer tends to doubt the serviceability of the product over a lifetime, if not its durability. Whereas, radios were once considered lifelong assets, televisions are designed to perform satisfactorily for just ten thousand hours or so. Consequently, customer satisfaction, in many cases, has shifted from lifelong durability to newer products with limited, yet acceptable period of performance. The implications of this on marketing have tended to become very uncertain. Product manufacturers, especially those that supply intermediate parts for the final product, have not only to assess the viability of the final-product-manufacturers in order to propose a supply link with them, but also has to keep on modifying their offerings over very short periods of time. Adaptability based on foresight and trend analysis has become a new 'mantra, and this poses useful analogies to the social sector.

The definition of 'value', according to the latest trend, has shifted from mere 'satisfaction' to 'delight' (*Business World*, 2000). In physical terms, this means that companies are setting up well motivated and trained staff to systematically collect data on all customers (not the market) and monitor their feedback, and take prompt action as may be called for.

Another new trend has been noticed in consumer durables. Cars, for instance, are not being sold only on their technical and performance merits vis-à-vis other cars, but the stress is on the availability of easy finances and after sales service. Long-term package sales are being offered in order to lure buyers. This approach is specially suited to markets where the need or desirability has been established and what is being sought is better value for money. This trend too, seems to have a special relevance to the social sector.

New technological development using the internet has enabled targeting of messages and incentives. South Africa's Transnet Health Care Train and Canada's Quit4Life antismoking campaign have been referred to as particularly innovative (Weinberg and Ritchie, 1999). Yet, in developing countries, this form is likely to become effective only for such programmes for which the reach is assured; most rural level and urban worker level issues are likely to be untouched.

Another trend that is becoming apparent in the social sector is the conflict of interest between organizations promoting private good versus organizations, including government, promoting public good. The example cited is the programme promoting the use of hand guns for self-protection in the US versus groups working to ban the proliferation of guns. The campaign on the use of fireworks during Diwali and its ban on environmental grounds is another close to home example.

Conclusion

The marketing exercise described in this chapter is the very basic followed in the commercial sector for influencing buying behaviour, satisfying needs with appropriate products and for keeping customers. *The treatment of the discipline has been limited to being just sufficient for it to be applied to organizations that are engaged in social planning and development, essentially because they too, have to look for markets and they too, desire to influence behaviour*. To paraphrase Kotler and Armstrong, 'Understanding, creating, communicating, and delivering customer value and satisfaction are at the very heart of modern marketing...' and should also be of social marketing. Indeed, this is the reason why these two experts emphasize that 'Business and government leaders (and non-profit organizations) in most ... nations are eager to learn everything they can about modern marketing practices'.

CHAPTER 2

UNDERSTANDING BEHAVIOUR

Behavioural science is a discipline by itself. Obviously, it cannot be treated adequately without extensive study and experience. Nor is it feasible to discuss all the major issues and ramifications in an introductory book on social marketing. Yet, because social marketing draws very heavily from the theories of behaviour and behavioural change, an attempt is being made to understand *just the surface characteristics* so that social marketers get a theoretical basis for their practical moves.

Buying behaviour (context: commercial marketing).

Commercial marketers have been trying to understand why a consumer buys a product. By doing so, they hope to develop appropriate strategies to mould behaviour in favour of their products over those of their competitors. But, even today, in spite of many studies and research, the answer is not clear. There are, however, some basics that influence 'buying behaviour', but it is largely undetermined how and to what extent or in what proportions.

The first pre-requisite in the buying process, quite obviously, is the *availability of information* regarding a product: what needs of a consumer it satisfies, and where it is to be found. Advertisement is the basic method of providing this information, but more important may often be other sources like word of mouth.

Just information may not be sufficient to influence buying behaviour. *Knowledge about the characteristics and functioning of the product;* indeed, how easy it is to use, and how it stands vis-à-vis alternatives are the next step. Product knowledge enables a buyer to equate and evaluate the offer with his or her needs *and the contributions required from his or her side.* Sale of personal computers picked up only when the operating system became compact, cheap and 'user friendly'. Yet, implied in its use was a modicum of 'new' learning. Availability of Oral Rehydration Salts (ORS) was not sufficient to induce its use till it was explained that its preparation at home was simple and inexpensive. 'Fill it, Start it, Forget it' is the slogan that reflected the ease and reliability of Hero Honda motorbike and set its sales soaring over others.

Need/ expectations > Product attributes → Rejection
Product attributes> need/ expectations → Acceptance

Just the mental acceptance of a product is most often insufficient to translate to positive action i.e., purchase. *Factors that induce movement from knowledge to overt action* towards the acquisition of a product include:

- The *'goodwill'* for the manufacturer of the product. A person satisfied with a product manufactured by Amul Dairy will be motivated towards another product from the same stable.
- *Impression* of the reliability and performance of a product among alternatives. Impression is actually a belief regarding a product rather than a person's attitude, which is a sustained belief in a larger context, developed over a period of time. For instance, a person's attitude towards products made in Germany may be based on impressions of reliability and sturdiness. Therefore, for these qualities, the person would go in for German made kitchen appliances or cars or other machinery. But within cars, a person may believe that Volvo, made in Sweden is the safest. A marketer would do well not to attempt to change an attitude for the reasons mentioned, but attempt to change a belief. A marketer of the small family concept likewise, should attempt to improve

the market's perception about the quality of products and service *on offer under this programme* rather than try to change market attitude regarding government programmes.

- It's *price or affordability*. Obviously, this will be market specific and often related to product quality. The lady in the popular advertisement for 'Surf' detergent, stating quite plainly that one should pay a little extra for good quality, is a case in point. This point will carry to a middle class and rich market, but may not to the poor sections to whom an extra coin saved is a coin earned.

- *Product availability*, nearest home or office, for ease in product inspection, purchase and service, will influence buying behaviour. Customers have been known to change banks consequent on the opening of ATMs near their work place or home.

- Impression of quality and promptness of *service*, largely gathered from the distribution and retail network and from social contact.

- *Advertisement* that induces a sense of dissatisfaction at the absence of the product; satisfaction at the acquisition and enjoyment of the product; and a fulfillment of a personal or socially perceived need.

(In real terms, these are the positive characteristics of the four Ps of marketing)

In effect, it is a combination of *environmental and psychological factors* that influences a consumer's decision to buy any product. Environmental factors in the form of tradition, culture and family upbringing will determine whether a product will or will not be attractive and acceptable in the first place. For instance, an Indian may want to buy a cricket set but a Chinese will not; to a Bengali, a book on Tagore will be a great gift but to a Punjabi it may not. The controversy regarding genetically modified foods, and the potential dangers thereof, may stop a consumer from buying 'atta' (powdered wheat) produced by a company associated with such research and technology.

In analyzing psychological factors, one needs naturally, to go deep into the buyer's mind. First, what is the cause for the buyer's gravitation towards a product? Does it satisfy his or her basic need or needs as per the hierarchy of needs enumerated by Maslow or deep, sub-conscious needs highlighted by Freud? A person may want to acquire a car to meet his or her basic travel need or just to keep up with the Jones'. The relationship is always not simple to detect. Indeed, numerous are the stories of painters who have devoted their entire time and energy in producing works of art, thus satisfying a sub-conscious, perhaps self-actualization need while according to Maslow, their dominant desire should have been the solution to problems of hunger and shelter. Then again, psychological factors are most often influenced by environmental factors. While self-actualization may be important to a person from the western world, social recognition may be more relevant to one from the Asian region.

To find a probable answer to the question of 'need', one should also attempt to get an insight into the domain of impressions that are built up within the buyer's mind over a period of time; impressions that tends to accept or reject some ideas regarding a product on a totally ad hoc and selective basis. Experts have called this behaviour 'selective retention' and 'selective distortion'. A customer may insist on buying a Nike shoe even if an earlier pair has come apart just after a year, justifying his or her action as only an unfortunate case, one in a million. Not insignificant may be the impressions of family members and close friends, especially if they have had some personal experience, towards a product. Incisive interpersonal interaction is the only way of ascertaining consumer impressions about a product and its manufacturer or distributor.

While complex thought processes and environmental influences precede expensive and infrequent purchases, relatively inexpensive purchases are generally the result of habit and repeated, reinforcing media exposures. A housewife is not likely to change the cooking medium, purchased routinely off the shelf, till she continues to receive assuring information about its good effects on the family health. For changing this habit, however, she needs startling information on the dangers of her habit and the availability of an alternative at a somewhat similar price.

'People differ greatly in their readiness to try new products. *Innovators* (some 2.5%) are venturesome – they try new ideas at some risk. *Early adopters* (some 13.5%) ...are opinion leaders in their communities and adopt new ideas early but carefully. The *early majority* (some 34%) are deliberate...they adopt new ideas before the average person. The *late majority* (some34%) is skeptical – they adopt an innovation only after a majority of people has tried it. Finally *laggards* (some 16%) are tradition bound – they are suspicious of changes and adopt the innovation only when it has become something of a tradition itself' (Kotler and Armstrong, 2001).

This view of pattern of 'product diffusion' needs to be modified in the Asian context as very few Asian consumers 'are prepared to take the social risk of being innovators by trying a new product first. The discomfort of being left behind, however, induces them to follow suit if they think that others have tried it...Referral is thus a very powerful way of expanding product trials by the first wave of consumers' (Schutte). The study on crop demonstrations by Ram Krishan, referred in Chapter 4, when he suggests that the number of farmers suffering from psychological inhibitions to new technologies and change can be as high as 20 to 30 per cent, confirms this postulate. *A marketer would do well to position a product and undertake the supporting activities, keeping this finding in mind.*

In the modern world, attracting attention in the first place – the battle for the eyeballs – is very crucial. Only then can the rest of the behavioural steps follow. Marketers are finding that time, like finance, is an 'investable' commodity and consumers are always weighing the pros and cons of investing 'learning time'. Only when the benefits are strikingly attractive, immediate, and tangible, do customer interests surge. When they are not, as is most often the case with social products, a marketer has to resort to other methods.

While the *source of the product*, i.e., the producer's goodwill and brand equity, influences a buyer's decision making process, does the *source of information* regarding a product have a similar claim? Apparently so, believe the communication specialists. According to them, information on a product emanating from an independent (of the producer or those directly interested in it) source such as the media or an expert body carries more persuasive ability. This explains why toothpaste manufacturers, for instance, often support their brand through endorsements from the country's premier dental association.

Understanding buying behaviour is the basis for influencing it. Market researchers and analysts attempt to do just that from the time they begin their market survey. The techniques they employ to influence opinion in favour of their products range from positioning to development to advertisement; conventionally identified as the four P's of marketing. In the following paragraphs, a number of additional issues will be discussed in the context of bringing about broader behavioural change, not just for inducing buying.

Changing behaviour (context: social marketing).

Influencing *buying* behaviour is not half as complex as introducing changes in *lifestyle*. The latter is steeped in inertia, justified over generations and traditions, psychologically disturbing, socially stabilized and therefore, more difficult to modify. Herein lies the challenge of social marketing. So, how does one go about changing behaviour and sustaining it over acceptable time periods?

According to one study (Blamey and Sutton, 1999), there are five distinct values that independently contribute to understanding and initiating compliance behaviour that need to be addressed. These values are identified as:

- Functional/economic (what is there in it for me?)
- Social (what do others say?)
- Moral (social approval/disapproval)
- Relational (what is fair?)
- Emotional (what do I feel like doing?)

Asking each of these questions and providing an answer is one way of proceeding. But, in order to relate – nay anticipate - the answers, it is necessary to remember that behaviour, its change and sustainability (though the rationale for its continuance and openness to change-stimuli vary from person to person), has always to be related to an understanding and analysis of two, often overlapping contexts not dissimilar to understanding buying behaviour:

- The person's internal environment (mental make-up), and
- The person's external environment.

The internal environment.

The hierarchy of human needs defined by Abraham Maslow, represented below, tries to understand a person's internal environment, i.e., his or her basic needs that shape behaviour:

THE MASLOW HIERARCHY OF NEEDS

NEED	EXPLANATION
Self actualization	(Personal) Sublime, sacrifice
↑	
Self Development	(Personal) Creative
↑	
Self Esteem	(Social) Recognition, status
↑	
Social	(Social) Love, belonging, relationships
↑	
Safety	(Physical) Self and family – shelter, clothing, property
↑	
Psychological	(Physical) Instinctive and basic –food, thirst, life, procreation

The Maslow hierarchy indicates that movement upwards is possible only when the earlier needs have been met (disregarding minor aberrations like selfless social workers, artists etc). *Hence, the first step is to identify the need status of a target segment*. Change stimuli can, thereafter, be designed for strengthening the basic instincts, the needs, and for moving towards the next. In the process, competition to change needs to be identified and annulled. (The modification of this hierarchy of needs in the Asian context may be read later on).

Understanding the stage of change in each level of behaviour based on need is also important in influencing change. According to the transtheoritical model (Prochaska & DiClemente), behavioural change is 'a progression through five specific stages including precontemplation, contemplation, preparation, action, and maintenance. Precontemplation exists when individuals are not thinking about changing their behavior within the next six months. Contemplation exists when individuals are seriously thinking about changing their behavior within the next six months. Preparation exists when individuals have tried to change their behavior within the past year and are seriously considering trying to change their behavior again within the next six months. Action exists when individuals have changed their behavior within the last six months. Maintenance exists when individuals have maintained their behavior change for longer than six months.' Consequently, 'individuals at different stages of readiness to change behavior will respond differently to specifically framed messages' (Greenlee, 1999). Research on this theory also indicate that 'for individuals in the precontemplation stage, the cons of changing the behavior are greater than the pros.. A cross-over effect between the importance of the pros and the cons occurs during the contemplation/preparation stages. With respect to individuals in the action/maintenance stages, the pros of changing the behavior in question are greater than the cons...' (Greenlee, 1999). Putting all this diagrammatically,

Precontemplation → Contemplation → Preparation → Action → Maintnance

Precontemplation →	Contemplation → Preparation →	→ Action → Maintenance
Cons > Pros	Pros = Cons	Pros > Cons
Intervention: Emphasizing Cons Providing information and knowledge/ skills	Intervention: Emphasizing both Providing justification to the five questions : *mic* (what is there in it for me ?) Social (what do others say ?)	Intervention: Emphasizing Pros Providing satisfation on the higher level hierachy of needs.

	Moral (social approval/ disapproval) *Relational* (what is fair?) Emotional (what do I feel like doing?)	Showing continuously that the decision was, indeed correct.

'These insights show that *consumers do not undertake high involvement behaviours rapidly and in one step*. They move towards the desired outcome in stages. So at any point in time, the social marketer's challenge is to move the consumers to the next stage of the process' (Andreasen, 1995).

The external environment.

Behavioural change rationale and stimuli often transgresses the border between the mental framework and the outside environment. Action, it is believed, is influenced by needs, opportunities and desires, in that order. In most cases, desires will not manifest unless there is an opportunity or rather a choice of opportunities. If the opportunity is singular, then the question of feasibility becomes very important and therefore, the desire may have to be postponed or become latent. If, on the other hand, there is a choice of opportunities, then economic, social and related factors can all be compared. If an option is logical then the desire for it is strengthened, followed by action if the desire crosses a critical stage.

An opportunity can be an availability scenario and/or a set of situations that can remove the causations for its absence. To illustrate, if a small, happy and healthy family is the goal, then the opportunity for achieving this may be the availability of positive factors like contraceptive services or the removal of negative influences (socio-economic, etc.). 'Opportunities are more basic than desires in one respect: they are easier to observe, not just by the social scientists but also by other individuals in society. It is usually easier to change people's circumstances and opportunities than to change their minds. In addition, ... the best way to change their minds may be to change their circumstances' (Elster, 1989).

Though opportunities are external to a person and desires are internal, each influences the other. Desires are influenced by a person's experience, perceptions and *a basic impression of feasible opportunities out of a set*. Hence, to a poor family that has always been unsatisfied by a product (poor quality food grains under a subsidy scheme) or harassed by a service provider (health or land revenue staff), an opportunity provided by the same set of product or service providers for preventive health practices may be ineffective in generating a desire.

Taking the preceding example a little further, if individuals reach a state of continuous and unbearable harassment, then they will be under a greater motivation to change. Availability of opportunities will make this shift easier. But, no business or social planner can gauge the level of harassment that becomes the overwhelming motivation for change. Further, it will be inhuman to plan for such a hardship to physically take place. Hence, in such cases and also in cases where the harassment is not yet obvious or has been taken for granted, a better way seems to be to effectively communicate the state of aggravation so as to make it apparent. This is another way of saying – create a demand or highlight a need.

Changing one's lifestyle and behaviour presupposes the availability of time and education to think of the problems and the solutions. The very poor do not have this. 'Innovation requires resources, time and costly investments with a delayed and uncertain payoff- but this is exactly what firms (read people) on the brink of bankruptcy cannot afford' (Elster, 1989). Social scientists also recognize that the real motivation for change comes not from the really oppressed but from the comparatively better off. 'The middle peasantry rather than the poorest form the backbone of peasant revolutions' (Elster, 1989). Also umpteen are the social change movements initiated by the youth and students; the recent in India being the agitation launched by the Manipur Students Union against the ceasefire deal between the Government of India and the Nagas. Their motivation comes essentially from ideology and a certain degree of frustration. *To a social scientist, both these attributes are 'harnessable' for a good* (sometimes political) *cause*. Indeed, the existence and nurturing of a youth wing by all major political parties is an indication of the proactive potential of youth.

Social scientists believe that literacy and broad-based education, especially education of women, *can alone* bring about progressive social change. To this line of thinkers, therefore, there is no alternative to more schools and more teachers (notwithstanding the mammoth task of training them to be excellent communicators). The empirical evidence of states showing high literacy and education and correspondingly high levels of social development are sited in support. But does education have to be 'general' and conventional? What about focused education on one or two additional, student-relevant items such as agriculture or trade or a small and healthy family? Why cannot information or 'education' on this be given by a non-traditional source, e.g., an agriculturist or a successful trader or a social marketer who is likely to be more trained to communicate with a customer? Indeed, the sense of marketing suggests that this be the behavioural change approach without waiting for total literacy and education to take roots as, for example, in Kerala.

The human mind, as has been suggested, is influenced at two levels. At the first level are his hierarchy of needs including disposition, attitudes, knowledge, educational qualification, skills and so on. At the next level is the influence his immediate surroundings, family members, friends, peers and the like have on him, as well as the influence of the society at large including the socio-religious-legal framework. According to one view, social norms and behaviour, through the process of organic development, represents an equilibrium that social marketing seeks to disturb in favour of a new equation, new equilibrium, new transactions, exchange values and consumer behaviour (Lazniac et al., 1987). Indeed, people and families behave in a way that enforces an established relationship with the other components of a society, including its institutions. A poor labourer, for instance, knows that he can meet his basic survival needs if:

- He can establish and continue a relationship with a rich landlord or a contractor (his market for labour),
- He can ensure that his family has enough hands so that the daily income does not dry up in case one working member is unable to go to work for any number of reasons including injury or illness,
- He can increase his family income for building a house or for saving for old age or bad times, if he can produce more working hands,
- He does not send his children to school.

So, any programme for inducing change, of social marketing (promoting children's education or a small family or whatever) *will be successful if it can actually disturb this balance.* The following contingencies, in the aforesaid example, may result in such change:

- The landlord mechanizes his agricultural operations on seeing positive benefits. In the immediate future, the labourer and his family may feel a loss and may seek alternate deployment of the children, including sending them to school, or

- Instead of the children, the father or the mother attend programmes in skill development, thereby enabling the family to earn a substantially higher income than would be possible through manual labour,
- The children are immunized and protected against killer diseases, thereby removing one reason for additional childbirth,
- The parents are covered under a social safety net that can see them through hard times, on their retirement due to old age or otherwise, and as an incentive for sending children to school.
- The government enforces the law prohibiting child labour.

It would be apparent from this discussion that the external stimuli for disturbing this balance will not only have to be critically planned and firmly executed, but also extended to many adjoining spheres. In contrast, *disturbing the equilibrium for a family that is not in such dire straits may be easier*. At the same time, 'it is important to assess whether it is realistic to overcome the external barriers you identify' (Mckenzie-Mohr and Smith, 1999). According to some thinkers like Alvin Tofler, conflict and change go hand in hand. Hence, just as one needs to tackle conflict in order to bring about change, so too does change continue to bring about new conflicts. *This postulate is the greatest rational for continuous interaction with programme adopters, often far into time.*

Behavioural change tools.

The nuts and bolts of behaviour change are very similar to buying behaviour. First is the availability of information that enables a person to compare whether his or her present position is advantageous over the promised or possible change. Just information and knowing the advantages may not be enough.

Indirectly and predominantly in this comparison comes in the question of competition i.e., what are the disadvantages that he or she will have to face in changing *both the mental framework as well as in adopting the specific actions*. 'Since the barriers that prevent individuals from engaging in sustainable behaviour are activity specific, community based social marketers begin to develop a strategy only after they have identified a particular activity's barriers' (Mckenzie-Mohr and Smith, 1999). If the perceived benefits are more and the steps towards the change, including the physical necessities, are available, a person is most likely to change. 'Good social marketers see consumers as making choices between action based on their perceptions of the balance between benefits and costs of present and proposed actions. Thus, they need to know what these perceptions are and what must change in their programme so that the balance turns in the marketer's favour' (Andreasen, 1995). Just financial comparison, studies show, may not be enough: 'As with information campaigns that focus on altering knowledge and attitudes, efforts that have concentrated on pointing out the financial advantages of a sustainable activity....have also been largely unsuccessful' (M. Costanzo et al 1986). Availability of 'investable time', on the other hand, is often of greater consequence. *Marketers, therefore, need to pay attention to 'enablers' i.e., steps that make it worthwhile for the prospects to spend* their time on learning, then progressing through the six identified stages of change.

Investable time is an interesting concept in understanding market receptivity. Persons may not be willing to listen to reasons why a small family is good for overall family and the nation's health and prosperity, yet they may devote considerable time in ascertaining the pedigree of a cow that they intend to purchase. What is the difference? Obviously, the link between the satisfaction of a need (be it nutritional or economic status) and the activity is immediate and tangible in the latter case while in the former, no such direct connection is apparent. Also, in the establishment of such a linkage, a behavioural change is often indirectly predicted (caring, feeding, grazing and so on), without being obvious. Establishment of a linkage between an objective and every preceding activity thus appears to be fundamental in social marketing. Oftentimes, there may not be any objection per se in accepting an idea like the desirability of a small and healthy family. The hesitation would generally be in taking the specific steps necessary for adopting the recommended behavioural pattern.

To further elucidate the earlier point, progress towards an overall objective may involve a number of intermediate steps either in relationship or independently. For instance, the objective of changing behaviour towards the adoption of a small family may be achievable by abstinence, contraception or abortion. Even within contraception, there exists a choice of methods. Adoption of any one method is a behavioural change contributing towards the overall goal. 'Deciding what behaviour(s) to promote should be based primarily on the answer to two questions. First, what is the potential of an action to bring about the desired change?... Second, what are the barriers and benefits that are associated with each of the potential actions ....whether the resources exist to overcome identified barriers and enhance perceived benefits?' (McKenzie-Mohr and Smith, 1999). *Social Learning Theory (SLT) suggests that self-confidence in the feasibility and possibility of changing behaviour is crucial for its sustenance.* Therefore, there is a case for highlighting similarly placed success stories, skill development, taking a person gradually towards the goal, and socially encouraging changed behaviour through recognition and/ or incentives. Viewing from a different perspective, in our example of contraceptives, the non availability of trained staff for IUD insertions may suggest promotion of condoms and oral pills. The convenience and therefore, the attraction for a semi-permanent method, rather than daily or activity specific protection, may suggest the need for holding

IUD insertion camps and frequent follow up camps. *The strategy may, therefore and ultimately, boil down to the enumeration of activity(s) – identification of benefits, identification of barriers, establishing opportunities and so on – that facilitate the taking of the desired steps.*

Very often, people find the alternative of inaction preferable to action essentially because they have grown used to such status quo. *'In social marketing, competition most often comes from habits or from inertia'* (Andreasen, 1995). In such situations, persons will argue that there are many daily necessities, which stop them from going to the medical center for an IUD insertion, for instance. In such situations, movement from awareness to contemplation to action can be possible only through a clear understanding of the chain of arguments, *in identifying the important ones,* and thereafter providing alternatives that are apparently more attractive. A housewife pleading the unavailability of time to go to a clinic because she has to prepare food for her husband when he returns from the field can perhaps be satisfied in one or more of three ways:

- If arrangements can be made to provide free meals to all the members of the family on such days. Indeed, similar arrangements can be made for all eligible ladies in a community, on particular days, or
- If the travel time can be reduced, or
- If such services can be provided at home.

In order to influence a change we must, therefore:

- Understand all the *perceived costs/ barriers/ competition to a product,*
- Understand all the perceived costs/ barriers/ competition to the *specific activities that precede the acceptance and adoption of the product,*
- *Reduce* or if possible *negate* the physical and socio-religious conditions that support the costs/barriers/competition, or

provide alternatives that are less of a cost/barrier/ competition,

- *Highlight* the benefits,
- *Strengthen* the benefits if possible,
- *Provide opportunities* for availing the benefits.

From the point of view of the market or beneficiary, one-to-one flow of information, experience and motivation is ideal. This is because a beneficiary tends to feel wanted and his or her compliance makes him or her a partner in the programme. Such neighbourly action helps to remind, as well as to avoid faltering on the way. Exercising by ourselves, indoors, is difficult but not necessarily so if done in a gymnasium or in a park with others. *Conformity to normative behaviour, as will also be highlighted later, is often a strong incentive towards sustainable change.* It is thus no coincidence that 'those who know about and adopt (progressive) agricultural practices also tend to know about and to adopt family planning practices' (Kivlin et al., 1971). Andreasen argues that 'in communities with 50 per cent adoption...(individual) movement from late Contemplation Stage to Action may be brought about by application of social pressure in addition to (or instead of) reductions in perceived costs' (Andreasen, 1995). From a positive point of view, if conformist behaviour is appropriately recognized, the change is, in a way, cemented. In Chapter 6, planning a distinct identity for programme adopters – umbrellas or bags or houses painted in particular colours - has been suggested.

'Often, we do not do things for pleasure, but because they give us pleasure. In these cases a certain form of behaviour has valuable or pleasurable consequences, and our perception or registration of that fact strengthens or reinforces our tendency to engage in it' (Elster, 1989). *In other words, pleasure being an essential part of sustainable behaviour, the pleasure of changed action should not cease once the action has been taken.* 'After sale service' and follow-up is exactly this. A 'pleasurable consequence' of a changed behaviour, in order that it be sustaining, must also be apparent, immediate and continuous. A customer will prefer to buy an air-conditioner from a company that promises an immediate incentive/ prize rather than from another that will refund a portion of the expenditure in the contingency of the buyer winning a prize – other things being equal. In the social context, the pleasurable part can come from increased attention, service, removal of problems or discomfort if any, and social recognition.

Conversely, *an adopted behaviour will be sustained if any of the adverse consequences of adopting the changed behaviour can be promptly mitigated*. In commercial marketing, this is rather easy: a television company that attends to problems promptly will have a satisfied customer who will prefer a second set from the same company. In social marketing it will be very difficult to demonstrate the immediate benefits of adopting contraceptive measures – say, in terms of improved health of the mother, leave alone intangible and long-term benefits. Fortunately, there will be no adverse consequences of adopting a small family norm. Complications arising out of adopting some contraceptive measures like IUD insertions or vasectomy/ tubectomy do arise, but prompt attention and medical care will be the obvious remedies.

Another way of fostering sustainable behaviour is what Doug McKenzie-Mohr terms as *'prompts'*. These are essentially reminders – could be stickers or letters or visits by programme participants or advertisements or such like, that enable a person to recall a message or an action to be performed. An eye catching sticker adjacent to the kitchen light switch would help a housewife remember to take her daily dosage of contraceptive pills, as she turns it off before retiring at night. A reminder by the family grocer regarding purchase of contraceptives, at the stage of weekly or monthly purchase of groceries would be another prompt.

McKenzie also advocates the *understanding and application of 'commitment' as a behavioural change tool.* A number of studies in the USA and Canada, according to him, have shown that 'agreeing to a small request lead people to agree subsequently to a much larger one'. It seems that people, in agreeing to a small request or activity feel involved and committed towards the overall goal. They appear to justify themselves in terms of behavioural consistency. Commitment is generally time independent i.e., a second request coming after a long period is also well received. Moreover, it is of little consequence if a different person makes the second request. 'That we will comply with a second request initiated by a new person suggests that these changes are not transitory; otherwise we would only feel bound to comply if the second request were made by the same person who had made the initial request' (McKenzie-Mohr and Smith, 1999).

Behaviour change can also be *'kick started' or 'pushed'*. Product distributors have been known to push products based on their commission margins rather than on product quality. Incentives, touched upon in the earlier chapter, are another way of motivating persons towards a particular, most often non-radical behaviour. However, such pushing is effective over a long term horizon provided the fundamentals of behavoural change have been observed. Or else, persons are liable to revert to their original behaviour once the incentives have been withdrawn or the programme pushers have lost their pushing zeal. Non-monetary incentives like public recognition, however, do not run this risk since these cater to the higher 'wants' of a person as defined by Maslow. Research has also shown that incentives work better than disincentives (McKenzie-Mohr, 1999).

Because social marketing may often require the disturbance of a social equilibrium maintained by the powerful, it can only be effectively done only if the marketing input is by itself powerful or is backed by the powerful. The role played by the powerful reformers in Operation Flood, described in the next chapter, is a particularly significant example. There are many such examples wherein social change agents had to take the help of partners who could effectively help isolate the machinations of the disturbed, vested interests. A powerful account of how local politics interfered with the running of a good school and the development of a village road has been reported in The Hindustan Times, New Delhi edition of the 25th of June, 2001. 'Our only hope is the higher ranks of a district administration miraculously upholding the rule of law against all odds' is what the author, Jugnu Ramaswamy asserts in 'A story for Mr. Bhattacharjee', the Chief Minister of the state of West Bengal.

What indeed, is the role played by 'outsiders' in generating group interest and positive action? According to members of one NGO, Svadesh, operating in the area around Vadodara, Gujarat, villagers rarely listen to members of their own group, even when such persons are academically very qualified and/ or have received national recognition. On the other hand, villagers are ready to accept the advise of the NGO whose members belong to another state. Somewhat similar was the experience of the KDCMPU, the milk cooperative whose success formed the basis of Operation Flood. Though local leaders formed the nucleus of the cooperative movement, the actual manager and presently recognized father of Amul was Dr Verghese Kurien, an outsider by place as well as profession (a metallurgist turned dairy engineer). Elsewhere, one has flagged the poor influence that government servants generally have on the people, whether insiders or outsiders. Yet, there are exceptions and exceptions. Why? What seems to be the difference?

It would appear that organizational or personal goodwill, as the case may be may have a great role to play. If the organization lacks goodwill or a positive brand equity, then the status of the motivator – an outsider or insider – is immaterial. If facilitators are identified and planted by outsiders – like a qualified or skilled mechanic – then the chances are small that the rest of the community will accept him or her as a 'teacher' or 'path finder'. *Consequently, it is best to ascertain from the community members themselves as to the persons they hold high in esteem, and then 'recruit' such person(s) into the social marketing programme.* Similarly, if there are organizations (commercial, religious, social, or simply sporting) operating in an area, the members of which have a good impression already, then they may be included in launching any new programme. All other persons, it would seem, have to prove themselves in terms of sincerity and empathy – often long term – before being accepted as influencers.

As regards messages aimed at fostering change, the Consumer Information Processing (CIP) model postulates that:

- A person's capacity to absorb and process information is limited, and
- A person tends to process information in bits and pieces as received from external sources.

Therefore, message construction calls for specific targeting with crisp and easily taken in and digested information/ knowledge from multiple channels. Scholars are, however, not unanimous regarding the efficacy of positive versus negative interventions. The majority opinion is in favour of negative messages to shake complacency into action. Messages, according to J.J Davis (1995) that emphasize disadvantages and dangers that follow inaction are consistently more persuasive than messages that emphasize savings as a result of taking action. However, it is well recognized that negative appeals must also highlight possibilities of corrective action. If the problems are posed to be mammoth, then a psychological barrier towards positive action develops. Fighting corruption on a national scale is a telling example. Though 'positive appeals are currently underutilized, perhaps because there is some doubt that positive appeals can be as effective as negative appeals' (Henley, 1988) they enable the alternative viewpoints to be appreciated, especially by those in the 'contemplation/ pre-contemplation stage. In the next chapter, it will be mentioned that *a combination campaign of both positive and negative media messages has proved to be ideal* in the Universal Immunization Programme (UIP).

Behavioural change can also be forced through legislation and fiscal disincentives. A smoker, for instance, can be denied access to cigarettes in non-smoking zones or the law can prohibit the purchase of liquor by teenagers. Duties on tobacco, likewise, may inhibit a smoker's natural inclination. Such behavioural restriction, however, is dependant on the degree of enforceability. But law or decree cannot tackle inaction in citizens not drinking safe water or heart risk groups not reducing weight or families not using contraceptives.

Community behaviour.

Promoting individual action in favour of a product is the aim of commercial marketing. Mass marketing is actually an aggregation of individual marketing rather than collective marketing. Even when commercial marketers target the very young or the teenagers, for instance, what they are aiming is the conformity by each individual to the projected group behaviour *rather than aiming to motivate the group as such.* When Harley Davidson advertises for its motorcycles, it is still aimed at the individual members, though within a larger 'clan'. Social marketing, on the other hand, needs to focus *primarily* at collective behaviour and action. Studies have shown, for instance, that 'adoption of an improved practice by a farmer is not necessarily based on his rational evaluation of the usefulness or the profitability of the practice alone. The farmer does not live in a social vacuum ..... His personality is a product of his group living (Kivlin et al., 1971). Indeed, social marketing considers a programme successful if it has been able to mould collective behaviour even if individuals within that group have remained unconvinced. From a practical point of view too, time, physical resource and funds may not allow individual based approaches. Therefore, 'social marketers recognize that to have maximum social effectiveness in a world of very limited budgets, one must focus on changing groups of consumers – not individuals and not mass markets, but carefully selected segments' (Andreasen, 1995). So, the short point is that the proper understanding of the nuances of *individual as well as collective behaviour and action* can result in the better development of social marketing programmes. Fortunately, it is the same market survey that commercial organizations carry out, with a perceptible bias towards social inter-relationships and net-workings that will enable the collection of such insights.

The first characteristic of collective action is that it may be against individual action. For instance, while it may be advantageous for an individual to have a large family, such action will be detrimental to a social structure where the resources are limited – the ration shops can dry up well before covering the population; the water from the irrigation channel may dry up before reaching the tail-enders; the community well may dry up and so on. *There is therefore, a great potential of harnessing collective opinion to supersede individual inclinations.*

Segment based behavioural change programmes are particularly successful when the bonding between members of the segment are very strong, for whatever reasons. The example of the success of the milk producers cooperative described in the next chapter is a case in point. In most homogeneous communities, divergent behaviour is frowned upon. Hence, though slow to react, the movement catches on involving each and every member.

Individual action, in spite of an obvious disadvantage to the individual, may remain suppressed in the face of collective action under three scenarios:

- Fear of reprisal from the collective body or another (could be the state if it is promoting collective social behaviour or norms),
- Fear of non-approval of the immediate social group. In the Asian context, this is very crucial. 'There is strong concern about acceptance by peers, anxiety about exclusion and a near compulsion to be always among the in-group' (Schutte), and
- The gains from collective behaviour are 'substantial; the gains from unilateral non-cooperation not too large; and the loss from unilateral cooperation small' (Elster, 1989).

Asian consumers, unlike their western counterparts, are 'fundamentally collectivist, meaning that the rights of the individual are subordinated to those of the group' (Schutte). Indeed, most Asians want to belong to a group, value what the group thinks of them, and finally relate their ultimate achievement to societal reference. Some time ago, the highest self-actualization motive was knowledge and education – that too, for the benefit of society. Equal in status were religious teachers providing comfort to their followers. Lately, money and power have overtaken knowledge as the highest need. Politicians, the emerging status symbol, feel satisfied if they can collect crowds, enjoy more and more privileges, and distribute largess at public expense. Bureaucrats follow next in stature. It is for these reasons that Hellmut Schutte (*Business* Standard, 2001) has suggested a modification of Maslow's hierarchy of needs in the Asian context, substituting self-actualisation needs with 'social affiliation, admiration and status'.

Conclusion.

For promoting behavioural change it is not enough to legislate or provide information and knowledge of the potential dangers and preventives. 'Numerous studies document that education alone often has little or no effect upon sustainable behaviour' (McKenzie-Mohr and Smith, 1999). In the final analysis, it is an understanding of the various ways that people and communities take decisions, the way their family and society influences their decisions, the benefits of action, barriers to action, the opportunities available for change, the effective manner of communicating and addressing each issue that hold the greatest promise of success. Indeed, this is the very basis of social marketing.

CHAPTER 3

MARKETING OF SOCIAL DEVELOPMENT PROGRAMMES

In this chapter, an attempt will be made to identify the broad manner in which organizations promoting social development programmes go about their task and, therefrom ascertain the use of marketing techniques by them, if any. Obviously, an 'across the board' picture will have to be drawn based on a few broad categories. In addition, three specific programmes undertaken by government will be studied somewhat closely, essentially because these have been held to be nationally successful. Finally, the concept of social marketing will be defined, explained, and the National Population Policy 2000 document will be analyzed, again in order to identify similarities with the concepts and principles of marketing.

Organizations that are involved in promoting social change can broadly be classified under:

- The government,
- The organized private sector, and
- The public sector.

While the Indian experience of these three will be briefly touched upon, the emphasis will be on the government sector. With the lessons learnt from some of these experiences, 'prescriptions' for social marketing will be suggested in Chapter 6.

The government sector

Government sponsored social sector programmes begin with a policy paper, items on operational strategy and action points for implementation. Planning is essentially a resource matching and deployment exercise. Areas specifically covered for this purpose include manpower, finance, infrastructure, training, and monitoring. There is a presumption, quite like the belief of educational institutions some time ago, that the objectives, being inherently desirable, need not be marketed. Hence, there is little attempt to include the context of the beneficiary in the planning process. Even where such interaction is specifically structured, it is mostly in the form of 'meetings' with local representatives. The programme planner or implementer purposefully interacting with groups of beneficiaries in order to understand their needs, hopes, and most important, the barriers to change, is conspicuous by its absence. Predictably, the implementation strategies *rarely* differ according to community differences. Areas having a very high incidence of landless labourers, for instance, are therefore, treated akin to areas having rich farmers. Whenever motivational concepts are discussed and stated to be important, these are not spelt out in clear-cut steps like that in the business sector. Social policy makers continue to think that they are knowledgeable and equipped to believe about and decide what is good for the people and therefore, are competent to devise social and development programmes accordingly. In the commercial sector, it may be recalled, this is rarely the approach and 'companies that design products they feel are good for the market without consulting the market beforehand often find they have few customers' (Kotler, 1975).

The implementation process relies on meetings and briefings down the line till it is left to the field level staff to carry out the programme objectives and provide feedback. Such 'cutting edge' staff is rarely trained to follow any management techniques, nor are their activities methodically supervised or guided. A plethora of schemes, as has been remarked earlier, results in dilution of effort. Involvement of the people, either through local bodies or through private NGOs is an exception. Successful implementation of programmes is mostly the result of dedicated work by key functionaries rather than systemic efficiency. Obviously, successful programmes falter when such key players exit.

A closer look at one of Government of India's programme i.e., for marketing contraceptives, though also termed as social marketing, show that it is just a truncated version of marketing. Actually it is selling - a common confusion among many organizations carrying out specific, advertisement boosted activities. Indeed, social marketing of contraceptives is nothing but 'supply stressed' and 'demand presumed' marketing. Such marketers believe that a product made available at a reasonable cost and promoted aggressively by advertisement will sell. They argue that by 'making possible what seems a relatively small difference in people's lives – access to affordable contraceptives and the information needed to use them correctly – we can provide services to millions of people at very low cost' (Harvey, 1999).

Government of India's social marketing of contraceptives (CSM) programme had its origin in the plan designed at the Indian Institute of Marketing, Calcutta (Kolkata) in 1960. The main components of the IIMC plan (Harvey, 1999) were:

- Mass production of condoms in order to bring down the price.
- Distribution through large private marketing channels with adequate distribution charges.
- Professional advertising and sales promotion campaign to create a demand for the product and market it successfully. 'A media blitz was essential to make it a genuinely large-scale undertaking'.
- Only available consumer research was considered in drawing up the plan but additional research by the advertising and distribution agencies was suggested as the programme progressed.

- Brand selection and packaging was undertaken and this was the birth of 'Nirodh'.

The plan was well received by the Government of India and the first step it took in 1965 was to rename and reorganize the Ministry of Health as the Ministry of Health and Family Planning in order to shoulder the perceived, new responsibilities. Several donor agencies simultaneously set up base in New Delhi to collaborate in implementing the plan. The first concrete step was a field trial in Meerut in 1966-67 in order to find out the response of the private distributors to condom distribution. Based on a favourable feedback, procurement of condoms (some 400 million from abroad, through USAID funding), and the designing of an advertising programme through professionals (J. Walter Thompson) was started. The Government of India's social marketing of contraceptive (CSM) programme was officially launched in 1968.

Interestingly, *there was a glut of condoms in 1973. There were no takers!* The sales estimates were too optimistic. In other words, supply by itself failed to generate demand. This situation and approach is what the proponents of social marketing, who do not believe just in supply side marketing, try to avoid. Free distribution of condoms, in order to generate demand was initiated, and the 'free condoms were packaged differently, in blue and white paper foil as opposed to the gold and red of the socially marketed Nirodh'. Oral pills were added to the programme in 1990. In 1995, the private sector (Population Services International and the DKT International) entered the field but by 1997, private sector involvement in retail distribution fizzled out. The CSM continues today under two streams – the government hierarchy distributed free condoms and pills, and the priced distribution by volunteer bodies (just thirteen of them). While the volunteers are expected to 'promote' the use of their products, mainly by advertisements, the government channel is expected to 'distribute'.

Barring this lone example of a programme that has some links with the practice of commercial marketing, social marketing in government is almost non-existent. The study of consumer preferences based on market segmentation, and the planning of a marketing mix based on the results is equally rare. The help of distributors and programme retailers is rarely taken in designing or implementing Government sponsored social development programmes. Such programmes do sometimes include advertisement as a motivational tool, but mostly at the national level where fund constraints are not very acute. Community level implementers on the other hand, hardly ever have the funds to design and publicize locally relevant messages using the appropriate media mix.

A number of interesting points are noticeable in government-sponsored advertisements:

- When they are distributed by the concerned organization, people rarely go through them, dubbing them as propaganda.
- When they come out as specific advertisements, especially in the print media, they are not sustained.
- Often a host of information is provided leaving the receiver confused about the operative message.
- The message in the print media is in a language that the target population is often unfamiliar with.

Social programmers generally have no guidelines on the optimal use of media. This is because the historical debate and the two divergent views regarding the role and influence of mass media on development continues, albeit covertly. Advertisement is meant for the commercial sector and is considered a waste in the government sector. The earlier referred perception that 'inherently noble' programmes need not be 'pushed' pervades.

Based on a study of mass communication in rural India, well before the entry of television, 'Hartmann et al. (1989:260) found that "interpersonal communication" was a much greater source of information than mass media, yet the latter *did* (italics is mine) prove to have certain development consequences' (Johnson, 2000). With the entry of television, however, most studies have acknowledged the strong influence it has had on social change and personal behaviour. At the same time, doubts continue to be expressed on the efficacy of advertisement over television; some stating that fifty per cent or more of advertisement cost is wasted but one does not know which fifty per cent! According to B.S. Baviskar of the University of Delhi, 'there are hardly any serious studies of the impact of television on Indian society and culture, particularly in the rural areas.' Even within this limitation it has become apparent to most that television has changed its face from being an educator, to an informer to an entertainer.

The introduction of television has brought about interesting social change. Yet, the need to note these for designing marketing programmes around them have not really surfaced. Though the following findings are from the study of two typical villages in Maharashtra (Johnson, 2000), a similar situation is likely to exist in most of the Indian villages (can be confirmed from the preliminary survey being prescribed as the first step in marketing):

* Television cuts across age groups and gender, bringing people together.

*With television, there is now greater equality among villagers in acquiring useful information.
*Consequently, the dominant role of some persons by virtue of their education or familiarity with the system and its rules has become diluted.

*Life in the village is now not organized entirely according to the position of the sun, but according to the schedule of television programmes. People adjust their work and other activities so as not to miss their favourite programmes.

*Urban consumerism has increased, especially among the young, thereby worrying the elders: as desires and aspirations cannot be met and there is increasing arrogance and lack of respect for elders.

*There is a palpable gap between verbal response to questions by outsiders and actual behaviour.

*Villagers have learnt to make politically correct statements but they do not practice what they state.

*Television has become an essential part of the dowry system. So its spread is likely to be fast.

*Television has restructured human relationship in a village.

*Television has aided the process of status change from heredity to achievement.

*Television has influenced changes in traditional age and gender relations.

*Television has promoted greater receptiveness to new values and norms.

*Television has reinforced the trend in delayed marriage and the desire for fewer children. Following are the responses from interviewed villagers quoted by the author (Johnson, 2000): "TV has taught us that marrying young is not so good". "There are many programmes on TV that explain to us that fewer children are better."

Though it is uncertain as to how enduring the influence of television in shaping human behaviour will be in India, there are studies (Kottak cited in Johnson, 2000) that show at least a three-stage impact. In stage one, the 'medium rather than the message is the mesmerizer'. In the second stage, which can last from ten to fifteen years, the viewers become more receptive to what they watch. In the third stage, the influence is all pervasive and the 'long term sociocultural effects become discernable'. This is also the stage when the 'strengthening of the nuclear family and the household at the expense of general community life' (Kottak cited in Johnson, 2000) is noticed.

(The role of television has been elaborated as its spread together with the Internet is expected to continue in the future, thereby opening up a huge potential for influencing behaviour.)

Government Departments and Directorates generally do not have a full- fledged marketing department. Some large organizations have positions that cater to their publicity, advertisement and public interaction needs, while others, like the government family planning department employ specific staff as their selling (as opposed to marketing) force. Then, there are some that assign marketing functions like surveys, advertising, and publicity to outsiders. Most, however, carry out motivational work based on government guidelines, by themselves and in conjunction with their regular, functional work.

Government organizations are generally better trained in planning than in efficient implementation. That is essentially because the socio-politico-administrative environment does not attach much importance to the efficiency of implementation, the need for regular nurturing and skill upgradation of its manpower, and the regular maintenance and upkeep of the established infrastructure. Organizational efficiency is often measured in terms of assets created and funds spent. Allocation of resource is mostly a distributive process based on the perceptions of the policymaker and planner and is rarely related to and derived from performance related data. The tools and techniques of management, including marketing, are generally considered inessential in this context. Notwithstanding the difficulty of quantifying marketing costs versus benefits, the fact that organizations can make rational investment decisions based on market response rather than by hunches has gone unrecognized.

The science of investments, it may be recalled, is based on market response under three different scenarios. One view holds that the relationship is linear i.e., that market response is directly proportional to investment; the other believes that it is a concave curve while the third thinks it is a 'S' curve. Those who subscribe to the second view justify it on the ground that the initial investments will be effective while the subsequent investments will not be optimum. The rationale for the third viewpoint is that small investments cannot change the market inertia while larger investments can.

Government sponsored social programmes suffer from the effect of 'negative demand' and therefore there has always to be a prior effort at 'de-motivating' beneficiaries from thinking that only government can and should take care of all their problems. This is often the greatest 'competitor' to social and development programmes. Most villagers, as is well known, will not organize themselves to look after and maintain their common assets, including their source of safe water. They would rather face drinking water shortage, and agitate on that. The business sector rarely comes across this obstacle. Their customers do not expect anything more from the product except perhaps a package of credit and after-sales service.

Staff who implement Government sponsored social programmers generally have a poor image among the beneficiaries – an issue which has been touched earlier and will be re-emphasized later on. Consequently, the programmes are accepted half-heartedly. Isolated examples of success, two of which will be analysed later on have, indeed, required Herculean efforts. Is goodwill so relevant? How do politicians manage to repeatedly win elections in spite of the fact that their reputation is certainly not at the societal peak? Instead of attempting to answer this question directly it is considered sufficient to identify the distinctive characteristics of a politician that are different from a government servant and enabling him or her to influence the voters (consumers). *What then is the foundation upon which a politician markets him or herself?*

The first point that comes to mind is that unlike most government servants, *a politician is rooted to a community or caste or constituency.* The politician campaigns from here, is elected from here, and if he or she does what the constituency expects him or her to do, gets re-elected from here. The politician understands exactly what his or her constituency expects him or her to do (and this may be different from what others, including political analysts think) and as long as he or she fulfills this demand/ need, he or she can reasonably hope to get re-elected. Most voters do not expect to personally benefit from the election of a politician. The direct beneficiaries are the party members/ campaigners who imbibe referral powers. 'On the other hand, many voters get quite involved in some election contests and act as if they anticipate personal benefits' (Kotler, 1975). A politician is a local leader. 'The charismatic candidate is someone who gives a great number of voters the feeling that they will personally benefit through the candidate's election' (Kotler, 1975). The government servant, on the other hand, is generally not from the area, not attuned to the needs/ demands of the community, and cannot provide leadership, leave alone a charismatic one. In fact, government servants tend to convey a feeling that they are aloof, unapproachable, and are wise enough to know what is best for the entire community.

Second, *a politician is with the community for good or bad.* A government servant, on the other hand, may not be around when a programme has gone wrong. Indeed, the common belief is that the coordinators and implementers are promoting programmes not because they are there for consumer/ beneficiary welfare, but because they are posted there. Unlike a politician, a government servant's survival does not depend on the welfare of the community and therefore, he or she is just a paid worker without any stakes. *A politician, on the other hand, is most often a stakeholder.* Third, the press plays an important role in the marketing person's espousing a policy, and in the process, the politician. The press does not evince similar interest in promoting social programmers, or the implementing body.

Finally, and this trend has surfaced in the recent past, even if the personal image of a politician, in a larger context is not flattering, the people of his or her constituency will still extend their support if they expect to benefit from him or her over another. This is the greatest example of the importance of the 'exchange' function stressed in the discipline of marketing.

The organized private sector.

This category covers major private sector business houses that have engaged themselves in social programmes in addition to their main line of business. There are two variations of this – one that restricts itself to its staff and employees, and the other that also includes the peripheral population. In taking up such activities, the organized private sector has certain in-built advantages, namely 'wealth of managerial and leadership talent', and for the first category, a market that is supported by better welfare facilities than the general population, and is therefore, more open to influence.

An interesting study on the implementation of the family planning programme covering 31 industrial units, however, showed that these organizations had approached the problem not on marketing terms but on the standard pattern of management. Their initiatives did not go beyond establishing housing facilities, support from the top management and unions, integration of family planning with health and welfare services, cash incentives, leave benefits, assignment of dedicated staff for programme planning, monitoring and management. No evidence of following commercial marketing techniques was available. Indeed, the 'educational and motivational methods used in industrial programme were found to be very similar to those being used in the national programme throughout the country. Incentives seemed to play a very important role in these programmes' (Murthy, 1983). There was however, one notable exception.

The family welfare programme carried out by Alembic Chemicals in Gujarat indicated a marketing approach. 'The programme was planned to be comprehensive, continuous and flexible, covering all the employees and their families. Emphasis was placed on effective communication, continuous promotion and freedom of choice rather than monetary and other incentives alone' (Murthy, 1983). The approach followed is described below:

- A social worker was appointed to draw up a motivational plan.
- A Labour Welfare Officer was put in charge of the implementation of the plan and for liaison.
- *A preliminary survey of the family status of each and every employee was carried out in order to classify him or her into different 'need groups'.* 'It was inappropriate to consider all Alembic workers as one large homogeneous group requiring the same treatment'.
- Leaders in each department were identified as family planning motivators.
- Leaders were trained in motivation for 15 days, and stocked for distribution of conventional contraceptives.
- 10 to 15 workers in each department were identified for *repeated group discussions* on the topic.
- *Special camps were held for non-acceptors.*
- *The services of acceptors were first recognized as a VIP and then made use of in motivation drives.* 'About 75 to 80 per cent of the sterilized cases in the following years were motivated by satisfied clients'.
- Posters/ messages and hoardings were specially designed.
- Regular distribution of literature, articles, wall posters, information booklets, and organization of film and puppet shows, talks, and exhibitions were taken up.
- *Follow up services were provided to sterilized couples both at their residence and in the factory premises.*
- Monetary incentives were sparingly used; *better hospital and*

after care services were offered instead.

- It was recognized that family planning motivation would be a long term effort and 'significant acceptance ... would take place after the passing of some threshold level of understanding' (Murthy, 1983).
- It was recognized that direct talks would have little effect in motivation. Hence, *creative and innovative communication was designed with the help of the Alembic marketing artist group.*
- No coercion was attempted. '... quality of acceptance was more important indicator of success than quantity of acceptors'.
- *The services of Alembic workers who had considerable influence in their own villages (in surrounding areas) were utilized in motivation.* Besides actual work in the peripheral villages, a baseline survey of eligible couples was carried out. A priority list was prepared for carrying out educational and motivational programmes. As State Government inputs of motivational messages were found to be inadequate, the material developed by Alembic was used.
- Substantial freedom was allowed to the local workers to develop the motivational programme.
- There were problems, in terms of rigidity, of working according to the government programme. The management therefore, considered going ahead with the programme independently.
- The organizers drew up specific indicators of performance. These covered (a) impact on the rate of growth between 1967 to 1973, (b) impact on the different segments (c) *performance as perceived by the family planning acceptors* and (d) performance evaluation by outsiders.

An early study, on the effectiveness of social marketing, in the sense of companies taking up one or more social programmes in the sideline, undertaken by G.D. Weibe way back in 1952 found that 'the more the conditions of social campaign resembled those of a product campaign, the more successful the social campaign' was. He also found five characteristics of effective campaigns:

- The Force : The intensity of the person's motivation towards the goal is dependant on the combination of his predisposition prior to the message and the stimulation of the message.
- The Direction : Knowledge of how or where the person might go to actualize his motivation.
- The Mechanism : The existence of an agency that enables the person to translate his motivation into action.
- Adequacy and Compatibility : The ability and the effectiveness of the agency in performing its task.
- Distance : The audience member's estimate of the energy and cost required to consummate the motivation in relation to the reward.

One would have expected that government planners, the private sector and the non-governmental organizations (NGOs) would have learned lessons from the aforesaid experiences; indeed, if they have, it has certainly not been apparent. Incidentally, the activities of the NGOs are not being discussed, as there are hundreds of them with variations in approach.

Private educational institutions have now come to the fore in terms of their marketing effort. They have identified a market need; have seen that parents are more than willing to make investments on their wards for gaining degrees in some 'in' disciplines; have also noticed the willingness of financial institutions to come forward for financing higher studies within or outside the country, and therefore, have advertised selected degrees and diplomas and often their 'international linkage'. As long as the demand lasts, such institutions can hope to prosper. However, since their marketing is actually 'selling', there is every chance that they will have to continuously adapt themselves to the market demand and offer courses accordingly. Information technology may soon have to piggyback on biotechnology; tourism management may soon replace catering management.

The public sector

The public sector, like the private business sector, has also to produce and market a product or service. There are however, two essential differences between the two. First, the public sector has both a profit as well a social objective whereas the commercial sector has only a profit motive. Second, the public sector, in most cases, receives both direct and indirect government support, including bailouts.

In general, the public sector has to cater to public expectations of social welfare in addition to its core business. Naturally, therefore, it invests substantial resources into social activities. In doing so, it generally follows the government and not the commercial marketing pattern. Some public sector units are forced to follow a different approach if so dictated by International Financial Institutions financing specific projects. Others like the Indian Petrochemicals Limited (IPCL) in Gujarat devise their own pattern of social involvement. IPCL has, for instance, joined hands with eight other chemical companies and formed a society (Svadesh) to undertake social work in identified villages around their area of operation. The movement towards the formation of such a society had started essentially from a desire to deflect the demand for jobs from each 'affected' or sometimes politically connected family into community development. So, with the help of persons trained in social welfare they have introduced a number of socially relevant, development projects. Community involvement and marketing of programmes has been possible through extensive inter-personal interaction -

mainly through plays and competitions, and the involvement of youth clubs in constructional activities, thereby successfully displacing traditional, oftentimes exploitative contractors).

As different from such instances, most other public sector units entrust one or more members of their personnel management group to liaise with the district administration to offer socially relevant inputs. These are mainly funding for schools, drinking water, rural roads, student scholarships and the like. Such social activities are more reactive than reflective of the basic needs of the community they hope to serve. To be fair, the basic need put across by most communities to such public sector units is of employment, but most units can never hope to satisfy this elastic need. So, these units try to do the next best thing: cater to the community need as expressed through the local administration, and often the politician.

Unfortunately, literature on innovative involvement of public sector units on social development is not easy to come by. Hence, only the very broad pattern has been discussed.

Case Studies – The Green & White Revolutions

In comparing the green and white revolutions with the family planning programme, it is useful to remember that both the 'revolution' dubbed programmes were almost totally dependant on forward, sideward and backward linkages. Somewhat akin to a major traffic roundabout, *scientific, technical and physical inputs* were expected from all directions - for the green revolution: improved variety of seed, adequate mix of fertilizers, pesticides, timely irrigation, other agronomic practices, etc.; for the white revolution: milch cattle, cattle feed, credit, machinery, skills and practices, etc., and a transport and marketing infrastructure for reaching the produce to the consumer at a price that is attractive to both the producer and the consumer. The family planning programme, on the other hand, is largely 'external-input' independent. True, improvements in educational and health status impact positively on curbing population growth, yet these are not crucial to the extent that availability of credit or a market for the produce is for the green and white revolutions. Conversely, if nutritional or conventional-education inputs are absent, one cannot emphatically suggest that family planning strategies will not be successful. Motivation and contraceptives is all that is wanted. Consequently, identifying reasons for success in the green and white revolutions, just from the point of view of bringing about a behavioural change amongst the beneficiaries will miss out the wood for the trees. Yet, just this is being attempted because the comparison with the family planning programme has this lone link.

There are a number of other areas of dissimilarity between the green and white revolutions on the one hand, and the family planning programme on the other. In both these 'revolutions', a drastic change in behavioural pattern (with intangible future benefits) was never the objective. Indeed, it was just the opposite. The promise held out was immediate returns in terms of food grains or milk, convertible into cash - through the introduction of improved practices, based on scientific and managerial principles. Both these programmes actually attempted to strengthen an existing and already established buying and selling function in the society – farmers have always grown crops and people were accustomed to keeping cows. While the green revolution aimed to increase production through the introduction of high yielding varieties, the white revolution aimed to increase availability by streamlining procurement/ distribution, and offering the product(s) to the consumers at an affordable price. In Operation Flood, the official name for the white revolution, '...dairy processing and marketing have been given higher priority over dairy production technology' (FAO: 1981) and it was 'designed less as a productive than a redistributive strategy'. The producers were not asked to break away from the past in the literal sense of the term 'revolution'. The family planning programme, on the other hand, aimed and continues to aim at introducing *a break from the past* through the adoption of a new behavioural pattern.

In one sense, the motivational effort towards a small family is easier than in the introduction of a new crop-related technology. This is because in the latter case, the extension machinery has not only to demonstrate that the recommended change is physically 'paying' in terms of increased production and, therefore income, it has also to overcome the natural hesitation of any farmer to invest on the recommended inputs, oftentimes by taking credit from banks, if not from money lenders. No such 'barrier' needs to be overcome in the former case i.e., for introducing a behaviour change towards a small family. Also, unlike any production-oriented programme, family planning is trader independent.

Both the revolutions began in the backdrop of overproduction in the west: wheat in the United States and milk powder in Europe. A shortage of domestic food production spurred the import of PL 480 grains on the one hand, while the pressure within the European countries to dispose their excess stocks of milk food resulted in their import for kick-starting India's Operation Flood. It was the foresight of the policy makers at that time that the 'donations' were not used to depress domestic prices, entrepreneurship or the overall market. Indeed, in a sense, both the green and white revolutions rode piggyback on western over-production to success. No such situation, one is not sure of categorizing it thankfully or not, has pushed the small family movement.

As regards similarity, all the three programmes - the green revolution, the white revolution, and the family planning - have been conceived as national endeavours: in terms of their relevance to the national economy, and therefore, the large scale organizational and planning requirement for technologically appropriate inputs, distributive mechanisms, trained manpower, infrastructure and mass mobilization.

The Green Revolution

When India became independent, it was producing just about fifty one million tonnes of foodgrains for a population of about 361 million (Chopra, 1985). The policy planners quite naturally were averse to the continuous pressure for importing food and so initiated a number of measures – a package of agronomic practices, programmes and the establishment of support institutions, collectively under the Intensive Area Development Programme (IADP) - to increase production. At the first instance, only seven districts in seven states were selected for the combined and coordinated application of a ten-point plan (for rice, wheat and millets) that included 'intensive educational efforts especially through scientific demonstrations, to disseminate improved agronomic practices' (Chopra, 1985). The basic operational strategy was the development of a 'good farm plan' for every cultivator and the linking of all inputs to the plan as opposed to the farmer (Chopra, 1985). The Pilot Programme was started in October 1959, and the seven originally selected states were increased to eleven by June 1960.

However, 'the package of practices promoted had one important missing ingredient, namely varieties which could respond well to good irrigation and soil fertility management. It was this missing ingredient that was provided in 1966 through the High Yielding Varieties Programme (HYVP) in wheat, rice maize, sorghum (jowar) and pearl millet (bajra) (Swaminathan, 1993). According to R.N. Chopra, this biological breakthrough rode well on the 'adoption breakthrough' introduced by the IRDP. 'In just one year, two million hectares were added to the land under wheat, productivity jumped from between seven and eight quintals to 11 quintals, and wheat production increased by five million tonnes to 16 million' (Chopra, 1985).

Participants of this revolutionary programme have identified three basic parameters that led to its success – Package of technology, Package of Services, and Package of Public Policies (Swaminathan, 1993). In discussing each of these in the context of this book, one is gratified in finding the application of many of the concepts of marketing and behavioural science.

First, was the assessment of the need. Indeed, this was largely a policy decision fuelled by the overall shortage of food production - necessitating regular imports, with all the strings tied with it – and the level of poverty of the Indian farmer. According to C. Subramaniam, the then Food and Agriculture Minister, the nation was at a crisis point. 'There was continuous drought during these two critical years of 1965-66 and 1966-76 and, instead of cutting down the imports, we had to import 10 and 11 million tonnes during these two years'. 'It was this crisis which, in my view, provided the atmosphere in the country to go forward with the new thrust in agriculture' is what he said in recapitulation. Interestingly, the other cause for the crisis, i.e., a faster growing population did receive recognition a decade earlier, but perhaps not a similar thrust.

Then came the product. Fortunately, work on producing improved varieties of seeds had been initiated some time earlier by scientists like Dr. N. Parthasarathi, and Dr. M.S. Swaminathan. With the active cooperation of Dr. Orville Vogel in the United States, and more significantly Dr. N.E. Borlaug in Mexico, a semi-dwarf, spring variety of high yielding wheat was obtained and grown in the fields of the Indian Agricultural Research Institute, (IARI) Pusa, Delhi, in Ludhiana and Kanpur. This was in 1962/63 and the results were very encouraging. Further trials with a wide range of high yielding, dwarf varieties followed together with an assessment of the agronomic practices that were needed for its cultivation in the farmer's fields. When Dr. Swaminathan's suggestion, in the year 1964, to 'introduce the farmers to the new opportunities' through a series of National Demonstrations was accepted and carried forward, the result in the minds of the farmers, to quote him, 'was electric'. The National Demonstrations began by taking the product from the laboratory to the demonstration fields through the first level scientists; then extended further by the second level scientists and agriculture extension staff to other village plots. 'Annually over 5000 demonstrations were conducted in the farmer's field by the scientists' (Prasad). In the process, the farmers witnessed the potential of the new variety and quite obviously, they were able to visualize the monetary gains they would receive if they planted these and followed the recommended agronomic practices. Opportunities also opened up for all 'downstream' business. The 'clamour for the seeds began and the area under high yielding varieties of wheat rose from four ha in 1963-64 to over four million ha in 1971-72. A small government program became a mass movement' (Swaminathan, 1993).

There is a general belief these days that the wheat revolution, or colloquially, the green revolution was not really a national success story but a regional one, covering just the states of Punjab (including Haryana those days), Rajasthan, western Uttar Pradesh and Gujarat to some extent. Indeed, that may be so geographically, but nationally the food grain output increased manifold – enough to make India self sufficient, with the contribution of Punjab being 'more than 60%' (K.S.Gill). This 'vertical growth in productive methodology' according to M.S Swaminathan, helped avoid an extension of 35 million hectares on the pre-1965 yield pattern; in the absence of which, 'even the remaining forests would (have) disappeared'. *But what is very important and tends to be overlooked is that the area specific introduction was intentional.* 'When the Green Revolution technology came on the scene in the country in the mid sixties, it worked better in north and southern regions because the conditions there were more favourable'. Deficiencies in infrastructure, administration and management in the eastern region would not have enabled the cultivators to obtain the needed inputs, and therefore the productive gains (Chopra, 1985).

A cardinal principle of marketing is that the market for which a product has been designed must be in a position to accept it – be it on account of personal, infrastructure or social reasons. A high yielding variety needs certain critical inputs ranging from what K.S. Gill calls 'no-cost or low-cost technology: seed rate, sowing depth, sowing time, adjustments in time and distance, shallow planting etc., to efficient and scientific application of fertilizers, pesticides, herbicides, and of course, irrigation. Hence, logic dictates that a programme on the adoption of the new seeds should best be directed or 'positioned' as marketers would call it, at areas and farmers who can make the most of it. 'A decision was taken', according to C. Subramaniam, 'which was criticized by many – that we should take advantage of places where the resources were favourable: the soil, water and, even more than these, enterprising farmers...Our strategy was to take advantage of these areas and push up production as fast as possible...People criticized it as a programme for big farmers, not realizing that once the big farmers took to it and succeeded, the small farmers would follow' (Swaminathan, 1993). This is also to say that a *practical* percolation strategy is the one that is aimed at the well to do so that they do not obstruct, but adopt. Seeing them, the others can follow. The National Demonstration Programme concurrently carried the technology to other enterprising farmers 'covering an area of 0.4 to 0.8 ha.' (Prasad et. al, 1987) and, therefore, the spread was wider. There is no doubt that the plan succeeded and interestingly, today, on the basis of that impetus and other extension programmes like Operational Research Programme in 1974-75, Land to Lab in 1979 and so on, we have problems of overproduction, much beyond our grain storage capacity!

Commercial and social marketers believe that behaviour and behavioural change depends on the capacity of a campaign to address the market needs as well as the 'enablers' i.e., the enhancements of the benefits and the removal of the barriers. The positioning of the green revolution at certain sections of the Indian farmers can also be viewed in this context. The following 'enablers' to the increase of farm productivity were identified:

Internal:

- Owner cultivation: suggesting that this allows appropriate investments on the factors of production, as well as interest in acquiring agronomic knowledge and *skills*,

External:

- Land consolidation; thereby opening up the potential of minor irrigation by tube wells,
- Rural communication,
- Rural electrification,
- A dynamic research and extension system,
- Policy support, namely remunerative price and assured marketing.

- 'these five (six) ingredients or pre-requisites', according to Prof M.S. Swaminathan, 'all existed in the Punjab when the new varieties were introduced, and therefore, took off very quickly'.

In contrast, in the eastern states, there was total lack of most of these enablers, if not all. In Bihar, for instance, according to B Sivaraman, the Agriculture Secretary at the time of the initiation of this programme, 'they certainly do not plough the land for wheat as it should be ploughed. A Punjabi farmer would be shocked by the way they run the plough and sow the wheat on the clods. You cannot expect any high yielding variety to respond to this sort of treatment' (Swaminathan, 1993). Mr. Sivaraman goes on to say that 'in both eastern U.P. and Bihar, the research base is very poor', and the top researchers do not work in the field unlike in Ludhiana! It is also, according to him, a problem of overall administration, and lack of labour (in the absence of compensatory mechanization) during crucial operations. Irrigation water from both ground and flow irrigation projects are not used. 'The soil is productive, the water is excellent; but there is no water management, the time of sowing is late, drills are not used, and fertilizer use is not correct', echoes Y.M. Upadhyaya (Swaminathan, 1993). Similarly, in West Bengal, according to R.S. Paroda, 'the universities are not at all attentive to the needs of these states, particularly in research and provision of useful technology and materials'. *In marketing jargon, 'one shoe does not fit all', and the green revolution planners showed how important it was to position the product appropriately.*

The second 'P' of marketing, i.e., 'Pricing' was not specifically planned for. Barring an incentive of five hundred rupees for each farmer participating in the national demonstrations, for all the other inputs, including the improved variety of seeds, unlike the present when the availability of credit is widespread, the planners expected the farmers to pay, and indeed, they did considering the obvious gains expected. 'The Green Revolution would have been a flop but for the fact that suddenly, because of two years of bad drought, the prices of all agricultural commodities shot up...the farmers experimented and were prepared to spend money' (Swaminathan, 1993). This heavy dependence on the farmer was noted by Norman E. Borlaug, the father of the original Mexican variety of dwarf, high yielding wheat. He put it thus: 'The farmer had to play an exceedingly large part in the introduction of the new varieties. We depended entirely on the farmer with irrigated land, and what enthused him then was the price factor'. The need for a support price for the producers, expected with an increase of harvest was considered and introduced for the first time.

The third and fourth 'Ps' of marketing, i.e., place/ distribution and promotion/ communication, if one can draw this analogy, were taken care of by the programme planners, policy makers and administrators. It was not just at the national level that there was total support, but also at the respective states and participating agricultural universities. Some have termed the effort as a 'cooperative movement among the scientists' but have also acknowledged the full support from all other participating sections with 'Dr Swaminathan acting as a catalyst for the whole exercise ...influencing the administration and the public' (Paroda). It was, according to him, the trio of Swaminathan (scientist), Sivaraman (administrator), and Subramaniam (Minister/ policy maker) who were instrumental in bringing about the green revolution. According to M.S. Swaminathan, unlike most Government programmes, the 'wheat revolution became a self propelling movement, because of the synergy generated by machining a package of economically viable technology with appropriate package of services and public policies'. The seeds procured from research institutions were multiplied, demonstrated in farmers' fields, and then offered to individual farmers mainly through the programme machinery.

The green revolution could be considered as a 'seller's approach' to the problem of hunger and self-sufficiency. The nation needed more food grains to feed its people; and the farmers needed to grow more in order to survive and indeed, prosper. So, the seller - in this case the combination of scientists, administrators and policy makers - had only to provide the appropriate product, and the associated inputs to the targeted segment of the market: those who were in a position to make the best of it. Simultaneously they had to transfer the required skills and practices for reaping the fullest benefit from the new technology. The market, thereafter, would take care of reaching the produce to the consumers – those in a position to pay for it that is – and the movement would grow as per its own, farmer driven momentum. A 'marketer's approach' came in when the same programme was specifically directed towards those *who felt no need for it*, e.g., the farmers in the eastern states. Obviously, the removal of barriers to its adoption would have to form an important part of the approach. It is interesting to read that the 'green revolutionaries' did wonder why there was so little response from states like Bihar. K.S. Gill, having found that the performance of high yielding varieties under late sowing conditions was good, if not excellent, was surprised to discover that 'when we wanted it to be adopted on a large scale, the farmers were not willing'. Likewise, B. Sivaraman questioned why, there being 'enough ground water to give you two crops a year' in the north Ganga region from eastern U.P. to West Bengal, 'quite apart from flow irrigation....Why was it not used?'. Demonstrations had little effect as 'demonstration is only a means to an end and not an end in itself...The initiation of a process of learning and the creation of an urge to change, are hardly sufficient by themselves. They must be accompanied by favourable environments, adequate supplies, easy credit, and proper and timely spot-guidance' (Krishan, 1965). Extension can only work to the extent that all the input supplies are available (Swaminathan, 1993). The administration in these areas then, and even today, was not geared up to provide even the basic requirements. Having said that, even if a product is successfully marketed in an area of low demand or latent demand, its continuous adoption will be determined by the anticipated benefit in comparison to the 'costs' that the farmer would expect. This partially answers the question why some farmers in West Bengal, shifted from high yielding wheat to mustard: 'A few national demonstrations in 1970 (of Sonalika), I recall, had great impact in the minds of the farmers in Nadia district of West Bengal. In the next few years it started spreading in West Bengal. Of course, now its use has shrunk again because with mustard crop, which needs less water, they get a much higher income' (Swaminathan, 1993).

It is acknowledged that the Green Revolution was not successful in the eastern states. The reasons offered span the entire gamut of socio-economic-politico-administrative environment. The natural tendency is to identify at least the essential technical, infrastructural, and financial basics and suggest that these be ensured in the lagging areas. A marketer's approach would be somewhat different. Within the specific requirements of the 'product', he or she would go straight to each segmented market (segmentation not having been done in an ad hoc manner) and ascertain their reasons for not carrying out the recommended agronomic practices. Such reasons, expected to vary between segments, would then be dovetailed with the standard ones and the respective 'enablers' found. The marketer's pattern would then look like this:

ESSENTIALS IN APPLYING HYV TECHNOLOGY
(Certified seeds, irrigation, package and prescribed quantity of inputs, crop- appropriate drainage, soil preparation, etc.)

+

LOCALLY RELEVANT BARRIERS
(Socio-economic, cultural, traditional, administrative, climatic, etc.)

↓

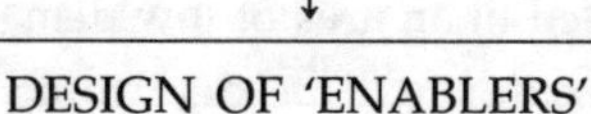

We can now come to the question as to how the interface between the extension personnel and the farmers was bridged, this being the ultimate 'taste of the pudding being in the eating' factor for the success of any programme. Researchers suggest that in the Green Revolution a two-fold approach was followed: through interpersonal communication and demonstrations. First and foremost, the information about the potential of the new seeds had to reach the farmers. Simultaneously, the growers had to be convinced that the promise of the new seeds was within their reach provided they followed a prescribed set of practices. Demonstrations were thus organized under four streams (Prasad et al., 1987): the ICAR extension system, the Ministry of Agriculture/ State Departments of Agriculture extension machinery, the Ministry of Rural Development/ State Development Departments, and the NGOs, business houses etc.. 'The agriculture scientists and extension personnel of these institutions were required to play first-line extension role...on a limited scale but forceful enough to have catalytic influence on other extension systems/ sub-systems' (Prasad et al., 1987). So, scientists of agriculture universities, as well as functionaries of the agriculture departments began to regularly interact with the identified farmers individually, and collectively in demonstrations, through radio forums and in Kisan Melas. 'This tripartite collaboration was important not only for transmission of technologies but also for getting a feedback' (Gill). Even though inadequate at that time, available literature on the new seed and the proper agronomic practices that were necessary for discovering its full potential was distributed. Not to be missed were similar interactions organized by the private sector interested in the sale of fertilizer, machinery, pesticides and related inputs.

> An interesting study (Kivlin et al., 1971) by four authors on 'Innovations in Rural India' has arrived at the following factors that obstruct/ favour adoption of agricultural innovations:
>
> *Traditional norms and beliefs remain a strong obstacle.
>
> *Urban contact was significantly related to adoption. Respondents who were exposed to information from the larger society, whether by extension contact, urban contact, or through contact with the mass media, were more likely to accept modern practices.

*Almost without exception, mass media access and contact, and contact with the agricultural extension agency were significantly and positively related to adoption. The impact of physical inaccessibility was, therefore, dependant on the performance of the latter.

*It is the larger and wealthier cultivators who are apt to adopt more practices and to adopt any given practice sooner. Reasons for this relationship lie in their ability to garner inputs, including financial, and their inclination to go for possible output advantages, including risk taking.

*Credibility of the source of information being material, the cultivator was naturally drawn towards 'demonstrations' over other forms of extension.

*Radio farm forums stood out as programmes of positive influence. (On the spot reporting has been reported elsewhere to be successful, again on the context of information credibility).

According to some, the crop demonstrations which 'began earlier, in the 1950s, with the community development approach' (IARI Seminar, 1990), were continued under the Green Revolution. Others suggest that the demonstration pattern was the one developed under the IADP (Chopra, 1985). Some others, including M.S.Swaminathan, draw a distinction between the new pattern of National Demonstrations and the earlier approach and state that the innovation was on four fronts:

- While 'earlier demonstrations were based on a patronage model identifying the so called "Progressive Farmers" which is an euphemism for rich farmers' (Swaminathan, 1993), the new extension was on the plots of 'actual cultivators with small holdings, so that high yield obtained are not attributed to effects of affluence' (Prasad et al., 1987).

- The area of the extension plots was 'about 1 ha so that the feasibility of raising a good crop can be strikingly and unquestionably demonstrated' (Prasad et al., 1987).
- There was a specific yield based target and there was no separate control plot, and
- The experiments had to be conducted in association with local extension agencies.

Notwithstanding the differing view points, it is apparent that extension measures introduced well before the beginning of the green revolution helped establish a structure for transferring scientific and agro-management practices from the scientists and administrators to the agriculturists – both for seeds and grains. Demonstrations had to be the programme catalyst as 'except in Punjab and perhaps in Haryana, and to some extent in western U.P., the farmer in India does not go out and seek information; he waits for it to come to him' (Sivaraman).

The 'transfer' of the high yielding seeds began on half-acre plots in various IARIs. All programme officers were assembled here for the demonstration, given 1 kg of seed, and advised to try them out in every state, in universities and colleges. Together with the multiplication of seeds, came the demonstration for grains. 'During 1966, 1000 national demonstrations in rice alone were conducted as part of the celebration of the International Rice Year. Being convinced of the merit of such demonstrations in popularizing new technologies, it was decided to continue these first-line demonstration operations, which were conducted by the researchers themselves' (Prasad et al., 1987). 'So it spread all over the country and became a mass demonstration. That was the starting point' (IARI Seminar, 1990). It was also the 'first time that scientists were entrusted with the direct responsibility of demonstrating n the fields of farmers, that the results obtained by them in experimental stations were of wide applicability and utility' (Swaminathan, 1966). Since the adoption of technology and practices is directly proportionate to the observable result, and the high yielding varieties, indeed, showed just that, the response was, to repeat what was stated earlier, 'electric'. 'Our high yielding programme became possible because it was not just a 10% or 20% increase but a 200% to 300% increase. The farmer's immediate reaction (was), let me try it!' (Subramaniam). At some places, the farmers went to the extent of way laying shipments and stealing the seeds!

The first lesson learnt in earlier organized field demonstration - that there is no 'across the board' approach and each extension body had to 'develop its specific objectives geared to the immediate as well as long term needs of the operational area' (Sevakram and Waghmare, 1986) - was carried over to the green revolution. The *segmented target,* in the case of the green revolution were farmers, whose entrepreneurship was noticeable, who had the means to procure necessary inputs, who were open to mechanization, and would follow the recommended agronomic practices, including irrigation. Having identified the market, the individual family needs and attitudes were surveyed in order to draw up a family specific operational plan. A good farm plan, as always, was expected to take 'stock of the farmers skill, knowledge and disliking and make room for sufficient flexibility in order that new opportunities such as new production techniques, a practice or a new post harvest method ...are availed of' (Sevakram and Waghmare, 1986). The scientists from the nearest agricultural universities and informed members of the district agricultural machinery, as has been stressed earlier, spearheaded the field demonstrations. A hierarchy of extension staff was specifically trained to motivate and transfer the prescribed agronomic practices directly to identified farmers and often through them to the potential prospects in each village. These 'contact farmers' were the opinion leaders and, in marketing terminology, the members of the distribution network. Training to the VEWs (Village Extension Workers) and a hierarchical pattern of work supervision were other important components of the programme. The VEWs were expected to visit the allocated families *as per a set schedule*. During such visits, as per an earlier established pattern, the VEWs encouraged the farmers to follow all the cropping recommendations, and at the same time, in order to generate a feedback, they were expected to 'listen as much as talk'.

Demonstration, the main tool used in agricultural extension continued to be stressed during the green revolution as it had the following advantages over other methods of motivation:

- It could be specifically targeted towards beneficiaries, who are similarly placed, if not on more than one criteria, at least in terms of physical resources,
- It could be based on micro planning – that is, through identifying the constraints in each area and developing strategies on that basis (somewhat akin to customer need identification),
- The beneficiaries could see for themselves the outcome within a finite period of time,
- They could also observe the entire process of achieving the result, and thereby comprehend the potential for similar replication in their own plots,
- The beneficiaries and observers could seek information and answer to their queries and doubts while the demonstration is going on, and
- The beneficiaries had not to change their traditional practice

and their feeling of time tested security in favour of something new; instead, the demonstrations could either be seen on someone else's land or on a portion of their own land.

- Provided research workers an 'opportunity to get first hand knowledge of the problems faced by the farmers'.
- Influenced all extension agencies working in an area.

> Approaching non-adopters within the target area and understanding the reasons for non-adoption is an important component of extension. The reasons discovered by Ram Krishan in 1965 still hold true in most situations today:
>
> *Some 25 to 40% of non-adopters belong to the class of subsistence farmers, with hardly any resources to deploy for improvement. Earning their daily bread is their main preoccupation. Credit facilities are also difficult to extend to them because of procedural requirements (eg., security or surety).
>
> *Some 20-30 per cent can be clubbed under the term 'psychologically inhibited'. These persons like to wait and see the result in other's fields. Sometimes, these persons like to go through 'mutations' rather than outright changes. Their children are often the change agents. (Notice the similarity of analysis with 'innovators, early adopters' etc. mentioned in Chapter 3)
>
> *Prevalent customs, traditions, and religious sentiments are another force against change. Ram Krishan found that *ex-military personnel could help overcome this.*

*Inadequate handling and motivation of influential persons of a community, resulting in them becoming 'behind-the-scene' de-motivators is another obstacle. 'It has been found that these 'progressive' individuals are progressive only when their own self-interest is concerned but are most unprogressive and conservative when it comes to spreading programmers to others' (Krishan, 1965).

*'Idle family members are also generally averse to new ideas'. These persons in a community are apt to discuss local issues over a hookah or cup of tea rather than pull up their dhotis and get to work.

Operation Flood

The white revolution or Operation Flood was the extension of the success story of the Khaira District Cooperative Milk Producers Union (KDCMPU) by replication, through similarly formed and operated cooperatives, throughout India. Some 170 such cooperatives have been set up, but their performance has not been alike; suggesting once again, that the basic raw material for any social programme is the people, and their receptivity and experience can hardly be replicated. At best, the techniques and tools of the trade can be shown, and some of the pitfalls avoided. In order, however, to understand the 'success' of Operation Flood, one needs to understand KDCMPU and its history.

India has always been a country with large numbers of livestock, comparable to the combined strengths of many countries. Yet, its milk production had not been as per international standards. Some pockets of India, however, have been managing their milk output better than the rest. According to researchers, one such area always rich in milk and ghee production was around Baroda, including Anand. As far back as 1892, 'Walter Reeves established a small butter manufacturing unit..' there, and the railway line between Anand and Bombay served as a very efficient milk marketing link (George, 1985). Including the military, Bombay was served by 'some 450 small dealers, each handling about a hundred litres daily'. At this time (1929), an enterprising private entrepreneur, Pestonjee Polson established a modern dairy with linkages to the hinterland producers. The name Polson's butter became household favourites, not only in Gujarat but elsewhere in the country. When the Greater Bombay Milk Scheme was inaugurated in 1945, the supply contract was signed with Polson.

According to Rameshbhai Patel, Chairman of KDCMPU, 'The prime objective of setting up Amul (the brand name for the cooperative and its products) was to free the milk producers of Khaira District from the clutches of private traders and their agents and protect their economic interests through this cooperative institution' (*Souvenir of Amul*, 1996). Tribhuvandas Patel, Amul's first Chairman, too was critical of the role of private traders and the inferior products offered by them. Private enterprise, prior to the establishment of Amul, had, according to him, 'things very much their way' and ' the result was that pure milk became impossible to obtain throughout India. Ghee that was not adulterated became an extremely rare commodity to find. No private dairy bothered very much to take steps necessary to help the farmers increase his production' (*Souvenir of Amul*, 1996). One researcher, (Shanti George), however, challenges this view point and suggests that the establishment of the KDCMPU was not actually on account of the assumed exploitative nature of private enterprise but because of other factors, primary of which, according to her, was the solidarity and clan feeling of the Patidar caste 'who perceived the marketing cooperative as a useful instrument with which to manoeuvre for economic advantage' (George, 1985). The Patidars, according to her are, and she quotes, 'a caste known for high mobility, a shrewd eye for business opportunity, excellent husbandry in agriculture, and above all a consuming ambition, combined with the necessary will to make money' (Nair, 1961). She also attributes this development to the initiative and support of national level figures like Sardar Patel and Morarji Desai. Neither of these explanations, for the purpose of this study however, provides a satisfactory answer to the question as to what sparked the milk producers to combine in the first place to change a social equilibrium. A cooperative was the mechanism, not the cause. Exploitation in any society is common; yet this is most often not enough to trigger a change movement. What was the catalyst, if there was indeed one, in Anand?

One possible answer could be that the basic desires of food, shelter, safety and so on (as per Maslow's scale) of the milk producers having been satisfied - as a result of the economic prosperity that milk production and marketing had brought about - they were at mental stage wherein they could receive, process and compare market information, and thereby come to the conclusion that the private traders were indeed pocketing as profit a major portion of what was rightly the producer's share. Because these producers, on account of their clan affiliations, behaved as a homogeneous segment, they could approach Tribhuvandas Patel, a self-less individual (a rare commodity even in those days) who had the foresight to suggest the formation of a cooperative. The fact that members of this caste had powerful political personalities, such as Sarder Bhallavbhai Patel and Morarji Desai, must have helped carry forward the 'felt need' of the milk producers into specific 'action'. Mr. S.S. Sunderan, Amul's Public Relations Officer agrees with this analysis. Indeed, so does Shanti George when she says that 'The KDCMPU may have grown out of the favourable soil of a rich milk tract near a thirsty metropolis, but it could not have reached its present dimensions without the nurturant sunshine and rain of political patronage' (George, 1985).

The story goes that the cooperative first began supplying milk to Polson's dairy, but then sensing success, it exerted pressure on its largest consumer, the Bombay Milk Supply Scheme, to procure its entire requirement from them and not from Polson. In order to enforce this, the producers stopped supply for about a fortnight, that is, till Bombay capitulated. On January 1952, the Bombay Milk Supply was forced to scrap the contract with Polson and entrust the entire supply responsibility to the KDCMPU. Meanwhile, anticipating the need for processing and preserving this perishable commodity, an ancient creamery lying unutilized was acquired in 1947, followed by the establishment of a new, modern pasteurization plant 1950. Then followed, what is known today as the successful Amul pattern of dairy management (which is not being discussed since it is not of direct relevance to marketing).

During the 1960s, when Europe was flooded with large stocks of unconsumed milk powder and butter-oil, India was considered the best outlet for it. India successfully negotiated with the European Economic Community to take the surplus as donation, but instead of simply flooding the market with these stocks, it was decided to route it through the National Dairy Development Board or NDDB. The NDDB thus came to be established in 1965 in the Anand district of Gujarat, the home of Amul. The NDDB would re-pack the donated milk and butter-oil after mixing it with indigenous production, and then distribute it all over India. In the process, it would make a handsome profit that would go towards the establishment of infrastructure for rural milk production-supply networks, pasteurizing and chilling centers, and for conversion into cheese, butter and so on. Indigenous milk production, it was planned, would be augmented by improving the quality of domestic stock and their feed. The established infrastructure would be able to take care of the increased production. Unforeseen or seasonal shortfalls only would be met through imports. In order to take up the financial aspects of the programme and to launch Operation Flood, the Indian Dairy Corporation (IDC) was established in Baroda in 1970.

The Anand pattern of village level producer's cooperatives, collecting and storing milk, and supplying to an apex level cooperative union for marketing was sought to be replicated nationally through the mechanism popularly known as Operation Flood. In the process, the traditional supply chains of petty traders was sought to be substituted by efficient management drawn on cooperative lines, with a network of motorized transport, backed by chilling and processing centers. The motivation to produce milk came by facilitating easy exchange (ready cash for milk twice a day at village level procurement points), by providing veterinary services at the doorstep, including stock upgradation through artificial insemination, and by supplying nutrient rich feed, again at the doorstep. Where the competition from food crops was not too overwhelming, producers set aside a part of their cropping area for growing fodder. Incidentally, it seems that the artificial inseminators, in the course of their work also carried the example and message of 'non-divinity of conception' and thereby promoted the concept of 'choice' in family planning. The Amul story is essentially the successful introduction of western, capital intensive, efficient, mass production technology to a well-experienced milk producing and consuming area with a receptive mind-set. Operation Flood was an extension of the Anand concept throughout the country. In general, the impression of success created by Operation Flood was due to the improved availability of milk in urban areas.

It has been suggested (George, 1985) that there were three pre-requisites for the efficient functioning of an organization like the Khaira District Cooperative Milk Producers Union (KDCMPU) and its dairy at Anand. Wherever such conditions have existed, the replication of the 'Anand pattern' has been somewhat possible. An analysis of the aforesaid three conditions, fortunately for this study, show distinct components of the marketing discipline, and to that extent, dilutes the author's disappointment at not finding overwhelming motivational inputs.

The first condition is that there should be a big market nearby to consume the milk. In other words, there is a 'need' and therefore, a 'demand'. The second condition is that there is a regular and substantial output of milk. This speaks of the availability of one or more product(s) to match the need and demand. The third condition is 'suitable facilities for procurement, processing, transport and distribution'. This component of 'marketing' needs no elaboration. In addition, there were two other conditions not mentioned in the quoted reference. First, there had to be a system of ensuring easy exchange between the producer and the procurer, and second, that replication would be successful where the psychographic conditions were similar.

Exact replication of the KDMPCU, however, can never be possible, as has been remarked earlier because social programmes do not deal with mechanical entities. In fact, the variations in milk procurement, even by similarly managed cooperatives has been substantial and not at all in proportion to their potential. Local innovations or lack of such have always played a major role. In recognition of this, according to Shanti George, milk cooperatives should 'evolve their own distinctive and contextually effective approach' and 'the 'real' KDMPCU formula, if there be any such beast, is simply this: to each locality, product, and group, the freedom to evolve its own pattern' (George, 1985).

'When discussing the re-creation of a cooperative like the KDMPCU, the human component is crucial: the physical elements such as collection centers, milk cans, and the tanker are less important than who the producers are and why they have decided to get together... On the other hand, when considering the replication of the dairy, technical considerations come to the fore...In purely physical terms, it is in fact easier to build a dairy than to create a cooperative, as buildings machinery and personnel can be procured with money unlike the desire to cooperate'. It is thus easy to identify managerial and infrastructural inputs in the white revolution, but not so easy to see the motivational components – motivation for the producer to join in the new set-up, to go in for improved strains of cattle, or to earmark a portion of cultivable land for fodder.

The real motivation for selling milk to the cooperative was the ready cash that it disbursed every following day. 'It may be asked why rural milk producers act against their own interests by selling fluid milk instead of ghee. The answer lies in their exigent need for cash on which agencies procuring milk can play' (George, 1985). Incentives have also been used for bonding the members to the cooperative. Milk producers are entitled to insurance against unforeseen deaths of their cattle, against accidents and ill health of their family members, and scholarships for their children. While the producer was happy that he or she was regularly getting a price that had been decided by the village cooperative and applicable equally to all, the consumers, mainly the urban housewife was happy that a semi-government agency was supplying her need for quality milk from convenient distribution points. No concerted motivational efforts seemed to have been made, or seemed to have succeeded if made at all, in weaning away all producers from the traditional supply-distribution chain.

In the context of KDCMPU, marketing inputs were necessary at two levels: at the time of motivating milk producers to join the cooperative pattern, including specific steps for increasing output, and at the consumer end. From available literature, it appears that the first part was tackled primarily through person-to-person contacts, enabling easy exchanges to take place (both price and place wise), by removing technical problems of short shelf life, non-uniform quality, and by offering a multiple set of processed products from the same stock. The second aspect, i.e., creating a brand name was achieved through easy availability (anytime, anyplace), product standardization, and by harping on the 'Taste of India'.

How did the traditional buyers take this change? As has been mentioned earlier, 'the main motivation' according to majority opinion, 'in promoting this organization [was] to exclude the traditional milk marketing agents (Nightingale: 1969). The traditional buyers of domestic milk [were] considered the 'leech sucking the blood of both the producer and the consumer'. Yet, the historical equilibrium was difficult to disturb and substitute. According to a World Bank study in 1978, 'Total sales of milk in urban areas presently approximates 15 million litres per day. Of this amount some 2.8 million litres per day is now being procured by cooperative and municipal dairies... The balance is supplied by traditional milk vendors'. According to Dr Kurien (1970) 'rural populations will continue to obtain their liquid milk and the bulk of their milk products from local and traditional sources'. In some areas, compromise solutions apportioning the procurement and distribution tasks, even including the traders as sub-agents of cooperatives were worked out. Operation Flood has not substituted the traditional distributive channels and producer-distributor-buyer equation and equilibrium. The study by Shanti George highlights that Operation Flood is certainly a gigantic venture in terms of investments, staff and expenses, yet 'this giant handles a pitiful amount of milk, some 6 percent of what is produced' in India, in 1978. It has now come to be accepted that traditional traders are not villains but players in a dynamic process that has grown over a very long period of time, need and consumer satisfaction/ acceptance.

KDCMPU has always faced another challenge. According to Dr. Verghese Kurien, the influence of local politicians and the bureaucracy was and remains the greatest challenge to the independent functioning of milk cooperatives. Most often, to the disadvantage of the milk producers, such persons cater to the needs of the urban consumers, thereby diluting the motivation to cooperate in producing and supplying milk. Likewise, the requirement of the government rules and regulations are restrictive rather than encouraging. 'We need genuine cooperatives, owned and controlled by their members and managed by real professionals (not bureaucrats). To achieve this we need new cooperative laws, laws that are enabling not prescriptive; laws that leave to the members the decisions that affect the resources they produce; laws that do not protect wrong doers; laws that do not allow political interest to hijack a business that is serving people regardless of language, religion, caste or political affiliation' (*Souvenir of Amul*, 1996).

The KDCMPU engages a large fleet of trucks to transport milk from village cooperatives to district and state and multi-state cooperatives and marketing outlets. On the return trips to the milk producers, such trucks transport cattle feed. *Yet, this business has not been organized in the form of cooperatives*! This absence perhaps lends credence to the suggestion that group similarity and therefore, cohesion may often vary even between programmes – a human trait that may be useful to remember.

Finally, from the point of view of this study, it is interesting to note that two of the stated objectives of the Operation Flood, relate to the satisfaction of *consumer's* rather than the *producer's* needs - this being the main criticism of the performance of the programme:

- 'To make available wholesome milk at stable and reasonable prices to the *bulk of city consumers*, including vulnerable groups, namely pre-school children, nursing and expectant mothers, etc. with major effects on protein intake;

- To enable the dairy organizations involved in the project to identify and satisfy the needs of the consumers and producers, so that *consumer's preferences* can be fulfilled economically and producers can earn a larger share of the price paid by consumers for their milk' (FAO: 1976).

It may be recalled that for the green revolution, the objective was increased production per se. The consumer's preference and the distribution network that will ensure that the produce will reach all consumers, far and near were not stressed. In Operation Flood, however, the 'dairy processing and marketing have been given higher priority over dairy production technology' (FAO, 1981) and it was 'designed less as a productive than a redistributive strategy.'

Characteristics	White Revolution	Green Revolution
Seed	Excess powdered milk and butter oil production and stock in Europe	Excess wheat production and stock in the USA
Coverage	Small, marginal farmers	Large, medium and enterprising farmers
Strategy	Capital-Intensive, Re-distributive & Market Oriented	Agronomy specific, technology based, irrigation and input dependent; producer oriented.

'The green revolution brought both augmented production and increased disparity; the white revolution promised the former without the latter, and further claimed to narrow the gap between rich and poor that the green revolution was responsible for widening' (George, 1985).

From the aforesaid history and working of Operation flood, we can pick up the following threads that may have a bearing on our social marketing study:

- One can *build on the strong kinship feeling* among the segmented market, even if it involves presently disgraced concept of 'castes',
- Social movements depend on the *attitudinal stage* of the targeted beneficiaries,
- It is worthwhile to strive for the consistent *backing* of leading public figures,
- It is impractical to disturb a long-standing social equilibrium by removing all those who gain from it and substituting it with an arrangement or organization that is perceived to be more efficient and transparent. A practical approach suggests the working out of a mutually beneficial compromise.
- Door-to-door motivational approach coupled with service can work wonders.
- Just because one programme has succeeded in a segment, it does not necessarily imply that other programmers will easily succeed therein. There can, at best, be a greater *chance* of success.
- It is easier to create infrastructure than influence mindsets. Physical achievements are easier to monitor and reflect as yardsticks of success. There is thus a natural tendency to build in all extension and expansion programmers whereas, success will depend equally, if not largely on psychographic similarity, motivation, training, team building and service.

The Universal Immunization Programme.

One Government Programme, which has been acknowledged to have achieved great success, is the UIP or Universal Immunization Programme. Launched in 1985, it aimed at providing immunization coverage to infants and pregnant mothers against diseases like polio, diphtheria, tetanus, and tuberculosis. The success of the application of the Oral Polio Vaccine (OPV), and the mass response it has generated, every time there has been a call (in spite of the fact that such calls are continuing with no consensus on the number of OPV doses required for full and permanent immunization) has been remarkable.

According to one study, the success of this programme can be attributed to a communication strategy that reached the individual as a part of a family, community, and as a part of the nation. 'Within such a media strategy there is little scope for any person to totally escape the message specifically addressed to him/her' (www.social-marketing.org). While the lay persons were addressed through messages carried by all the presently recognized static and active forms, question-answer booklets 'which did not read like prescriptions sent from the top and without outright discrediting the anxieties of the readers' (Singh and Bharadwaj, 2000) were designed for the semi-educated as well as the educated. Alliances between the family and the community were established by organizing immunization programmes during social and religious occasions and functions. The media messages were so structured as to represent health and the absence of disease on the one hand, and easy cure through simple means on the other. Often 'shock therapy', depicting the horrific effects of vaccine preventable diseases was resorted to (www.social-marketing.org).

According to a pediatrician (Dr. P. Chowdhury of the Maulana Azad Institute of Health Sciences, New Delhi) directly involved in the OPV programme, there were two main reasons for the mass acceptance of the programme:

1. The fear of polio, a lifelong, crippling disease, and

2. A hassle-free preventive:

   a) requiring just a visit to a nearby school/ health center, and

   b) a trouble free application.

Like all social development programmes, the UIP too has faced competitions in the form of misinformation and rumour campaigns. According to Satyajit Sarkar, an official of the WHO, 'there are rumours that polio drops cause impotence, AIDS, paralysis and even death. Believing these, patients in these states (Bihar and Utter Pradesh) have stayed away from the immunization programme' (*Times of India*, 2001). On the other hand, the UIP is the programme for which, the Shahi Imam of the Jama Masjid of Delhi has publicly come out to lend his full support. The UIP coverage in the country, according to Mr. Sarkar, is a phenomenal 98.5 per cent.

New Programmes- The National Population Policy 2000

Background.

It was the Bhore committee report of 1946 that first suggested a high priority to maternal and child health services. But India's population control programme owes its origin to the first All India Population and Family Planning Conference held in Bombay in 1951. Though this conference was followed by debates in the national media and Parliament on the subject, it seems that there was divergence of views at the policy making levels as to the relative importance that this should be given vis-à-vis other programmes. Pandit Jawaharlal Nehru was of the opinion that there is no conflict between economic growth and population control. He wrote that,

'I do not agree with those who suggest that we should attach even more importance to population growth than to economic growth', and believed that, 'an increase in the standard of living of the people will help in reducing the rate of population increase' (Chandrasekhar, 1961). Others believed that, 'excessive population growth defers or nullifies most programmes for improvement in education, public health, sanitation and rural recovery' (Chandrasekhar, 1961). According to Sir Julian Huxley, way back in 1955, 'it is a mere wish fulfillment to suppose that such measures (agricultural and industrial development), either singly or in combination, can solve India's population problem'. In other words, population control strategies remained non-focused.

The first Five Year Plan (1951-56) that followed the aforementioned conference 'cleared the air by conceding that the country had a population problem and that Family Planning was an acceptable solution to it' (Chandrasekhar, 1961). 'While many of the suggestions and recommendations of the First Five Year Plan were shelved for various reasons, important experiments in the rhythm method were carried out during the plan period. These experiments were useful in the sense that they demonstrated the ineffectiveness of the rhythm method, which therefore could be put aside as a serious method of Family Planning for the nation' (Chandrasekhar, 1961). The main recommendations of the first plan covered the following (Chandrasekhar, 1961), and to that extent is in consonance with modern marketing management:

- Collection from representative sections of the population of information on reproductive patterns, attitudes and motivations affecting the size of the family. (Need for Survey)
- Study on the inter-relationships between socio-economic factors and population changes. (Survey output analysis, perhaps segmentation)
- Progress in the field of family planning would depend upon

the creation of a sufficiently strong motivation and inculcation of need for birth control. Development of suitable procedures to educate different sections of the people on family planning methods. (Promotion and communication)

- Conducting field experiments on, collecting and studying information about different methods of family planning. (Product analysis)
- Provision of acceptable, harmless, cheap and efficient methods for birth control. (Product availability)
- Making such information available to professional workers, especially in the health centers so that they can provide the necessary advice to married couples and especially women visiting these centres. (Establishing and strengthening distribution mechanisms)

The second Five Year Plan (1956-61) recommended the continuation of the programme which was started in the first plan, but on an increased scale (Chandrasekhar, 1961). It was realized that the rural sector had to be catered to in terms of reach. The following would continue to be the main areas of focus:

- Demographic research, including socio-economic inter-relationships, attitudes, motivations affecting the size of the family.
- Research in human fertility for the purpose of regulation.
- Training of personnel.
- Public education on family planning and population problems.
- Grants to State Governments, local authorities and voluntary organizations for opening family planning clinics.

During the sixties, beginning with the third Five Year Plan

(1961-66) the family planning programme was extended on the earlier pattern with one important change: family planning was integrated with general health service and a Department of Family Planning was established.

> This Third Plan document also highlighted issues like:
>
> 'It is the poor and underprivileged with large families who desperately need assistance in family planning, but who are denied access to it because of poverty and ignorance and cultural inhibitions. They are the least equipped for the rearing of the nation's future citizens; and yet, often, it is these poor families who contribute more than their proportion of the next generation. Thus the under-privileged, who are a majority in all these areas tend to become greater majorities through progressive differential birthrates. And the children are usually even more handicapped than others' (Chandrasekhar, 1961).
>
> 'In rural societies, from the communal point of view, the advantages of large families seem to outweigh the disadvantages. Every mouth brings with it a pair of hands' (Chandrasekhar, 1961).
>
> Surveys from as far back as 1951 (Chandrasekhar, 1961) show that a majority of couples are in favour of avoiding or postponing pregnancies and were keen to know how this could be done.
>
> 'Thus an extended family (the Kibbutz in Israel is an extreme example) is a cultural barrier to birth

control in the sense that the children do not effectively compete for time with various other activities in which the parents might be interested. In large, traditional families such as the joint family in India, and the extended family in China, the normal economic deterrent to the arrival of the extra baby does not operate' (Chandrasekhar, 1961).

'Though religious attitudes, which are fluid and flexible, towards family size are equally if not more important in moulding certain patterns of behaviour, they are not insuperable barrier to family planning' (Chandrasekhar, 1961). The example of Indonesian clerics supporting wholeheartedly that Nation's family planning programme is a telling example. The Church blessing religious wars is another example.

'A barren wife is considered an inauspicious person in all religious and ceremonial functions, even when the sterility may not be her fault' (Chandrasekhar, 1961).

Following the important change in strategy i.e., inclusion of family planning within considerations of overall health, the seventies saw an emphasis on the improvement of the nutritional status of women and children through an improvement in the primary health infrastructure in the country (*Ninth Five Year Plan Document, Vol II,* 1997-2002). Doses of Vitamin A, anaemia prophylaxis, food supplementation to pregnant mothers and children, distribution of contraceptives and sterilization were all offered through the primary health structures set up far and wide. Even though the 'census of 1971 showed that population explosion was no longer a potential threat but a major problem to be solved', family planning was included as a priority sector. Subsequently, the 'programme was renamed as Family Welfare; increasing integration of family planning services with those of MCH (Maternal and Child Health) and nutrition was attempted (*Ninth Five Year Plan Document*, 1997-2002). The adverse high point of this decade was the political backlash of the drive and attempt at compulsory sterilization (1976).

The eighties showed a greater thrust at reaching the integrated family welfare services to the doorsteps. Health infrastructure at all levels was increased and strengthened. The achievements during the eighth plan were not noteworthy in terms of goals. Between 1992 and 1996, the number of sterilizations remained unaltered; there had been an increase in IUD and OC (Pills) till 1995-96 and condoms till 1994-95 (*Ninth Five Year Plan Document*, 1997-2002). However, the combined effect of all the plans was a reduction of the Crude Birth Rate (CBR) from 40.8 in 1951 to 29.5 in 1991. *The nineties saw the recognition of the need for 'flexibility in programme planning and implementation'* (*Ninth Five Year Plan Document*, 1997-2002) *in view of 'area specific socioeconomic, demographic and other differentials.* The steady decline in CBR in this decade in spite of a slow rise in Couple Protection Rate suggested that there was a 'qualitative improvement in providing appropriate contraception at the right time'. An important revelation during the formulation of the ninth plan was that the country's demographic pattern is such that 'the number of births will not alter during the next two decades' (*Ninth Five Year Plan Document*, 1997-2002). It was, therefore, decided that during this period the stress should be on *providing 'high quality of services'*. This, accordingly, was the main thrust in the ninth plan (1997-2002). A table indicates the critical aspects of the family planning status on the eve of the ninth plan formulation, the strategy adopted, and the proposed action plan:

9th Plan Vol II, 1997-2002

STATUS	STRATEGY	ACTION-PLAN
*High growth rate due to size of population in the reproductive age group (estimated contribution 60%) * High fertility due to unmet need (estimated at 20%) *High IMR, therefore high 'wanted fertility'	* Assess needs for RCH at PHC level and undertake area specific Microplaning. * Provide need based, demand-driven, high quality, integrated RCH care.	* Bridge gap in infrastructure and manpower. * Invest in Social behavioural and operational research. * Ensure uninterrupted supply of essential drugs, vaccines, contraceptives, adequate in quantity and quality. * Promote male participation in the planned parenthood movement. * Increase participation of general medical practitioners in voluntary, joint sectors and from alternative systems of medicine. * Involve Panchayati Raj Institutions in planning, coordination, monitoring and management. * Involve industries, organized and unorganized sectors, agriculture workers, labour representatives.

It would be seen that the items included in the action plan have many marketing oriented inputs. These need, however, to be extended and structured in a sequence, and that will be proposed and attempted later on. The most noteworthy output during the ninth plan period was the formulation of the National Population Policy 2000. This also subsequently, will be discussed in detail. It is in the background of the afore-discussed programmes and plans that one can introduce the concept of social marketing.

What is social marketing?

Social Marketing is the design, implementation, and control of programmes seeking to increase the acceptability of a social idea, cause or practice among a target group (Kotler and Armstrong, 1994). A more operational definition for the purpose of this study suggests that it 'is the planning and implementation of programmes designed to bring about social change *using concepts from commercial marketing*' (www.social-marketing.org).

Kotler and Zaltman are reported to have introduced the term 'social marketing' with the publication of an article in 1971, as an extension of or another dimension to conventional marketing. Yet, it may be recalled that the marketing of contraceptives on commercial lines took root in India as early as 1960 with the publication of a document called 'Proposals for Family Planning Promotion: A Marketing plan' by the Indian Institute of Management (IIM), Kolkata (Calcutta). According to Philip D. Harvey, the President of DKT International, 'the "proposals" spread back to business and management science circles in the United States through MIT's Sloan School of Management and Harvard Business School connections. Through the Ford Foundation, the proposals quickly reached major donors and population study centers, to whom Ford was often the major donor' (Harvey, 1999). *It would thus appear that though Philip Kotler and Zaltman were the first to introduce social marketing as a concept in 1971, the basic work on the subject had been initiated in India some eleven years earlier!*

Marketing interventions at the social level have, however, been made for quite some time, without labeling them as part of a discipline. 'Social marketing is a new way of thinking about some very old human endeavours. As long as there has been social systems, there have been attempts to inform, persuade, influence, motivate, to gain acceptance for or new adherence to, certain sets of ideas; to promote causes and to win over particular groups; to reinforce behaviour or to change it – whether by favour, argument or force. So, social marketing certainly has some deep roots in religion and politics, education and even, to a degree, in military strategy. It also has intellectual roots in disciplines such as psychology, sociology, political science, communication theory and anthropology. And practical roots in disciplines such as advertising, public relations, and market research, and in the work and experience of social activists, advocacy groups and community organizers' (Young, 1988-89).

During the 70s, the social marketing concept was explored and discussed, and accepted as an adjunct to broad-based marketing. By the 1980s, the 'academics were no longer asking whether marketing should be applied to social sciences, but rather how should this be done' ('What is Social Marketing?' www.csm.strath.ac.uk). It became obvious that just inputs from diverse disciplines like sociology, religion, political science, information and communication did not directly result in a change of behaviour. All these had to be assimilated in a discipline, and applied on the pattern of business marketing. It is only since the 90s, that the concept transgressed the domain of the academics into those of the practitioners especially 'in the public health field, generating lively debates about its applicability and contribution' ('What is Social Marketing?' www.csm.strath.ac.uk). Lately, it has been suggested that social marketing must distinguish itself from commercial marketing in that its primary aim is the interest of the society, rather than the interest of the marketer (Andreasen, 1995). The bottom line, however, remains the market, and social marketing aims to change market behaviour in tune with a social cause, and for doing this, it needs to follow a set of techniques perfected by the world of commercial marketing.

'While for generic marketing the ultimate goal is to meet shareholder objectives, for the social marketer the bottom line is to meet society's desire to improve its citizen's quality of life' ('What is Social Marketing?' www.csm.strath.ac.uk). Indeed, social marketing can have different objectives. For instance, it can aim at introducing an *understanding* of a social theme like the need for preventive health or nutrition, or seek to *change the behavioral pattern* like use of tobacco, or seek to bring about a *change in a fundamental belief* such as a large family may not be the best social security for parents in their old age, or aim to trigger a *one time or short time action* like cleaning of a village or de-silting of a tank. Some may market (actually sell) socially relevant commodities like improved wood burning stoves, solar cookers, condoms, etc., but not just for profit. When a business organization markets a social idea without any linkage to organizational profit (a family planning programme for its workers for instance), it is social marketing. If, however, it markets an idea, which indirectly helps in marketing its product (dental hygiene for the purpose of marketing toothbrushes for example), it cannot strictly be termed social marketing.

As has been remarked elsewhere, 'exchange' is an essential component of marketing. 'Exchange is easily understood as the exchange of goods for money, but can also be conceived in a variety of other ways: further education in return for fees; a vote in return for lower taxes; or immunization in return for peace of mind that one's child is protected from rubella' ('What is Social Marketing?' www.csm.strath.ac.uk). *Hence, exchange in the social marketing concept is an exchange of modified behavior in return for good health or good living.*

Quite obviously, social policies and programmes that aim to bring about a change in the lifestyle and value system of a person are most difficult to market. In the case of family planning, it could involve not only major changes in behaviour and family life; it can also go against entrenched social equilibrium and religious beliefs. While social marketing acknowledges that social norms are influenced by a multitude of factors and most often, a simple solution is just not there, yet it suggests a systematic and structured approach to a problem, and *offers solutions that are essentially people-centric.* 'Social marketing acknowledges the fundamental difficulty of promoting social change, and so it views the process as one that requires careful analysis, effective planning, sustained effort and a broad array of tactics' (Young, 1988-89).

Various organizations work for the social sector. However, one rarely comes across any that goes through the rigours of the marketing discipline for marketing a social sector programme or idea. Behavioural change in all such programmes have been sought to be brought about by techniques variously termed as 'extension' as in agriculture, or education, or participation, or promotion (as in health), or information-education-communication, and so on. Each of them assume the predominance of a particular aspect of change, and stress on that rather than consider behavioural change as an integrated effort, keeping in mind the 'stage of change' as the approach to the market focus. The educationists, for instance, believe that informing and educating individuals can bring about change. Conversely, they assume that people are not changing because they are unaware. What moves the aware into action is left unsaid. The extension approach believes that change can be brought about through examples: seeing is supposed to be the best motivation. However, these are the essentials of the 'seller's approach' and in this lie the danger of pushing something which the participant may never see to be important. This technique has worked well in promoting the green revolution, but only where the ground and the mind was fertile; it could not motivate farmers in the eastern part of the country. Similarly, the 'participationists' believe that the people themselves, urged by a trained facilitator, must realize their problems and also the solutions. How the change will come about, they believe, will emerge organically in the process. The Information, Education & Communication (IEC) group believe in the combined strengths of information, education, and communication. Again, the understanding of the process of shifting from one stage behaviour to the other, overcoming the 'barriers' to change, and finally to change-action is left unstructured.

Social marketing has elements of all these techniques and approaches, but never looses sight of the following:

- That it is cost efficient to deal with homogeneous groups of people rather than individuals. Hence, *market segmentation is essential.*
- That *obstructions or competition has to be addressed* before any change from awareness to positive action can be brought about.
- That *the product or idea to be put across must be relevant to the market* – predominantly from the customer's point of view; indeed, some would assert *only* from their point of view.
- That the effort the consumer is being asked to make, and the monetary price to be paid will be well worth the perceived benefit.
- The product and services should be easily available, thereby offering a choice.
- The most logical use of media and personal communication should be used for the entire exercise.
- That all action should be pre-tested, systematically monitored during implementation, and the emerging and necessary changes be incorporated.

Social marketing relies heavily on understanding behaviour and on fostering behavioural change. Social marketers believe that 'because influencing behaviour is social marketing's fundamental objective, the discipline can be applied to a wide range of topics and audiences' (Andreasen, 1995). *The techniques and tools are not elemental in its application or importance.*

The National Population Policy 2000 has been studied from the point of view of the marketing concept. The following Table 4-1 indicates the result in a tabular form. The policy approach vis-à-vis the prescriptions of social marketing, are commented below. In Chapter 6, the family planning programme will be suggested on the social marketing format. (It is emphasized that there will be no attempt to comment on the family planning programme as it is being run; it is just an exercise in applying the social marketing techniques with its help).

Comments:

- It would be seen from the Table, especially under strategy and action points, that most of the essential components of commercial marketing have indeed, been included. To be sure, the number of items under distribution and communication/ promotion are overwhelming in comparison to the rest. The issues, however, are not in the sequence dictated by the marketing discipline. From the point of view of social marketing, something more crucial seems to be missing – the overall need to focus on the needs, aspirations, problems (competitions) of major and locally relevant segments of the market, and the layout of solutions as per their expectations. The NPP 2000 approach is what could be considered 'organization centered'; whereas the social marketing approach is customer centered.
- A policy document, understandably can only suggest a broad pattern based on an overall assessment of the problem and the prospects. According to the Action Plan for One Year 2000-2001 document (the portion dealing with the recommendations for the Corporate and Private sector), the 'National Population Policy, 2000 should be used as a blueprint to enable all partners/stakeholders to guide their

own efforts. The implementation of NPP would require imaginative thinking and coordinated effort from all stakeholders. Just outlining the policy is not enough.' It would thus appear that national level action plans have to be translated to field level plans. The Policy conceives that this is to be done by the Panchayati Raj Institutions, under guidance. There is thus a case for initiating social marketing plans.

- The Policy appears not to have commented on the need for surveys at the implementation level and of the beneficiaries/ market, so as to selectively carry out the strategy and action plan for optimal effect. In the absence of this, one is apt to miss out at the very least – and if one may put it thus - the affected trees for the wood. However, this aspect has been included in the ninth plan strategy in the form of 'operational research' and hence should be read together.
- In the absence of a survey, the greater danger is that the locally relevant reasons why persons are not availing the population stabilization measures will not become apparent. Unless the disadvantages or costs of the suggested behaviour change is reduced and the benefits increased, the shift of the market having taken place from knowledge to action, that too in a sustained manner will be difficult.
- Survey would also identify the 'stage of behaviour and need' perception of the segmented market. In the absence of this, effective communication strategies will be difficult to plan. Moreover, the opportunities for redress, at the right time and with the right product(s) will be ad hoc.
- The importance of regular and continuous field-testing and feedback need also to be in focus.
- The importance of the 'product', including the service component has been referred to in both the policy document as well as the plans, but does not come out prominently. Product quality, after sales service especially, and issues of

'atmospherics' are important components of commercial and social marketing.

- Specialised medical help at village level is contemplated. Yet, this is known to be impractical as doctors, after rigorous medical study, are generally not willing to serve in rural areas. Their 'competition' needs to be squarely addressed. Local administrators should be encouraged to go beyond the suggestions made in the policy document.
- Appendix IV of the Policy document projects the following shortfalls in infrastructure and qualified manpower:
  - Health infrastructure:
    - 23190 sub-centres
    - 4212 primary health centers
    - 3776 community health centers (1st referral unit)
  - Trained manpower:
    - 27501 ANMs
    - 64860 male multipurpose workers
    - 4224 lady health visitors
    - 5126 male health assistants
    - 2475 medical officers in PHCs
    - 1429 surgeons
    - 1446 gynaecologists
    - 1525 physicians
    - 1774 pediatricians
    - 6635 other specialists
    - 1171 radiographers
    - 6045 pharmacists
    - 12793 laboratory technicians
    - 18851 nurse mid-wives

These shortages have increased in the last decade and are likely to increase further according to the increase in population. Hence, the practicability of basing a population control policy and plan on fully meeting the shortfall in the 'distribution network' is debatable. Strengthening distribution, even if physically and financially possible, is a residual of the 'selling' approach – believing that a product will sell if made available. According to Philip Kotler, 'the number of births averted may be higher if the Indian government spends its funds to advertise family planning nationwide rather than using all its money to set up efficient distribution' (Kotler, 1975). Moreover, even if 'lack of infrastructure' has been identified as the cause for unmet demand for family planning services, it does not address the root issue and therefore, does not guarantee that doctors will be available when such infrastructure comes into being.

Investing in infrastructure is a measurable way of programme achievement and reflects the thinking prevalent in many social programmes (including Operation Flood) that physical infrastructure improves performance. So, even if the desirability of re-working the population-infrastructure-work norms is not stressed for the present, an alternate approach could very well be to go for home or community based contraception – condoms and pills to begin with; IUDs with trained staff; and injectables and implants as and when these may be permitted by the law in force – supported by the existing government and private infrastructure.

- Hands-on social marketing requires effective communication and promotion. It not only believes that the demand for a product or service has to be generated, the entire process of movement from 'knowledge' to a positive 'attitude' to a change in favour of positive 'behaviour' is more relevant and essential. While the Policy document has a lot of suggestions on communication and promotion, unless such activities are related to the specific requirements of the target, there is every possibility of a lot of expenditure being incurred on the subject without commensurate results.

- The 'Objectives' stated in the Policy document suggests that the motivational work is over ('achieved universal awareness of the need for and methods of family planning' – p.1) and only 20% is the estimated 'unmet' need (B9). This statement and the figure need re-confirmation at every working level. Since only 44% of the eligible couples are protected, the rest 55%, even if fully aware, have to be motivated towards specific action. Further, within this, there are about 20% couples in the reproductive age group who are neither contraceptive users or come under the category of unmet need. They are the 'fence sitters' or probably in the contemplative stage. This group has also to be targeted. Social marketers would pay attention to all the different categories including the programme adopters, and would design different approaches for each of them.

The population control policy takes a wide, integrated view of family welfare and therefore, prescribes objectives and strategies that cover the entire range: from the pre-natal, post-natal, adolescent, girl-child, women, and men, to geriatric care. The logic is that an integrated approach will indirectly result in motivation for and adoption of a small family norm. In marketing terms, the 'product mix and range' is very vast and it has to be cautioned that taking up the promotion of too many products should not become counter productive or competitors to each other (Weinberg and Ritchie, 1999). *It may be justified from the point of view of optimal resource utilization to include in the package just those items that the localized survey indicates are crucial for achieving success in the family planning programme.*

From the discussions in this chapter, it would be seen that organizations promoting social programmes are, indeed, following many of the techniques and tools of marketing, but either randomly, or non-sequentially, or superficially. Bits and pieces do not help make a whole picture. Social marketing suggests that the marketing exercise be taken up systematically. The last chapter illustrates how.

CHAPTER 3 TABLE 1

Conventional Marketing Inputs	National Population Policy 2000
Market Analysis	
Segmentation Geographic Demographic Psychographic	Available data used. Need for segmentation and targeting at district levels not discussed.
Analysis & Market positioning	(B9) Momentum of population increase will continue because 58% of the population is in their reproductive years. India has 168 million couples. 44% are effectively protected. 20% needs are unmet. Another 36% not covered. High IMR. Therefore high fertility need. 50% of girls marry before 18. Therefore, early introduction to fertility. 33% births occur at intervals of less than 24 months. (C27) Men play a critical role in determining the education and employment of family members, age of marriage, besides access to and utilization of health, nutrition, and family welfare services for women and children.

Marketing Programme Development	
Image and goodwill	Not discussed
Product decisions Idea generation Concept development Product development Test marketing Product launching	Not discussed except for suggesting more contraceptive technology research.
Price decisions Profit maximization Cost recovery	Not discussed
Incentive pricing	(G44) Preventive and promotive services will continue to be subsidized. Increase compensation for tubectomy from Rs 200 to Rs 300 and vasectomy from Rs 180 to Rs 200.*
Disincentive pricing	Not discussed
Place/Storage/ Distribution decisions	(C12) An equipped maternity hut in each village. (C25) Provide mobile clinics for tribal communities, hill populations and displaced and migrant populations. (H46) Wider, affordable choice of contraceptives with counseling services will be available at diverse delivery points. Creches and child care centers will be opened in rural areas and urban slums.

	(20/14)Develop maternal hospitals as First Referral Units (FRU)s at sub-district levels, for complicated and life threatening deliveries. *((20/17)Create a national network of public, private and NGO centers, identified by a common logo for providing free service, on the basis of a national standard and, reimbursable rates.*
Intermediate agents	(C12) Promote mobile services. Involve voluntary and non-governmental sectors, in partnership, to increase static and mobile services. Increase in the number of trained birth attendants to at least two per village. Listing of village level functionaries for coordinated service delivery.] *(16/2) Implement at village level a one-stop, integrated and coordinated service delivery package.* (C21) Services of a National Technical Committee to be set up for neonatal care. (C22) Extension of the services of the Baby Friendly Hospital Initiative (BFHI) to the sub-centre levels. (C23) Encourage and strengthen local initiatives for ambulance service. Encourage innovative social marketing schemes for affordable products and services. (C25) Provide mobile clinics for tribal

	communities, hill populations and displaced and migrant populations. (H46) Soft loans will be provided for running ambulance services. (C28) Increase and diversify the categories of health care providers. Accredit private practitioners to provide beneficiary specific health care services, revive the system of licensed medical practitioners after appropriate certification by the Indian Medical Association (IMA). (C30-31) Mainstream the resource available under the Indian System of Medicine through appropriate training and skill development etc. (C32) Strengthen the International Institute of Population Sciences. (F40-43) Following structures recommended for set up: *National Commission on Population *State/UT Commission on Population *Coordination Cell in Planning Commission. *Technology Mission in Department of Family Welfare for focused attention, particularly on weaker states. Self-employment to girls through vocational training will be encouraged.

	Soft loans to ensure mobility to ANMs will be increased. *(24-25/1)Explore contractual engagement of private medical practitioners whose credentials are certified by the IMA, with proper monitoring and checks and balances. Their services can be payable by designated agencies.* *Involve retired defence personnel, retired school teachers etc. in advocacy and counseling.*
Communication & Promotion	(C24-25) Spread awareness, through education campaigns, about health care facilities available for urban slum population, and tribal communities, displaced and migrant populations and hill peoples. (C26) Information, counseling, education to adolescents who constitute about one fifth of the population. (C27)Information and education campaigns focused on men for promoting the small family norm. (C23)Encourage advocacy for affordable products and services in locally relevant and acceptable dialects. (C36) Information and education campaigns to be taken up on the model of total literacy campaigns. (E38) Enlist the support of prominent

	public personalities to the small family norm. *(19/10) Support community activities on Information, Education & Communication (IEC).* *(22/13)Promote primary education and through education, promote awareness, late marriage, small family norm, child survival etc.* *(28)Converge IEC efforts across the social sectors and encourage:* • *Optimal use of every possible media.]* • *Extend coverage and outreach through established organizational networks, and their field functionaries.* • *Fund nagar palikas, panchayats, NGOs, and community organizations for interactive and participative IEC activities.* • *Support to the small family norm by political, community, business, professional, and religious leaders, media and film stars, sports personalities and opinion makers, including by personal example.* • *Involve the civil society for IEC, counseling and monitoring.*
Advertisement Media selection Theme selection Evaluation	[Special campaign through TV and radio including spots, folk music programmes, plays etc., Production of two full length feature films by eminent Directors, one in Hindi, one in Tamil and theatrical

	release of two feature films produced last year, Special mass media campaigns on non-scalpel vasectomy, Workshops, orientation and study tours for journalists, Parliamentarians, and Legislators .... will be initiated. Consultation with social editors and media representatives recommends: • That electronic media need to dwell more forcefully on the negative consequences of population growth. • Extensive use of local radio channels. • Professionalize the IEC works by involving people from the media as the quality of health communication programmes broadcast and telecast through the radio and TV is too poor. • Mere advocacy through TV and Radio on general issues was not enough and advertisements should be directed at specific segments of the population, that needs close attention.]*
Personal contact Selling	(C14) Panchayats should seek the help of community opinion makers to communicate the benefits of smaller, healthier families, the significance of educating girls, and promoting female

	participation in paid employment.
	(C21) Promotion of breast and complimentary feeds by BFHI.
	(C36) Effectively convey family welfare messages on the pattern of the literacy campaigns, involving artists, film stars, doctors, vaidyas, hakims, nurses, local midwives, women's and youth organizations.
	(1913) Educate on, and expand availability of, safe abortion facilities. Strengthen control and enforcement mechanisms.
	(21/4) After birth of a child, provide counseling about contraception, encourage adoption of a reversible or a terminal method.
	(21/10) Motivate mothers below poverty levels to have their first child after 21 and to adopt terminal methods of contraception after the second child.
Servicing, and feedback	(22/1) Strengthen, energize and make publicly accountable the cutting edge of health infrastructure.
	(C12) Convergence of service delivery at village levels.
	(C21) Training of birth attendants by BFHI.
	(C22) Significant improvements in the quality and coverage of routine immunization programme needed.
	(C23) Strengthen, energise and make

	accountable the cutting edge of health infrastructure to improve facilities for referral transportation. (C35) Sensitize health service for geriatric care *(19/8) Improve monitoring of:* ❏ *Incidence and coverage of anti-natal visits* ❏ *Deliveries attended by trained personnel.* ❏ *Post-natal visits.*
Incentives	(C11) National recognition to Panchayats demonstrating exemplary performance. (C26) Enforcement of the Child Marriage Restraint Act 1976 (disincentive). (H46) Cash incentive to first and second girl child @ Rs 500 will continue. Cash incentive to mothers aged 19 years and above upto two children @ Rs 500 will continue, but subject to compliance with antenatal check-up, institutional delivery by trained birth attendant, registration of birth and BCG immunization. Health insurance for couples below poverty line that undergoes sterilization with not more than two children living, to cover

	hospitalization and personal accident insurance not exceeding Rs 5000. Reward to couples below poverty line, observing certain norms of marriage and childbirth. Revolving fund to village self-help, health care *and neighbourhood acceptor groups (16/1)* for setting up income generation activities. Creches and child care centers will be opened in rural areas and urban slums. *(23/8) Link the continuance of facilities to urban slum dwellers to the observance of small family norms.* (disincentive/ incentive)
Atmospherics	Not discussed.
Programme Administration	
Organisation Level	Focus on village levels through village panchayat; support from district and state. Partnership with non-governmental bodies.
Planning and control	(C11, F39) Bottom-up planning from panchayati raj and nagar palika institutions in coordination with State and UT administrations. [Workshops will be organized to prepare the District action plan.]*

	(Other items are indicated under 'Action Plan'.)
Objectives	(A1)The overriding objective of economic and social development is to improve the quality of lives that people lead, to enhance their well being, and to provide them with opportunities and choices to become productive assets in society. (B1) Immediate objective is to address the *unmet needs* for contraception, health care infrastructure, and health personnel, and to provide integrated service delivery for basic reproductive childcare. Medium-term objective is to bring the TFR to replacement levels by 2010, through vigorous implementation of intersectoral operational strategies. Long-term objective is to achieve a stable population by 2045. (B8) Goals for 2010: (1) Address unmet needs for services, supplies and infrastructure. 2) Make school education upto age 14 compulsory; reduce dropouts at primary and secondary school levels to below 20% for both boys and girls. (3) Reduce infant mortality to below 30 per 1000 live births.

	(4) Reduce maternal mortality rate to below 100 per 100,000 live births (5) Achieve universal immunization of children against all vaccine preventable diseases. (6) Promote delayed marriage for girls; not before 18; preferably after 20. (7) Achieve 80% institutional deliveries and 100% by trained persons. (8) Achieve universal access to information/ counseling, services for fertility regulation and contraception with a wide basket of choices. (9) Achieve 100% registration of births, deaths, marriage and pregnancies. (10) Contain spread of AIDs, promote integration of management of AIDs, RTI and STI (11) Prevent & control communicable diseases. (12) Integrate Indian System of Medicines into reproductive and child health services and in reaching out to households. (13) Promote small family norm to achieve replacement levels of TFR (14) Bring about convergence of social sector programmes to that of family welfare.

Strategy	(C11) Decentralized planning and programme implementation by panchayati raj institutions. (C12) Convergence of service delivery at village levels. (C15-19) Interventions for improved women's health and nutrition. Empowerment of women. Involvement of voluntary organizations in both. (C21) Intensify neo-natal care. Setting up of a National Technical Committee for prescribing perinatal audit norms, developing quality improvement activities with monitoring schedules, facilitating continuing nursing and medical training to all perinatal health care providers. (C23) Meet the unmet needs for family welfare services in both rural and urban areas. (C24) Provide basic health, reproductive and childcare needs to nearly 100 million people who live in urban slums, and tribal communities. (C26) Specific programmes to cover the needs for education, counseling and services for adolescents. Enforcement of the Child Marriage Restraint Act 1976 (C28) Increase and diversify the categories of health care providers. (C29) Need to put in place a

	partnership of non-government voluntary organizations, the private corporate sector, government and community. (C30-31) Mainstream the resource available under the Indian System of Medicine through appropriate training and skill development etc.. (C32)Advance, encourage and support medical, social, demographic and behavioural science research on contraceptive technology and reproductive and child health care. (C34) Promote old age health care and support in order to reduce incentives to have large families. (C36) Effectively convey family welfare messages on the pattern of the literacy campaigns, involving artists, film stars, doctors, vaidyas, hakims, nurses, local midwives, women's and youth organizations. (D37) Introduce the 42nd amendment to the Constitution, freezing the number of seats to both houses of Parliament till 2026. (Indicated against each item wherever possible) *Converge service delivery at village levels:* • *Integrate with existing Centrally Sponsored Schemes.*

	• *Organize and utilize self-help/ acceptor/ neighbourhood groups.* • *Train and motivate these groups to become primary contacts at village level.* • *Organize fortnightly meetings of these groups.* • *Guidance to groups by panchayat appointed health staff.* • *Groups to provide six services:* • *Registration of births, deaths, marriages, and pregnancy.* • *Weighing of children.* • *Counseling, advocacy of contraception plus free supply of contraceptives.* • *Preventive health-care and provision of common medicines including ORS.* • *Provide nutrition supplements.* • *Advocacy and encouragement of school enrolment upto age 14.* • *Aanganwadi centers to cater to all health and contraceptive care needs and activities.* • *A fully equipped maternity hut to be established in every village. A panchayat appointed mid-wife, supported by volunteers will look after the maternity hut.* • *Trained birth attendants (TBA) will*

	be trained to respond to emergencies and for supporting Auxiliary Nurse Mid-wife (ANM)s at health sub-centres. • *Maintain a village-wise list of persons trained in various aspects of health care, including in the indigenous systems of medicine.* • *Provide a wider basket of contraceptive choices to reach household levels.* *Empowering women for improved health and nutrition:* • *Provide cluster services for women.* • *Open more child-care centers in rural and urban areas.* • *Pursue programmes for access to fuel-wood and drinking water.* • *Reward schemes to households to aim at empowering households, especially women.* • *Improve district, sub-district and panchayat level coordination especially in neo-natal and obstetric care, including referral network.* • *Improve accessibility and quality of maternal and child care services through:* ❑ *Deployment of health providers at village levels.* • *Strengthening primary health centers.*

	❑ *Involve professional agencies to develop training and management modules.* ❑ *Improve supervision.* ❑ *Improve monitoring of:* ❑ *Incidence and coverage of anti-natal visits* ❑ *Deliveries attended by trained personnel.* ❑ *Post-natal visits.* ❑ *Etc.* • *ANM to be accountable and responsible for all registration, neo-natal and post- natal services.* • *Improve technical skills.* • *Support community activities on Information, Education & Communication (IEC).* • *Develop a health package for adolescents.* • *Educate on, and expand availability of, safe abortion facilities. Strengthen control and enforcement mechanisms.* • *Develop maternal hospitals as First Referral Units (FRU)s at sub-district levels, for complicated and life threatening deliveries.* • *Create a national network of public, private and NGO centers, identified by a common logo for providing free service, on the basis of a national standard and, reimbursable rates.*

	• *Child health and survival- issues of neo-natal health and nutrition to be focused.* • *Set up a National Technical Committee on neo-natal care.* • *After birth of a child, provide counseling about contraception; encourage adoption of a reversible or a terminal method.* • *Pursue rigorously the pulse-polio campaign.* • *Ensure 100% routine immunization, especially tetanus and measles.* • *Motivate mothers below poverty levels to have their first child after 21 and to adopt terminal methods of contraception after the second child.* • *Encourage NGOs and voluntary groups to implement special schemes for vulnerable groups like street children and child labourers.* • *Explore the possibility of national health insurance for children below 5 years, of parents who have adopted the small family norm, to cover hospitalization expenses.* • *Promote primary education and through education, promote awareness, late marriage, small family norm, child survival etc.* • *Provide vocational training for girls.*

	Meet the unmet needs of family welfare services: • *Strengthen, energize and make publicly accountable the cutting edge of health infrastructure.* • *Address unmet needs relating to infrastructure, trained personnel and availability of equipment and drugs.* • *Increase outreach and coverage of products and services through innovative social marketing Ñ schemes.* • *Improve facilities for referral transport/ ambulance services.* • *Provide soft loans to ANMs for increasing their mobility and for ambulance services.* • *Provide loan schemes for setting up village level, basic medicine shops and first aid.* *In urban slums:* • *Promote net-work of retired government doctors, paramedics and others, on remuneration basis, to provide health care.* • *Strengthen social marketingÑ programme for non-clinical products and services.* • *Initiate specially targeted# information, education and communication campaigns.*

	• *Promote inter-sectoral coordination to deal with unplanned settlements.* • *Streamline referral systems.* • *Link the continuance of facilities to the observance of small family norms.* *In tribal communities, hill area population, and for displaced/ migrant populations:* • *Introduce information and counseling on infirtility.* • *Provide mobile clinics for regular coverage and outreach.* • *Need for standardization and distribution of indigenous systems of medicines.* *To adolescents:* • *Provide information and counseling.* • *Provide package of nutritional services under the ICDS scheme, especially to females.* • *Enforce Child Marriage Restraint Act, 1976.* *For increased participation of men in planned parenthood:* • *Organize IEC campaigns.* • *Re-popularize vasectomies.* • *Explore contractual engagement of private medical practitioners whose credentials are certified by the IMA, with proper monitoring and checks and*

	balances. Their services can be payable by designated agencies. • *Revive the earlier system of licensed medical practitioners.* • *Involve retired defence personnel, retired school teachers etc. in advocacy and counseling.* • *Modify under/post graduate medical, nursing and professional courses to reflect the concepts of the national population policy.* • *Augment the services of specialists in FRUs.* *Collaborate with the non-government sector:* • *To augment services and advocacy.* • *To strengthen management information systems.* • *To run professionally sound advertising and management campaigns.* • *To provide markets for income generation activities.* • *Help promote transportation to inaccessible areas.* • *To promote reproductive and child health care among its employees.* • *To create a national network of health care centers, under a common logo, for delivering reproductive and child health care services.*

	• *To support primary educational efforts.* *(27) Utilize Indian System of Medicine and Homeopathy practitioners and institutions for population related programmes.* *(27) Promote contraceptive technology research.* *(28) Provide for the older population through:* • *Sensitizing, training and equipping rural and urban health care centers on geriatric care.* • *Encouraging voluntary organizations to make the elderly economically self-reliant.* • *Explore tax benefits to encourage children to look after aged parents.* *(28)Converge IEC efforts across the social sectors and encourage:* • *Optimal use of every possible media.* • *Extend coverage and outreach through established organizational networks, and their field functionaries.* • *Fund nagar palikas, panchayats, NGOs, and community organizations for interactive and participative IEC activities.* • *Support to the small family norm by political, community, business, professional, and religious leaders, media and film stars, sports personalities and opinion makers, including by personal example*

	• *Involve the civil society for IEC, counseling and monitoring.* [At local levels, the Mahila Swastha Sangh (MSS), existing self help and other grass-root groups to be mobilized.]
Budgeting	(G44) The annual budget for the Department of Family Welfare will be doubled. The programme is 100% centrally funded. Preventive and promotive services will continue to be subsidized. Priority allocation for creation of health care infrastructure at village, sub-centre, primary health center and community levels. [Consultation with social editors and media representatives recommends investment of more funds on communication issues]
Information system and Feedback	(C14) Panchayats should involve the civil society in monitoring the availability, accessibility and affordability of services and supplies. [Mechanism for computerized monitoring will be strengthened. Workshops will be organized to prepare the District action plan.]

Key: (C27) refers to Para C27 of the Policy chapter. (E 23) refers to Para E 23 and so on.

(16/1) and the portion in italics refers to page 16, para 1 of the Appendix on Operational Strategies. Similarily 20/17 refers to page 20, para 17 and so on.

Action Plan for One Year: August 2000-2001 document. Department of Family Welfare. Government of India.

In using the term 'social marketing' what is perhaps implied is innovative selling and distribution. To illustrate, "in addition to free supply of condoms and oral pills, these are also supplied at subsidized costs to NGOs and companies under the name social marketing" (Action Plan for One Year:August 2000-2001 document).

The word target has been used, implying the need for segmentation.

Should include health and family welfare too.

Such action plans can rarely be taken up at field levels.

CHAPTER 4.

DISSIMILARITIES
SEARCH FOR SIMILARITIES

Introduction of a new method of working always entails doubts and cynicism. Traditionalists and specialists are generally reluctant to see beyond their domain. Yet, the 'power of one' is really to push new ideas, encourage its experimentation, incorporate local sensibilities; and adapt and adopt till it succeeds. It is on this belief that this chapter discusses the major functional differences between private and public sector bodies and still arrives at the conclusion that notwithstanding these differences, there is a common, important thread – indeed rope - between the two; a rope that strongly suggests the applicability of the marketing discipline – developed over fifty years or more for products and services - to the marketing of ideas.

Dissimilarities.

The most glaring difference that comes to mind between the private sector (meaning organizations engaged in business or commerce) and the public sector (meaning thereby, the government and government undertakings) is one of employee accountability, a summation of which indicates organizational performance. In a privately held company, all activities are geared to the profit - ambitions of the owner or majority stockholders. Hence, the employees and workers have either to perform or depart. Good workers are adequately compensated; workers with an indifferent attitude can leave with or without notice. Horizontal mobility is standard, including at the higher levels. Even in large, transnational companies, the top managers are answerable to the shareholders, including the public, and it is not uncommon to hear of non-performing Chief Executives being forced to quit.

Employee accountability in government or in government organizations on the other hand, it may not be an exaggeration to say, is neither transparent or direct; nor is there an effective system of removing the insincere, leave alone offering any meaningful incentive for meritorious work. The system also does not allow any lateral input of expertise or substitution of the inefficient by the efficient in any other way. Organizational interest and employee interest may not be the same. Likewise, employee interests are unlikely to be unaffected by organizational inefficiency. Sectarian, bureaucratic and political interests may count but not necessarily the welfare of the customer – the programme beneficiary in this case. When logic dictates, for example, that disadvantaged peoples and areas should get the services of persons with extraordinary zeal and efficiency, it is not unusual in government to post incompetent persons to such areas, as a form of 'punishment'! While in the private sector, most transfers and changes in assignment and responsibilities are decided within the overall objective of the organization, in the public sector, this is generally decided on the personal agenda of the senior bureaucracy and the politician. Consequently, government programmes may falter or even fail to perform, and yet can continue indefinitely. Security of service coupled with unpredictable tenure of postings is the greatest challenge to uninterrupted and planned good work.

When competition is the driving force in the private sector, if not a matter of survival, no such compulsion exists in the public sector. Though this trend is changing, at least it is under debate and in isolated instances units are being hived off, there are many instances of public bodies – hospitals for instance – continuing to exist even in the face of out-performing competition from the private sector. Whether a government organization performs its mandated task or not, albeit the difficulty of social work and its survival is generally never called to question. Interestingly, in all such situations the hierarchical position of the staff remains unaffected;

indeed, it remains assured. Wherefrom, social administration analysts have wondered, can the drive to perform, leave alone excel come?

Social programmes generally need an integrated approach. Family welfare is thus not just population stabilization but health, nutrition, education, agricultural production, income earning opportunities, empowerment of women, enforcement of rights and so on. The lucky commercial marketer does not have to contend with all of these – he can concentrate on just the competitions to the product or service that he hopes to market. Likewise, environmental considerations are simply to be taken note of in manufacturing the product; its long-term consequences can be glossed over. 'The process of positioning a social product is much more complex than positioning a commercial product because commercial marketers are not necessarily concerned with the social consequences of their actions. On the contrary, the social marketer is attempting to solve social problems and it would be counterproductive to create a new social problem or to reinforce beliefs which are detrimental to progress while positioning a social product' (McKee)

As has been remarked elsewhere, social marketers often have to encounter public cynicism regarding government's motives or the insincerity of its servants. Commercial marketers have rarely to face such a contingency, and organizations with a negative brand image will not enter the market in the first place. In addition, the social marketing target groups generally being the most disadvantaged and least educated, the consequent motivational efforts seeking a change in their lifestyles need more time, investment and planning. Indeed, social marketers have the difficult task of being innovative and at the same time 'careful not to overwhelm their target audience' ('What is Social Marketing?' www.csm.strath.ac.uk). As opposed to this, commercial marketers, in most cases do not need to ask their customers to do anything very serious or dramatic; they just have to promote products, the acquisition or non-acquisition of which *may not* really be of any consequence e.g., buying a shirt or a particular brand of TV. Social marketers, on the other hand, have to urge the change of habits and lifestyles that have been carried on traditionally and over many, many generations. The 'exchange' offered by social marketers is thus more difficult to persuade.

Conventional marketing draws upon voluntary market behaviour whereas social marketing operates mostly in a regulatory context. Consequently, for every major programme trying to introduce a break in behaviour from the past, the social marketer has to contend with issues of 'fairplay' and 'procedural justice' (Blamey and Sutton, 1999). Viewed from another angle, social marketing campaigns can be supplemented by appropriate legislation whereas commercial marketers cannot use this method.

Pricing of products is a factor for competition in the commercial sector and pricing strategies are a studied mix of price and volumes. In government promoted social programmes, the price at which a product or service is provided is of little consequence; it is either supported by a system of 'stretchable' budgeting, or administered so that beneficiaries are forced to pay in the absence of alternatives. The performance of a government programme is rarely driven by considerations of input-output costing. In fact, an administrator of social programmes is given credit for spending all the budgeted money and not for curtailing costs and therefore, expenditure.

Marketing limits itself to the use of promotional and communication channels; it does not encourage the use of marketing tools by the market itself. Social scientists, on the other hand, working on participatory movements advocate the use of communication tools *by the beneficiaries themselves*. The Bangladesh Grameen Bank for instance, encourages and facilitates the enthusiastic members of their collaborative community, especially the women, to use video cameras to document success stories as well as social maladies for social viewing, discussions and action. In many Indian cities, women's groups, youth clubs and schools collect rural experiences and publish newspapers that 'move'.

Similarity.

The aforesaid discussion raises the pertinent question that everything being so dissimilar, how can any of the management techniques being followed by the private sector be applied to the governmental sector? The answer is not easy but receives emphatic support from just one crucial point. *Keeping in mind the logic that behind every product lies an idea or a message, what has worked all these years for marketing a product should also work for an idea per se.* This reasoning, coupled with the positive experience of countries practicing social marketing e.g., Canada, the USA, Australia, and the Philippines suggests very emphatically that similar experiments in all other countries are likely to be successful.

> Philip D. Harvey has argued that social marketing programmes should be carried out by private agencies. He advances arguments to show how government functioning is hostile to the basics of marketing. 'Social marketing sales staff, for example, normally get paid a commission based on the number of contraceptives they sell. The commission scale can often be a vital part of a successful social marketing effort, and the best salesmen and women often make very substantial incomes. This very idea is antithetical to government operations; it is considered vaguely immoral to have anyone on the government payroll making a lot of money' (Harvey, 1999). It is also argued that marketing is a job for professionals, not generalists.

However, social marketing is only a discipline, and there is no reason why its basics cannot be learnt by government functionaries. Professional help can always be taken wherever needed and the programme adjusted to suit the application. There is, per se, no reason why government functionaries cannot apply the concepts, at least most of them. Indeed, there are two very strong reasons why they should: first, they are the ones responsible for most social programmes (private agencies can take up limited areas or small countries), and second, NGOs are fund-insecure. They do not know just when their financiers will pull out, leaving the people literally high and dry. The example of US government withdrawing funding for USAID population stabilization programmes during the incumbency of President Reagan (1984), and more recently on the appointment of President Bush (Jr.) is particularly telling. Government involvement in their own social development programmes is more far sighted, especially in India. Likewise, in supporting the private sector 'for-profit' social marketing companies, smaller funding agencies proclaim that they are emphasizing the free market but actually ensuring that they have an 'exit strategy'. All the major multinational funding agencies, on the other hand, support funding governments.

In the final analysis, since a consumer and a producer would be willing to enter into an exchange as long as both consider the deal to be fair and in their mutual interest, there should be no problem of systematically enabling or preparing the grounds for this exchange. The techniques of marketing aim to do just that.

CHAPTER 5

PRESCRIPTIONS FOR SOCIAL MARKETING – IF, FOR INSTANCE, APPLIED TO INDIA'S POPULATION STABILIZATION PROGRAMME

Social marketing, it may be recalled, is the application of commercial marketing techniques to facilitate the adoption of programmes in the social sector. However, it has to be remembered that *such techniques can best be applied if a mindset that puts the customer before everything and everyone else is already in place*. In other words, for the proper application of marketing methods to the social sector, there is first and foremost, a need to create a similar mindset among social marketers. Social marketing requires that a governmental organization, which is bureaucratic, and is therefore, accustomed to emphasizing the perceived merits of rules, organizational growth, impersonality, and so on, readjusts its vision and functioning so as to recognize the overall objectives of all social programmes i.e., to *satisfy customer (public) needs and expectations*. Social marketing, to put it plainly, reminds government functionaries that they exist for the welfare of the people, and therefore, public as well as individual opinions and inputs have primarily to be taken into account in implementing development programmes. 'Social marketing asks not "what is wrong with these people, why don't they understand?" but, "what is wrong with us? What don't we understand about our target audience?"' ('What is Social Marketing?' www.csm.strath.ac.uk). 'Social marketing provides a rich conceptual system for thinking through the problems of bringing about changes in the ideas or practices of a target public. It appears to represent a bridging mechanism which links the behavioral scientist's knowledge of human behaviour with the socially useful implementation of what the knowledge allows' (Kotler, 1975).

Enlightened marketing recognizes the difference between a consumer and a product. Thus, it allocates targets for products and not consumers. *Marketing pushes products, but before doing that, it empowers and enables consumers to pull products.* This difference is worth remembering in social marketing: You can push a product (idea) *only after* you have generated a pull for it. Marketing also acknowledges that there is a face behind the term 'consumer'. Hence, one has to recognize the face, its smiles, its frowns, and its look of satisfaction. In order to do this, a marketer must interact with the face and not treat it just as a number(s). *What does a marketer do when the faces are many? He or she tries to group them on the basis of available or collected data into workable categories – a kind of large face.*

Administration of social development programmes has always been an individual, hunch based activity. The administrators have rarely been trained to understand why their customers behave in a certain way, or why they find it difficult to accept a change, or just to listen to the wishes of the beneficiaries. Even in situations when the nation's needs, as perceived by the people's representatives, have been projected, a dialogue with the beneficiaries has not been attempted. In its absence, influencing the minds of the beneficiaries and convincing them of the merits of a programme, thereby gaining optimum response for any scheme, has been difficult. Government promoted social sector programmes have most often flowed hierarchically through the medium of meetings till finally the interaction with the beneficiaries (customers), the implementation, and the first stage of reporting has been effected by the largely untrained and neglected village level workers. True, training programmes in government are routinely organized, but again for the senior members of the hierarchy, and most often not for the 'cutting edge' workers, the beneficiaries, or their 'opinion leaders'. Training programmes have rarely been structured to gather regular and objective oriented information on beneficiary needs and aspirations. Whereas, the private sector has long ago accepted that 'market information is.....a superior tool than institutions and hunches for decision making' (Mehta, 1973), and they spend millions of dollars the world over for harvesting this knowledge, in the social sector it is still the personal plan of the implementer(s) down the line.

A coordinated, and structured marketing approach towards social programmes has not been pushed essentially because different programmes have their respective 'subject matter champions'. Health programmes, for instance, have thus had strong health, nutrition, epidemiological or clinical approaches and solutions. Educationists have designed educational and literacy plans just as agricultural scientists have designed programmers for bringing about increase in production or diversification of crops, sometimes linked with nutritional overtones. But social marketing is essentially a behavioural science based approach – it seeks to introduce lifestyle changes. It attempts to create and maintain a demand. The social marketing approach is therefore, the most relevant for the acceptance and integration of all other approaches (Grifiths, www.unu.edu/unupress). One commentator puts it rather bluntly: 'Development programmes are often irritating given the closed minds of their planners. Such persons will simply shut out concepts they have not evolved themselves, or those from other fields, however relevant. So public health work is imperially led by epidemiologists, though the projects themselves are behavioural in substance, being about change in attitude and practice. Social psychologists and pedagogues reign in literacy programmes, though the task usually has much to do with economics and, once again, with people needing to adopt new practices'. In all these, including the Reproductive Child Health programmers (RCH) – once family planning - programme, the commentator argues, lies the need for straightforward demand creation. For that, 'the required ideas and strategies must surely come from commerce, not the medical sciences' (De Cunha, 2001).

In Chapter 4 it has been pointed out that social policy and programmes are often designed and developed for the country as a whole whereas one of the basic prescriptions of marketing is: *application through segmentation*. National level social programmes suffer from this inherent defect and therefore, call for local level adaptations. This very important lesson learnt in commercial marketing flies against the common refrain aired at many fora that successes in one state could straightaway be replicated in another. At best, tips can be taken, as has been reflected in discussing the three nationally successful programmes, but the basic plan and implementation has to take into account local sensibilities. Thus, while the concept of marketing is relevant and applicable to social programmes, it cannot be presumed that the design of marketing plans would be uniform for all situations. Indeed, it just cannot be, considering the substantial difference in the context and content of different social programmes. *The creative challenge is in selecting these contexts and contents and matching them with the general principles of marketing*. 'In population control too', according to C. Subramaniam (cited in Swaminathan, 1993), 'the important question is, how to bring about an impact. A national plan is of no use; it has to vary from area to area'. At best, a national plan can be a guideline. Indeed, the Population Policy 2000 - the social programme that will be considered in designing a marketing plan in this chapter[1] - advises that the broad, nation-oriented strategy and action plan needs to be translated to suit field level situations. Two of the recommendations contained in the page 18 of the Action Plan for One Year document emphasize this by stating:

- "National Population Policy, 2000 should be used as a blue print to enable all partners/stakeholders to guide their own efforts." and
- "Implementation of NPP would require imaginative thinking and coordinated effort from all the stakeholders. Just outlining the policy is not enough."

The practice of social marketing.

The fundamental concepts behind social marketing are:

* What is relevant is not what you want but *what the consumer wants*.
* If you can find out what the consumer wants, but it does not fit into your programme, find out if and where you have gone wrong.
* If you can find out what the consumer wants, and it fits into your programme, provide all opportunities for its satisfaction.
* If you think that there is something worthwhile for the consumer, but the consumer is not aware of it, provide information about its benefits, knowledge and skills regarding its use and the opportunities for availing that 'something worthwhile'.

What specific steps you take, on the pattern of commercial marketing, to ensure all this is the rest of social marketing. The introductory prescriptions are:

1. Know your market so that you can establish a long term link between the customer and the product/ idea.
2. Apply the techniques and tools to satisfy, maintain and if need be, create a demand.
3. Provide products, services and opportunities (including the removal of barriers) for the behavioural change to take place (an exchange), and finally
4. Monitor the performance, and adjust according to the feedback

The organization proposing to undertake the social

marketing exercise needs first to familiarize itself with the essentials of marketing. Thereafter, it has to formulate its plans, and action so as to be in consonance with these fundamentals. Since, however, the social marketing 'pioneers-to-be' are most likely to be already a part of a social development organization, *no basic structural changes are being suggested*, nor is it desirable. Only the few major aspects and issues that need to be specifically addressed are being elucidated.

Marketing Programme Administration

Organizational mindset, structure.

That marketing begins and ends with the customer is the fundamental principle of marketing and, therefore, of social marketing. *It is essential for every practitioner of social marketing to feel in his or her veins that 'we are not doing him (the customer) a favour by serving him, he is doing us a favour by giving us the opportunity to do so'* (Bean). Only from this can the rest of marketing follow. Social marketers must also get out of the feeling that the programmes that they are espousing are noble and should, therefore, be forced down the throats of people. 'Too many organizations that think that they are practicing social marketing are really mired in an organizational centered mindset that sees their mission as inherently good', and therefore, their 'lack of success as their customer's fault'. Such persons are also liable to 'think that marketing is just really communications, that research is seldom necessary, that customers can be treated as a mass, and that competition can be ignored' (Andreasen, 1995).

It is also important to realize that in marketing, *the term 'customer' is used in a wide context*. Besides the obvious end-of-the line market towards which the product is being developed, the term customer also applies to the programme staff, the partners, the donors, and so on. 'A dealer who stocks a company's washing machines and fridges is as much of a customer as the housewife who buys them' (Dutta, 2001). For all such customers, the objective of social marketing is to bring about a behavioural change in support of the programme. Therefore, *the first step really is in understanding the attitude of the participants towards the programme* and, especially why a section of the participants is behaving in a 'non-conformist' manner, either towards its objective(s) or the strategy or the action plans. Addressing these attitudes effectively would, in the ultimate analysis, reflect on the success or failure of the programme

The concept of marketing has to go well beyond the marketer and further than just one or two members of the organizational leadership. It is a *conceptual change* that needs to be brought about *within the entire organization, as well as in those partner-bodies with whom a linkage has to be established.* It has to be remembered that 'if social marketing has to be done well, there must be a strong organizational commitment to doing it' (Young, 1988-89), and that marketing is 'more than a set of add-on activities' (Kotler, 1975). In effect, this would mean that the Chief Executive, be it the Panchayati Raj Officer/ Block Development Officer, the Sub-Divisional Officer, or the Zilla Parishad Officer/ Collector, should first be convinced that this discipline which has made sense to the private sector, has important application possibilities in the social sector. Thereafter, he or she has to organize a series of 'concept imbibing' discussions with the staff and colleagues in the linked departments - like the medical officers if the project to be given first priority is population stabilization and/ or preventive health - as well as academicians and resource personnel available locally. *Indeed, the chief social marketer has to enthuse everyone, including his or her peers, on the relevance of the marketing discipline for the social sector.*

The next step will be to entrust an officer to head the marketing function and thereby support the Chief Executive. In the present system of government, getting an officer to perform this function independently may not be possible. Hence, someone will have to shoulder additional responsibility. Hopefully, when the results are apparent, the system will allow full-fledged staffing for this important function. A core social marketing team, consisting of officials and non-officials need to be in place. Opinion leaders and stakeholders have to be included in this team for the reasons to be elucidated later on. *The team will provide continuity even if individual members are absent or replaced, as is likely to be.* It needs to be ensured that the size of the team is lean, and its members are *activity rather than debate oriented.* The first important task of this team is to identify one, or at most two programmes, that will be taken up under this endeavour. The application of the marketing discipline to the promotion of these programmes, on the basis of a set organizational and implementation pattern will not only help in popularizing it but will also introduce the basic elements of continuity.

Companies marketing more than one product usually organize them as distinct units, operated more or less as different business and reporting finally to a holding company or board. Some companies form category management teams only at the field level for different products, but such teams are generally structured and supported by all the standard management functionaries. The question that arises is how should a social marketer for different programmes carry out his or her marketing function? One suggestion could be to follow the aforesaid, former model i.e., earmark the subordinate marketing functionaries product wise but coordinate at an appropriate level. In the context of Indian administrative structure this would be at the level of a sub-division and the district. The marketing strategies would remain the same but there would be scope for combining steps such as survey, distribution and feedback but perhaps not communication as this needs to be programme specific.

The strategy (C11) prescribed by the NPP 2000 of decentralized planning and programme implementation by Panchayati Raj Institutions needs to be fully supported. Studies in social marketing have shown that 'interventions designed and directed by community members are far more likely to succeed than those planned and executed exclusively by outsiders (Green and Kreuter, 1991; Minkler and Wallerstein, 1997). The Community Based Prevention Marketing Model (CBPM) 'places social marketers and academic based researchers in a collaborative partnership with local public health professionals, other local health and education agency representatives, lay leaders and activists, representatives of local business, churches, voluntary organizations, and residents. A primary goal ... is to build the community's capacity to work together to achieve consensus about critical issues, set goals, and solve problems. ....during the process, indigenous leaders are developed who can stimulate critical problem solving activities and direct sustainable change activities (Bracht, 1990; Minkler and Wallerstein, 1997).

Later on in this chapter, the importance of partnerships has been stressed. At the very beginning, presuming that the programme coordinator will be new to the subject, *it would make sense to find and involve marketing practitioners from near-by public or business institutions, or at least an academic body for assistance in organising surveys, if not for the entire social marketing exercise.*

- So, the first set of Prescriptions is:
    - Read and convince yourself that social marketing is sensible.
    - Convince your working colleagues - official and non-official.
    - Organize the Panchayati Raj bodies if in existence and form a working team.

- Try to find and involve partners in undertaking the social marketing exercise.
- Include local stakeholders and opinion leaders in the social marketing team.
- Be sure to apply the marketing concept, techniques and tools to all participatory levels.

Planning and control.

Since most organizations already have a planning and control structure, only such aspects of planning that are critical for social marketing are being highlighted.

As has been stated in Chapter 2, marketing and social marketing begins with an idea of the product to be marketed. In our case, the idea – the objective - is to promote the concept of, and the adoption of a 'small and healthy family'. The way to achieve this objective is through an appropriate strategy. The NPP 2000 has already laid down, quite elaborately, the national strategy. Hence, these can be adopted or better still *these may be discussed, modified and reduced in numbers so as to make the task more manageable, and to suit local conditions and sensibilities*. 'The preparation of a sound strategic plan is critical to any successful social marketing programme or campaign. Without it, the enterprise is rudderless. An operation with only a vague sense of its strategy can careen dramatically from programme to programme or campaign to campaign, trying this, trying that' (Andreasen, 1995). Therefore, there is practical merit in identifying just a few *locally appropriate* items within the ambit of 'strategy' while leaving the rest to the action plan. The precise strategy, for example could be to make all *aware* of the objective or it could be to *provide outstanding service* to promote this idea or to reduce if not remove most of the *obstructions in the path of change*, or it could be a combination of all of these *on an inter se priority* basis.

To decide what is locally appropriate, and to initiate the 'action plan' a market survey, even if a very preliminary one, has first to be undertaken. Only after a survey can the first prescription of marketing i.e., segmentation be conceived, and the next operative steps planned. In addition, based on the findings of the market survey, the reachable goals, keeping the national goals in mind, can be set. The subsequent steps in the social marketing action plan can now be conceived and implemented, *leaving no ambiguity about the responsibility of each participant, on a short as well as a long term basis*. The responsibilities should, inter alia cover:

- Implementation related to budget, personnel and infrastructure support,
- Supervision – content and schedule,
- Expenditure control,
- Coordination with partners including specified meetings,
- Training programmes and schedules,
- Performance monitoring with clear-cut parameters for both products and services, and
- Channels for and periodicity of feedback on programme performance as well as market attitude and response.

This exercise i.e., the drawing up and implementation of the social marketing plan, needs to be done in a bottom-up-top-down manner so that all the players as well as the participants are fully involved, and feel accountable. The process of discussion with key players and partners has at least three advantages:

- It enables programme partnerships to develop.
- It brings about consensus on the strategy. Conversely, *it identifies discord.*
- It enables action plans to be drawn up on the basis of a common strategy.

In drawing up the strategy and the action plan, the planners must not forget that 'marketing does not occur unless there are two or more parties, *each with something to exchange,* and both able to carry out communication and distribution' (Kotler and Zaltman 1971). The second aspect that needs to be remembered is that *people behave in a manner they justify.* In other words, recalling the discussions in Chapter 3, for any exchange to take place, the benefits of the exchange (or change) have to be made quite apparent. Conversely, the disadvantages or costs of not changing need to be highlighted. These two fundamentals of social marketing, in the context of the population stabilization programme can be illustrated as below:

THE 'COST-BENEFIT EXCHANGE' MODEL

OBJECTIVE:

ACHIEVE AN *EXCHANGE* BETWEEN THE CUSTOMER AND THE SELLER (SOCIAL MARKETER)

* SELLER promises 'Good Living', 'Good Health', 'Social Standing and Usefulness', 'Good Citizenship feeling'
* CUSTOMER agrees to a 'Behavioral Change', Self Restraint', 'Inconvenience or Discomfort'

THEREFORE,

THERE IS A NEED TO FIRST UNDERSTAND THE CUSTOMER'S CONCEPT OF THE EXCHANGE FUNCTIONS AND THE OBSTACLES IN THE PATH OF CHANGE. THEREFORE, THE NEED FOR SURVEY AND ANALYSIS.

THEREFORE,

THE SIMULTANEOUS NEED FOR THE SELLER TO ASSESS AND IMPROVE HIS/HER CAPACITY TO FACILITATE

AND DELIVER THE EXCHANGE

THEREFORE,

THE NEED TO UNDERTAKE ALL THE NECESSARY STEPS TO:

-MAKE THE EXCHANGE LESS DISTURBING AND MORE ATTRACTIVE (Home delivery. Good service, Incentives, introduce 'enablers' etc.)

-EFFECTIVELY COMMUNICATE THE EXCHANGE BENEFITS AND NON-EXCHANGE COSTS

-FACILITATE AND ENABLE BEHAVIOURAL CHANGE BY REMOVING/ REDUCING COMPETITION.

It is worth emphasising that *the action plan needs to have a direct link with what is attainable within the time specified or desirable, and budget supportable*. Open-ended programmes cannot be controlled. That is why the setting of attainable goals, and a periodic *evaluation* of the achievements is imperative. It is also necessary to introduce the concept of *'pre-tests'* at every activity stage of the action plan. Pre-tests can avoid time and resource wastage. Finally, at periodical intervals after the initiation of the marketing exercise, the *feedback* needs to be discussed by the strategic planners and the action plan re-modeled to the extent necessary. This entire process continues till the conclusion of the programme.

The essential steps involved in drawing up a social marketing plan are:

A. Survey:

For segmentation.

For psychographic data.

B. Position the idea/product based on the decided strategy.

C. Strive to improve organizational image & goodwill.

D. Decide on the product and service to be delivered.

E. Decide on the price/ rate for the product/ service.

F. Decide on and set up the distribution network including and especially the involvement of the opinion leaders and stakeholders.

G. Develop and carry out a communication and promotion programme.

H. Develop and carry out all enabling functions.

I. Pre-test, evaluate and correct.

Each of these essential components of social marketing will be elaborated in the context of the population stabilization programme.

Strengthening of available infrastructure and support systems

The social marketing action plan would have taken into account the hierarchy of health related staff and the facilities available to them for delivering the goals. In consultation with them, the targets, the budget-backed activity sequencing, the optimal utilization of equipment and consumables available, the feedback mechanism, and also the possibilities for performance, including service-cum-quality improvement would also have been spelt out. *The availability and status of infrastructure, upon which the plan rests, would point out to the options and priorities just as the hitherto untapped resources will determine the way the programme can be strengthened.* For instance, partnership programmes with NGOs, educational institutions, and public and private sector organizations can take care of planning and survey inputs, emergency requirement of consumables or transport, training, management information system development and, indeed many other areas that need support on a regular or occasional basis.

An input worth stressing is training. It is unwise to begin a programme without adequate training. Training time is not wasted time. Training must be participatory, simple and often repeated across all the steps in the process. In the course of training, it is worthwhile examining whether the delivery organization is clear of its strategy for achievement of the national goals, if enunciated, or its own goals. Are the strategy items direct, sequential and practical? Are they in agreement with the objectives and the plan? Can they agree to specific market-segment-wise targets and a time frame for achievement? Can they suggest improvements based on their field experience and feedback? How to ensure optimal output from all and every equipment? Can the indenting process be streamlined so as to ensure that commitments made are honoured?

The training method and process is actually the social marketing concept in a capsule form. It begins with the beneficiaries – the segmented market. In advanced stages, representatives of different segments may be included. The beneficiaries interact with the SHOPs and the programme staff in order to understand the market needs and aspirations (that have to be identified or have already appeared as an outcome of the market survey). In the process, what should come out forcefully are the obvious advantages that will accrue if the needs and the aspirations are met – a healthy and educated family, for instance. Only when the common objectives have been identified, and reinforced in everyone's minds, can the next step begin.

The second step is the identification of 'competition' - the reasons why the needs are not being met. The reasons may be social, economic, religious; family oriented or community decided;

apparent or hidden. In other words, the pinpointing of the competition needs prolonged discussions, but this time spent will be essential for the rest of the programme.

The third step is the identification of the ways by which the competition can be overcome. In the process, the group can also suggest and devise methods by which the 'ways' can be publicized so as to involve those who could not be included in the training programme as well as for constantly reminding those who could. Volunteer groups to spread the message through inter-personal interaction, through locally relevant and popular media and methods may also be formed and self tasked on a specific area and time frame.

The final, but not last in the sense that this step continues as long as needed, is the feedback and review. The entire programme and process, what went right and what went wrong, what new initiatives are needed, and so on are all to be discussed so as to start afresh. The most important part of this stage is the inclusion of social groups who were found to be interested in obstructing the programme. An open but non-acrimonious discussion with them may bring out solutions, both immediate and long term. Another important part of this stage is the identification of the form of recognition that is due to persons or groups or institutions for exceptional work.

It would be seen that such training is also an adjunct of planning. Hence, during the entire process, the availability of physical and financial resources, and the untapped resources are to be kept in mind in order to match the scale of action with the resources. No one, especially the programme coordinators, participates with any pre-conceived notion of the outcome or from a position of authority. Each comes with a willingness to learn and share skills. The programme staff, for instance, may be equipped to share financial resources but may be unaware of the social nuances that may resist change. The beneficiaries may be aware of their needs and problems, but may have never had an opportunity of thinking through them, in partnership with others. The SHOPs may find that some of the attitudes of the people that they took for granted may not be true or are changing fast in favour of something else.

In trainings, it is desirable to invite the staff from adjoining marketing areas. This can have two distinct advantages:

- Exchange of information and success stories, and
- Observing of the programme; recalling that often a spectator sees more of a game than the participants.

Information systems.

As has been remarked earlier, planning and control functions are possible only if an organisation has a well-established information and monitoring system. The system should be able to *gather* useful information from the 'macro' as well as 'task' environment, link it with *available* information, *analyze and process* it for use by the marketers, and *obtain feedback* for effective control. Taking the family planning example, the broad components of the management information system would look like:

Information from the

MACRO Environment:	TASK Environment:
Economy	Customers/ Beneficiaries
Technology	Distributors & SHOPs
Government & Law	Partners
Culture	Programme staff

↓

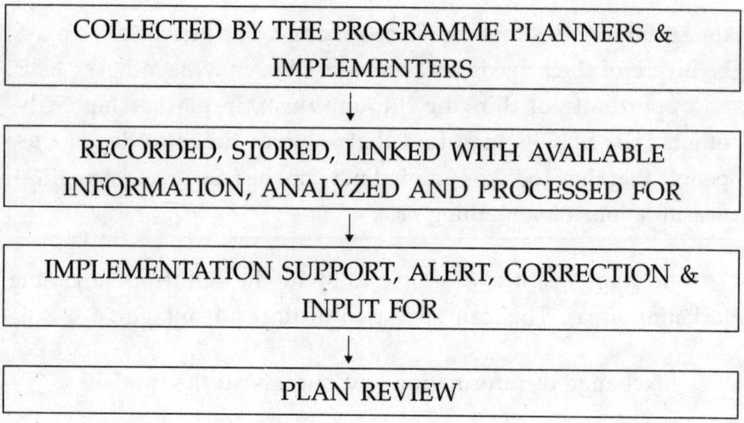

COLLECTED BY THE PROGRAMME PLANNERS & IMPLEMENTERS

↓

RECORDED, STORED, LINKED WITH AVAILABLE INFORMATION, ANALYZED AND PROCESSED FOR

↓

IMPLEMENTATION SUPPORT, ALERT, CORRECTION & INPUT FOR

↓

PLAN REVIEW

A likely outcome of a successful social marketing programme will be the increased demand for information, products and services. Full use of modern information technology (with the assistance of partners, if in-house expertise is not possible) to record each activity and for obtaining a feedback/ analysis at, and for every level needs to be built in. Staff and volunteers involved in the programme must be adequately trained and equipped to handle the expected rush for information and services. Indirectly, it will be wise to limit the reach of the programme to the extent the resources permit. *This is an argument that will recur throughout this chapter in favour of conventional contraceptives rather than sterilization or medical termination of pregnancy – the latter requiring and dependant upon elaborate infrastructure, manpower and financial support.*

Programme evaluation, described at the end of this chapter, is an essential adjunct of the information system because it helps benchmark the status of the activities at the launch of the programme with mainly the short term goals. In simple terms, the following table indicates the design:

STATUS	GOALS	EVALUATION (based on feedback)
Performance parameters:		Planned/achieved/ Shortfall –why? Increase –how?
No.of persons in the productive stage (M/F)		
No of persons under protection(M/F)		
No.of families with one child		
No.of products being sold		
No.of queries received		
No.of persons attending camps		
No.of media items appearing/ month		
Etc.		
Process parameters		
No.of teams reaching products.		Planned/ held/ new revelation
No.of teams holding trainings.		
No.of trainings being held.		
No.of product & service camps organized		
No.of houses visited.		
No.of media interactions		
No.of interactions with partners		
Etc.		

The nucleus formation.

While the planning should be for the entire market, the action plans, as will be shown later, must be segment oriented. *Within segments, the activities should begin in a limited way and then expand outwards*. The first step in this direction is the selection of special groups who are likely to respond better than others. These can be members of an existing, cohesive organization involved in social change or groups that can be motivated to become one. In relation to such groups or bodies, the supporting infrastructure can be focused and linked for providing the social marketing output. In a way, this is a kind of pre-testing (for corrective action wherever necessary) on, as well as for launching the main, large-scale programme. From this nucleus, and around it; and on the tested pattern, the programme can expand – in a kind of franchising exercise.

◆ So, the next prescription is:

- Draw up a marketing plan with the available and reachable resources in view.
- Train the staff to efficiently implement the plan, receive and honour regular feedback, and modify implementation as per need.
- Decide on a 'nucleus' to begin a pilot exercise.

A. SURVEY

a. To list out the market segments.

> This survey is essentially a demographic and situational survey aimed at segmenting a wide market on the basis of common characteristics, for a preliminary idea as to the task involved, the resources available and homing on to one or more segments for marketing the social idea.

Categorizing the market into sub-groups is essential because no society is a homogeneous mass, but consists of self-evolved lifestyle clusters based on various criteria. The search for such lifestyle clusters, to re-emphasize what has been stated in Chapter 2, is an approach 'based on two underlying assumptions: Birds of a feather flock together. People living in the same neighbourhood are likely to have similar lifestyles...similar health behaviors. A neighborhood cluster will have the same lifestyle characteristics regardless of the cluster's geographical location' (Taylor et al. 1999). Therefore, efforts to influence behaviour must be designed for each lifestyle cluster. Conversely, 'target audiences (being) seldom uniform in their perceptions' are unlikely 'to respond to (uniform) marketing efforts' (Social Marketing Institute Web Page). One offered size cannot be expected to fit all, to use marketing jargon. Segmentation enables focused attention, prioritization of effort, optimal application of resource and development of segment-specific action plans. Cluster-wise approaches can also effectively exploit subtle relationships of interests as well as status. 'A mother with a baby in her arms', for instance, 'will freely talk to another mother (although a stranger to her) with a baby in arms in a train or a ship' (Francis, 1978). Segmentation, social marketing experts argue, *'is one of the most powerful contributions that commercial sector marketing has to make to the solution of social problems'* (Andreasen, 1995).

On this principle, since population stabilization is the programme under consideration, it would make sense to classify the beneficiary population into rural/ urban, their respective avocations (e.g., nomadic/non-nomadic/ tribals/landless labourers/ small landholders/ large landholders/ artisans/ service holders/ industrial workers/ etc.), the numbers/ families under each, and so on. Suppose the data showed that:

- 70% are rural and 30% are urban,
- Of the rural, 60% are landless, 40% are landholders,
- Of the landholders, 70% are tribals,

- Of the urban population, 50 % are industrial labourers,

then, in absolute terms, the primary target should be the landless, the tribals, and the industrial labourers. The secondary data collection i.e. Survey B will have to concentrate on these categories.

In the urban areas, the survey might show that a large section consists of employees of one or more business organisation either in the private or the public sector. The marketing programme can, therefore, be organized in conjunction with the concerned organization. *Presence of military or para-military establishments in an area should be considered to be a bonus.* Not only will the disciplined members themselves be receptive to progressive ideas, they can very well form the extension force in their immediate neighbourhood and in the villages/ towns from where they hail.

A very important feedback for the planning of population stabilization programmes is the demographic profile and trend. If it turns out that a particular segment will, in the near future, have a majority of members in the age group above fifty, then the planners need not pay much attention to them. Instead, this information will be relevant for programmes on social security and health, including cataract and blindness control – issues that subtly impact on parental desire for the male child.

An important information that would come out of the survey is the category-wise usage of contraceptives. Indeed, the distribution aspect of marketing will depend heavily on this feedback. A simple collection sheet may take this form:

Category	Sex	Age Groups	Method	Users %*	Nonusers%
Landless		15-24	Rhythm		
			Local methods		
			CC		
			OP		
			IUD		
			Vasectomy		
			Tubectomy		
		25-39	as above		
		40-59	as above		
Tribals		as above	as above		
Labourers Rural		as above	as above		
Labourers Industrial		as above	as above		
Etc					

(The age grouping stresses 'eligible and just married', 'novelty worn off couples' and 'aged couples'.)

*This can be further broken down to the period of use. People using contraceptives for three years continuously can be considered to be 'adopters' or clients — a very special place given to such persons in marketing.

While eligible and just married couples should be the first group to be interacted with, if the survey also shows that there are a good number of non-users among the other two groups, it will be advisable to target them too.

It has been mentioned elsewhere that *it is always advisable to inculcate the services of satisfied customers first than to seek new ones.* The key to a successful business, it is said, is key customers. The survey on family-wise details of contraceptive methods used would help identify this important group. Likewise, data on the NGOs operating in the market area would be useful not only for the point of view of identifying partners, but an idea of their 'reach' may help in optimizing collaborative costs. Identification, recognition and partnerships with functional NGOs is a good way of turning potential competitors into collaborators.

This survey will also identify all the opinion leaders[2] and / or stake holders (SHOPs) – a group whose help will be shown to be crucial in carrying out a successful social marketing programme. It seems possible to establish a *co-relation between societal values and opinion leaders.* Ranking of opinion leaders together with the values that people perceive in them could give a direction to the marketing strategy.

> Just how important it is to identify the appropriate SHOP for effectively attracting market attention was demonstrated in the context of a recent television serial. Star TV, the promoters of the super successful Kaun Banega Crorepati (KBC) chose a senior film-star to anchor their programme – thereby achieving the highest viewer ratings for more than a hundred episodes - instead of the pattern followed elsewhere in the world using communication professionals.

The initial survey should bring out the *opinion leader within every family.* In general, as has been remarked earlier, this will be the mother-in-law or the father-in-law in a joint family or the father in a nucleus family. Students and children often have a great influence on their families for positive action. They are influenced in turn by the media, and enlightened schoolteachers. It is not uncommon to hear teenage students arguing with family elders about social reforms and progressive behavioural changes. While men and women in the age group of 25 and above are likely to have already matured with well-formed value judgments - and would therefore, have become more difficult to de- or re-motivate – *the minds of school children are easily influenced.* (By the time they grow up to be adults, progressive ideas, including the benefits of a small family would have been, hopefully, engrained in their minds). A case will also be built up later for designing messages aimed at parents referring to the benefits that will accrue to their children.

While opinion leaders can be found within a family, their influence is likely to be limited. On the other hand, *opinion leaders across many families* are the SHOPs who have to be specifically identified. Beyond the family, the important opinion leaders are the village leader (and his wife), the village priest (especially in traditional and conservative societies), the practitioners of 'other' systems of treatment, the non resident villager (NRV) who has migrated to the town, but still maintains contact with the village and brings fairy tale news of 'modern' life as lived by townspeople, the village-outside-world interface that is the postman, the land revenue staff, the policeman, the forest guard, the members of the defence and paramilitary forces hailing from the village or locality, etc. *It is not very well known that some thirty to forty thousand members of the military, the level of a Junior Commissioned Officer and below, retire every year. They are a disciplined work force, charged with patriotism and enthusiasm, waiting to be gainfully deployed for social service.* Indeed, programmes that have included them, like the desert a-forestation in Rajasthan, have reportedly been immensely successful. The conclusion of the earlier mentioned study (Kivlin et al., 1971) regarding increased adoption by persons exposed to urban contact also supports this suggestion.

Innovative ideas can extend to the 'hidden' opinion leaders – the village merchants (*Feriwalla*), including the traveling kind who seems to have an exclusive audience with the village ladies otherwise shy of strangers or the men-folk. It should be a worthwhile challenge to train and draft the traveling 'Churiwalla' (Bangle seller), the artificial 'jewellerywalla', and the 'sariwalla' into the programme, and get them to talk about social programmes in the way they promote one form of cosmetic or soap over another.

One is not aware of any social programme that includes all these people in influencing minds but *this is an advantage available to the social sector and not to the private sector.* Surveys must, therefore, not miss the potential and influence of such persons. Indeed, it is desirable to be always on the lookout for *potential leaders* 'and allies who are motivated by a zeal for common good' (Krishan, 1965). The private sector builds in a system of commission for such motivators. Surely, social sector programme promoters can also do something similar; but this aspect will be touched upon later.

> Innovation:
>
> In an innovative experiment, according to Dr. D. Anand, President of Sakshi, a NGO, the spread of a message has been hastened in one area of Uttar Pradesh by identifying and carefully training a set of 'gossipers'!
>
> A popular form of transport in both urban and rural India is the cycle or human powered rickshaw. One can conceive a programme involving the rickshaw pullers: in adopting contraceptive measures as well as promoting family planning. Participants can be distinguished by colour or banner and may be encouraged to sell condoms at subsidized rates to passengers. A commission on sales, besides the pleasure in participating in a social cause (basic, plus self esteem needs) could well be their motivation.

One is apt to, but *should not forget the health worker as an important opinion leader, especially if he or she is also a local stakeholder.* In spite of the general lack of goodwill of government functionaries, government staff who are also members of the local community hold a special place in the consultation process, and therefore, should not be neglected. Any measure that helps to increase the image of such persons is likely to be productive just as the 'improvement of the image of the health worker in the minds of the beneficiaries was cardinally important for the success of the UIP' (www.social-marketing.org).

In identifying SHOPs – the 'movers and shakers' of society - the essential characteristics of whom have been highlighted in Chapter 2, one should not miss out those who have emerged as a result of the attitudinal changes that have taken place in modern life. Till recently, education and religious standing were characteristics of prominent village level SHOPs. Now, those who have amassed wealth, whatever their educational standards, and therefore, wield more power are the neu-SHOPs. One should also not dismiss as unimportant those SHOPs with relatively localized spheres of influence. In a large market, it is quite possible that a SHOP for one group may not hold influence over another – just as in the commercial world, a retailer of high end products wielding influence over the rich members of a posh colony may rarely cater to or be visited by, and therefore, have any sway over the rest of the community.

Some social scientists believe that 'it is communication that creates a community'; others believe that 'communication nurtures a community'. The latter view seems more practical since communication helps to relate, and therefore, bind people who have flocked together on account of their common interests or physical needs or characteristics or apprehensions. Communication 'enables people to define their own problems, set their own goals, come up with their own solutions, and optimize individual and group abilities to learn, resolve their differences, and to act on their behalf' (White, 1999). *Entering this 'community communication network', therefore, seems to be an essential element in bringing about behavioural change in a community.* Social and religious organizations, sporting bodies, academies promoting art and culture, and the like are the places where the networks are generally anchored. Hence, during survey, the existence of such networks needs to be discovered.

As mentioned at the outset, the findings of this survey will help the planner identify segments that need to be prioritized for designing the marketing programme. However, before embarking on the work, one should take into account the data that may already be available from national, state or local level surveys carried out earlier. Unless very outdated, these could be of help, especially in reducing survey costs.

◆ Prescription:

- Conduct a survey of the market in order to determine:
  - ❑ The dominant segments.
  - ❑ The characteristics of the segments.
  - ❑ The organizations working in the market and their influence.
  - • The opinion leaders and stakeholders.
- Hone on to the identified segments for the next part of the plan.

(The different approaches to survey as well as the main techniques have been explained in Chapter 2.)

b) Psychographics Survey.

> This survey is aimed at ascertaining the needs, aspirations, attitudes, experience of the customer, segment wise, so that appropriate marketing programmes can be drawn up on the basis of available opportunities, existing and perceived barriers and threats.

This second part of the survey is the one that effectively addresses issues that will decide the marketing approach. This will also provide an opportunity to carry out the first step in 'hinting' and leading the participants up to the programme objective – something that has been explained in Chapter 2. Ideally, therefore, this targeted survey should be carried out individual or family-wise. Most often, however, time and resource constraints will not allow such a detailed exercise to be undertaken. *So, the next best thing is to carry out representative survey of families forming a cluster or through focus groups.*

What do the members of the 'homed-on' segment consider important for their well-being? Do they feel the overwhelming need for family planning or are they more concerned about irrigation, for instance, that will enable them to grow vegetables in their homesteads? Would this increase family income and thereby, reduce the psychological pressure for additional working hands? Would this, in effect, empower the women towards family welfare? The results that may be thrown up may indeed, surprise the marketer. Programmes that are helpful and meaningful to women, for instance, may not necessarily relate to issues of their health 'but more related to understanding the lifestyle context in which they are operating and making decisions...... what a woman wants from life, her aspirations for herself and her children, what her dreams and fears are, what makes her feel inadequate or happy, how much she feels she is in control or can influence things' (Grifiths). *A thorough understanding of these issues, even if the solutions to them may not be clear or immediately possible, is essential in designing the social marketing programme; and it is at the survey stage that these attributes can be detected.*

Survey may bring out that a particular community does not welcome contraception on religious grounds. They might, however, be inclined to try out abstinence on grounds of maternal health. Ascertaining this is important and the marketing approach for this group will obviously have to be different from another group that relies on more children to take the village cattle for grazing.

In urban or semi-urban areas, the survey might throw up aspirations in every household to own a television set. If there is already an existing cable network or there is likelihood of one coming up, then communication of the benefits of social development programmes through television advertisements, plays, invitations to successful families to participate in live programmes, and so on are feasible options. The influence of television in moulding behaviour, it may be recalled, has been referred to in Chapter 4.

> 'We found that caste, education of both respondent and wife, level of living and literacy of the respondent were all positively and significantly related to knowledge, approval and adoption of vasectomy and the loop' (Kivlin et al., 1971)

How do families take or make social decisions? This crucial information can come out of an organized survey. Are family decisions taken in-house or do they seek the help of others? If the majority answer is that they seek the advice of the Panchayat, then obviously, the marketing design should stress on approaching the community leaders. 'The existing leaders may be good or bad, progressive or conservative, motivated or unmotivated, but they dominate the village thinking and action, and therefore, cannot be ignored' (Krishan, 1965). If on the other hand, most of the family members say that they are most influenced by their elders or their spiritual leaders, then the marketing approach would have to be different. It is advisable that the surveyor, in order to avoid programme bias, holds up different social issues in seeking such information. It may also be possible to get an indication of the time taken, on an average, for taking such decisions by a family, based on which the communication density can be planned.

During this survey *it is appropriate to interact with the acceptors and adoptors of social programmes* in order to ascertain why they are different in their attitude and behaviour from the rest. Why did they change their behaviour? Was it on the basis of a social message? Who were their motivators? Do they regret? What changes would have made their experiences better? Will they act as opinion leaders? Indeed, partners? It might, indeed be very useful to identify adopters at the very beginning of the survey process and involve them in all the marketing activities till the very end.

This survey will also throw up the special characteristics of SHOPs identified. Do they believe in the programme? What, according to them, are the problems faced by the segmented market in accepting the programme? How can these be overcome? Will they agree to join in the effort? What are the physical and financial resources that they can bring in? And so on. A word of caution though. Since research shows that 'if in addition to the goal of the message, an organisation has other apparent conflicting goals in sponsoring the message, individuals may have less favourable attitudinal responses to the message' (Blazing, 1999). As the advice applies equally to individuals, the attitude of the SHOPs towards the programme needs to be carefully collected. Will their help be overtly forthcoming or will they act as saboteurs? There are two approaches that one can take regarding SHOPs who are personally a bad example for the programme. Either, one can shun them, in which case the possibility of them becoming programme saboteurs cannot be overlooked, or they can be involved as 'failed-but-now-repentant-persons'. The latter approach is obviously tougher, but certainly better.

Social marketing involves *issues of opportunity costs*. A beneficiary, in order to avail population stabilization services, has often to forego opportunities: for earning an income or investing in agriculture or timely completion of household chores, and so on.

The obvious question is why should he or she do so? The answer that will be discussed and suggested later on lies only in making the real or apparent exchange comparable, if not better. Similarly, opportunity costs will also have to be incurred by SHOPs. It may be more difficult to arrange or facilitate an acceptable exchange for them. *Social service does not seem to carry conviction in the present context unless the SHOPs are members of a group – religious or otherwise – rather than individuals.* Maybe, such activities will further their political ambitions. Discovering this at the time of survey, not underplaying the difficulty, would be invaluable in planning the delivery of the product.

Social marketers must also understand the benefits to individuals and families of errant behaviour, and thereafter, devise strategies and marketing plans to counter these. Hence, this group even if a small minority has to be recognized, studied and appropriately approached with the objective of:

- Changing their behaviour in favour of the programme, and
- Getting them to admit their mistake (thus convincing others for not making the same).

This survey is also the *time to recall the concepts discussed in the chapter on behaviour*. The collection of the following information is of particular importance:

- The perceived costs/ barriers/ competition to the concept,
- The perceived costs/ barriers/ competition to the specific activities that follow the concept,
- The stage of behavioural change in a person according to the trans-theoretical model.

Also of crucial significance is the opportunity that is provided during a standard survey to apply the laddering or grand tour techniques. These, in addition to the understanding of life-style characteristics, influence thinking; and thereby motivate prospects towards the programme objectives. 'Whenever we design a method to learn about customer relations, we should do it with the alteration in mind that we would like to happen.' (Kennedy and Schneider, 2000) Academicians may take objection to this suggestion. However, it must be remembered that practical marketers, and indeed social marketers do not have stretchable time and resources. A social marketer is not also a researcher. The survey is being carried out with an objective in mind, and the quicker this is achieved, the more effective will be the overall programme. For example, it can be ascertained from the beneficiaries, through well-designed questions, whether the addition of an extra mouth in the family increases their responsibility, and expenses (on an annual basis for easy computation), besides affecting the health of the mother. The surveyor can guide the discussions along items that are likely to be strained on account of additional childbirth: land ownership, housing, health expenses, sanitation, and of course, food and clothing. Besides leading the discussion towards the justification for a small family, depending on the nature of the feedback, effective follow-up programmes can be designed. This is what can be termed as 'objective oriented survey'.

Objective oriented survey can determine an important component of marketing that addresses behavioural change i.e., *the stage of change* most members of the targeted group are in. Are they aware of the problem? If they are, are they aware of the possible solutions? Do they have the knowledge/ skills for properly adopting the solutions? Have they decided to try out any of the solutions? Would incentives/ samples help in a try-out? If the persons already have an experience, do they plan to continue with it? If not, why not? Would long term adopters like to join in the programme as brand ambassadors? The classification of groups on the basis of the answers to these questions is crucial for the designing of the action plans.

Since social marketers are likely to be under finance-and-time related pressures, it might often be necessary, as has been touched upon earlier, to undertake *observational and focus group surveys* instead of regular ones. Indeed, focus group surveys, for their stated advantages, are recommended at every step of the marketing effort. Observational surveys too, are recommended for the validation (or modification) of the results of the person-to-person survey. Persons may say, for instance, that they do not like to use condoms, but observation at selected outlets may show a large number of them asking for or buying condoms. The conclusion, to be verified, may be that either the persons were embarrassed while reporting or the condoms are being used for something else (as happened amongst handloom weavers in the city of Banaras who used the lubricant from the condoms for easing the spindle movement!).

A word about survey timings; indeed *all village level interaction timings*. The convenience of the villagers should decide this, not the convenience of the survey staff. 'Generally when a government agency sets up a family planning office in a village, its employees fail to realize that ideas on family planning may fail to take roots without long discussions' (Ray, 1986). People cannot abandon their work for discussions. Discussion time has to be snatched from them regularly and periodically.

An expected reaction from administrators of social development programmes would be the difficulty of organizing such surveys in the face of a nonexistent survey machinery and a budgetary provision in most organizations and departments. A definite suggestion on how to get over it cannot be given unless each situation is studied. However, it would seem reasonable to state that most organizations can locate funds for specific activities, including from programme partners. A partner body, be it a NGO, a University or in the Public Sector, may very well be able to organize the survey, perhaps in a manner akin to the one described in Chapter 4: (IPCL). What about the machinery? One does not need an elaborately established one; again, the members of a partner organization will do very well, especially if they already have an influence in the area. The members of the government hierarchy already available for programme implementation, though not specifically for a survey, may also like to join in if the idea can be appropriately marketed to them. *A new suggestion that has been floated is the involvement of the programme adopters or clients from the very beginning, and through all the intermediary steps, including the feedback.*

- Prescription:
  - For each segment identify the dominant behavioural traits and stages, their needs and aspirations, and the perceived costs and benefits of adopting the programme.
  - Verify the results using short, focus group/ observational/ phone surveys.
  - During the process of survey, encourage and cherish the objectives hoping to be promoted.
  - Involve the adopters from the survey stage itself to the very end of the marketing exercise.

B. POSITIONING OF THE PRODUCT/ IDEA

> Positioning is the linking of an idea and/or a product or a set of products with the needs and aspirations of a target market.

Positioning is indeed the beginning of the conceptual exercise that applies the theories and precepts of behavioural science to the identified market(s). *Basically, it is at this stage that the marketer attempts to link selected market segments to specific interventions, keeping in mind the behavioural characteristics of the segment and the potential of the product*. For instance, positioning would take up macro issues by linking particular groups with particular programmes, or micro items like:

- Linking those who are adopting population control measures to programmes on service support, social recognition etc.,
- Linking those who are productive and yet presently issue-less to programmes aimed at delaying their first child: through the spread of relevant information on the need and use of conventional contraceptives, etc.
- Linking those having one child to programmes on social recognition, community action, regular information on the benefits of a small and healthy family, the need to continue using conventional contraceptives, etc.,
- Linking those with two children with motivational programmes showing the desirability of adopting a permanent method of contraception, and
- Linking those having more than three children with persuasive drives for adopting a permanent method of contraception.

Similarly, linkages can also be in terms of other demographic-cum-psychographic or just psychographic characteristics. If, for instance, it transpires following a survey that couples tend to engage in physical intimacy during periods of stress or agricultural inactivity, and yet the wife is apprehensive of unwanted pregnancy but cannot insist on her husband wearing protection, it bears logic to push oral pills during such periods; indeed, if need be, under cover of some other health or nutrition drive.

One can take another instance from available literature on family planning in India. This data, surprisingly, shows that there is universal awareness about contraception, and that:

- 40.6% of currently married women use contraceptives, and
- The unmet need for contraception is 18.5% — 11% for spacing methods and 8.5% for terminal methods (Working Paper Series 2/2000-PC, Govt of India).

Logic, therefore, would point out the need to:

- *Move the 'aware' group from awareness to action* Never assume that awareness alone can lead to changes in attitudes and behaviours. In other words, provide the motivation and opportunity to the group concerned to cross over to action,
- *Nurture the 40.6 % to continue using contraceptives.* In other words, ensure regular follow up services *to this group,* and provide opportunities to switch methods, if such inclination is perceived,
- *Motivate the 59.9% of married women* (who do not use contraceptives) *to use any form of contraceptive,* and
- Provide information, knowledge, physical products, choice, opportunities, motivation and the strength to overcome personal, family and societal barriers, if any, to family planning *to the 18.5% of cases under 'unmet needs'.*

If just the concept aspect of the product is considered, and the intention is to spread awareness then, in tune with the suggestion made earlier, and indeed, that will continue to be made subsequently, the positioning should be *prioritized* on:

- The students
- The 'marriageable'
- The newly married, and
- The one child family.

(Good positioning will avoid time and energy to be spent on people whose behaviour and beliefs – couples with many children, for instance - have hardened over time).

As the earlier examples show, positioning in the minds of a targeted market is both in terms of the 'idea' as well as the individual products, including service, that support the idea. One should remember that *in social marketing, the physical product follows the idea* and not vice versa. 'Family planning marketers who say that their product is a condom misunderstand their market. Even those who say that their product is family planning may be out of touch with what target adopters are readily seeking in birth control and family planning' (Kotler and Roberto, 1989). *It is also not enough to link; it needs to be ensured that the link remains.* The tools that enable such linkages to be established are to be found in the rest of the social marketing exercise.

Recalling the experience of the UIP, product positioning should not only be in the mind of a customer, but should also spread from an individual, to an individual as a member of a family, to a member of a community, to a member of a state and finally the individual as a citizen of a nation. In other words, an individual, in accepting the idea or the product should ideally feel pleased as a person, as a member of a family, and so on. The longer the chain, the more enduring will be the product-person linkage.

◆ The next prescription is:
  - Link the product with the target segment for imbedding the idea and for initiating the marketing exercise.

C. IMPROVE IMAGE & GOODWILL

> A positive image and goodwill is the basic requirement for any organization to carry out social marketing.

This is perhaps the toughest job for a government or government related organization to tackle. Not only have the historical impressions of insincerity and inefficiency to be overcome, but also the continuous perceptions of insensitivity and corruption. However, a beginning can surely be made with the following steps – *the goodwill goals*:

- Ensuring that only such commitments that can be fulfilled are made. A promise must be a promise.
- Commitments must be fulfilled within the time indicated or even before.
- Service and delivery schedules are adhered to.
- Service and quality must be synonymous.
- Service is with empathy.
- Staff linkages are established so that the consumer is not inconvenienced by unforeseen absenteeism.
- Mistakes are acknowledged and followed by an all out effort to correct the damage done (to the extent possible).

The aforesaid suggestions may appear idealistic. These would, indeed, require the full support of the entire organization, if not more. Yet, these provide a direction. *Can, incremental steps be taken*? Yes, as has been urged earlier too (nucleus formation). To repeat, the way could be to enlist the services of staff or volunteers who are already members of a social or religious organization that enables them to imbibe in them a sense of dedicated service. Another way could be to associate with institutions or organizations that have a good image, and get them to play a prominent role, if not spearhead the programme. Over a period of time, the 'referral impression' will wipe on to the promoting organisation. Once the programme takes off in an ideal manner, it would make sense to 'enable' the media to study the achievements and lend their support to it, thereby progressively building up a positive public image both of the programme as well as the participants .

In the ultimate analysis, it is under the leadership of the chief social marketer that the entire team will have to strain for achieving the identified goodwill goals; and, indeed, there are many examples of chief executives who have brought about image improvement in spite of, and within the overall system. If the beneficiaries know that an organization – in this case offering family planning products and services - is honest and sincere, their response towards the programme is likely to be commensurate and may even be overwhelming. Corporate sincerity and honesty, according to Azim Premji, Chairman of Wipro, goes beyond contractual obligations.

Brand identity, as has been discussed in Chapter 2, is an important concept in commercial marketing. It is generally associated with the goodwill of an organisation and its products. 'A promise is implicit in a brand'. But promise is not only of consistent product quality, but also of service. According to Nicholas Ind, 'an organization – through its reported activities, communications and employee behaviour – provides us with an approximation of organizational reality. Then, if the signals we receive are proven by experience, our anxiety is reduced in subsequent interactions and we may come to trust the brand and even become advocates for it'. What this statement stresses is that a product and service must not only be reliable to begin with, but these must continue to live up to all expectations and promise; likewise, with social marketing products and services. The various and many ways that can be locally devised to facilitate this will decide the success of the programme.

The advantages of branding have been stated earlier. One more aspect of branding becomes important as any programme picks up momentum, especially when there arises a case for a second or multiple branding, in addition to the main one, for multiple products or service(s). This is based on the natural tendency of persons to avoid taking decisions - a statement that may sound contradictory to what has been discussed in Chapter

3, but is actually not. *When we are exploring, we need options for making choices in tune with our perceived needs. But having arrived at a conclusion: that a certain behaviour is in our interest, we would like to be guided by an expert or a body/ organization of repute. Product branding enables this.* So, if a person believes that a condom is needed in deciding a product among many alternatives, the person is likely to go by his or her impression of the brand identity of the product and its manufacturer. So, according to Nicholas Ind, in deference to the statement that the 'primary function of brands is to reduce our anxiety in making choices', *it makes sense to find out the brand equity (brand value) of the products on offer and push those that are positive.*

Logos are the most popular expression of brand identity, hence the population control programme should be carried out with the 'red triangle' logo already popularized throughout the country. All connected events and programmes should display this identity – as publicity materials, stationary, uniforms, incentive gifts, and so on. *In addition, one may decide to build up an impression of quality service that the social marketing body is engaged in. For this, as opposed to the product, it might be advantageous to create a new brand in order to distinguish the programme the social planner is hoping to carry out from the rest.* Since the product brands are already decided nationally, it is only the service brand that the social marketer can promote. In order to do this, the following steps are essential:

- Identify persons – official and non-official – who are likely to be 'brand ambassadors'.
- Train and motivate them on a continuous basis. Their behaviour must be obviously and apparently different.
- Decide on the centers where quality products and services are guaranteed to be available. Such centers may start with a few, but gradually build up to many.

- Decide on an identity – a name and a logo for the new 'superior' service, and a badge for each brand ambassador and service center, in consultation with them.
- Publicize the identity and the product/ service on offer. Encourage the market to contact them and others to join in.
- Dovetail the reaction with the rest of the programme monitoring system

- Prescription:
  - Take as many steps as possible to continuously improve organizational image and goodwill.

D. DECIDE ON THE PRODUCT TO BE DELIVERED

A product is what is offered to the market, in due recognition of its needs, in exchange for something.

The primary component of any social marketing product is the 'idea' or the concept. This is what is to be offered to members of a segmented market as something very desirable and in their interest. In exchange, the acceptors are expected to modify their personal behaviour and adopt measures that enable the crystallization and growth of the idea. A choice of tangible products and services is thereafter needed to nurture an immediate exchange, even though in most social programmes the long-term goals are not so concrete. *So, in social marketing, the term 'product' dons its widest mantle – encompassing the idea, the supporting physical products, and of course, the services.* It is also seen that the development of the product and the positioning of the product becomes very related in social marketing.

PRODUCT = IDEA + PHYSICAL OBJECTS + SERVICES that satisfy a need.

In offering contraception as the main plank of the population stabilization programme, as the item for exchange, one should not miss the fact that the offer flies against the *underlying motivation and desire for sex and progeny in all human beings*. 'The increase or decrease of human populations resolves on the axis of two, sometimes opposite, impulses – desire for mating and the desire for an offspring'. At the initial stages of marriage, the dominant motivation is sex, resulting in childbirth while later on, often under the persuasion of the family elders, it is the desire for succession. *To put it differently, the product should support the desires – the desires themselves being unobjectionable – and enable the participants to control it as per their free choice*. Conception control products (condoms, IUDs, pills, injectibles and sterilization) do not interfere with the first desire i.e., mating. So, satisfying this desire without resulting in unwanted childbirths is not difficult. The second desire for offspring needs to be addressed— essentially by communicating the advantages and the desirability of a small and healthy family, and how this is in overall individual, family, societal, and national interest—only if it results in numbers beyond the national norm;

In some cases, individual members of a family, in spite of family or social pressures, may desire *not* to have a child. There are, indeed, instances when rural ladies, already burdened with children and household chores, have approached doctors for a contraceptive that will be unobtrusive. 'Sometimes, the woman wishes to limit but the husband is either unwilling or opposes contraception. In such a case, a woman might be willing to quietly try out a method and reveal it to her husband, when the time is appropriate' ('The Ten Year Copper T', 2000). India's population stabilization programme has not encouraged such items – mainly injectables and implants – and so, the closest to their desire is[3] the pill (that may be taken surreptitiously). The question that can be considered while discussing the action plans is whether such secretive intervention as this can be facilitated? Perhaps at a place where women have to gather everyday for some other need or work?

(The latest, approved method in the U.S.A., the small body patch that releases hormones through the skin into the bloodstream to prevent pregnancy, costing as much as a pill, known as 'Ortho Evra' may be most convenient, but it is visible and not secretive).

There is no particular problem in offering condoms to all. Simple training, even leaflets, on its use is just what is wanted. Many practitioners believe that condoms are the best product to be spread in most rural situations devoid of qualified and trained medical personnel. Offering oral pills, on the other hand, however simple, needs some precautions. The initial use should be on medical advice since there could be discomfort, requiring a change in the type. Forewarned, there is less chance of the product being discarded. Thereafter, for a regular user, the distribution procedure would be easier, akin to the condoms. IUDs, naturally have to be implanted by trained and approved persons. *It is worth recalling that the success and the mass acceptability of the pulse polio programme suggests the need for offering a product that is easy to deliver and effective over a reasonably long period.* If and when skin patches and injectables arrive on the scene, the acceptance may, indeed, be greater. The issue of 'choice' is also very important. Multiple products encourage wider acceptance.

Service.

Service is also a product under its broad definition. However, what is meant by service here is the interrelation aspect between the marketer and the customer that, in the ultimate test, converts a person into a prospect, and finally into a partner.

PEOPLE → PROSPECT → CUSTOMERS → CLIENTS → SUPPORTERS → PARTNERS

Service, as is well understood, can 'follow' a physical product or be independent e.g., consultancy. Service for the population control programme would range from medical advice before, and after the use of a contraceptive device. Hence, in order to decide on the service to be delivered, one needs to 'begin at the beginning', that is, by recognizing that no one likes to go to a dispensary or be hospitalized. Therefore, as has been mentioned in Chapter 2, the distribution network should ideally reach all the products to each doorstep. *The service to be aimed for is 'doorstep' or 'near doorstep' or 'mobile delivery'*. However, since this is not always practicable, the success of a marketing programme will depend largely on how well the programme coordinators come close to the 'reach home' concept. When the patient needs to be hospitalized, the service in the hospital, if it cannot be painless, should at least be clean, private, pleasant and caring.

> 'Since the rural mother cannot afford to come to the city clinic, the contraceptive services must be taken to the village'.

> 'Illiteracy and ignorance of our women is a formidable obstacle. We cannot entrust mothers with a contraceptive and some printed instructions...Without a clinical demonstration and without absolute cleanliness and without proper knowledge, birth control may do more harm than good' (Chandrasekhar, 1961).

Service has many faces. It may, for instance, appear in the form of 'exchangeability' or 'buy-back' facilities - an attractive aspect of present day consumer durable marketing. On the same analogy, in the context of the population stabilization programme, if the customer knows that a product – an IUD for instance – would be removed if she is not satisfied, then the desire to try out the product in the first place will be stronger. 'Apart from good quality of care, an IUD service must respect women's right to adopt or discard the Copper-T at will. Critical to this is a liberal policy of Copper-T removal as per the client's wishes – service providers must not sit in judgement over the correctness of women's reasons for removal...' ('The Ten Year Copper-T', 2000). This would, indeed, be an example of quality service and quality product going hand in hand.

Service is dependent on available infrastructure including static and mobile sites, equipment, consumables, and trained manpower. The NFHS 92-93 had found that 'in spite of obvious constraints and inadequacies, the government network can and does, provide most of the MCH and contraceptive care'. Though the NPP 2000 has projected additional requirement in tune with the growth of population, the earlier statement would imply that the *infrastructure available, even if non-optimum in relation to the growth of population, is yet adequate. Hence, it would make sense to concentrate on the other aspects of service like customer care at home and in camps and hospitals.*

A very useful guide for customer-oriented reproductive health quality care in medical institutions suggests nine areas for attention:

1. Access to services
2. Equipment and supplies
3. Professional standards and technical competence
4. Continuity of care
5. Service environment
6. Client provider interaction
7. Informed decision making
8. Integration of services
9. Women's participation in management

Source: UNFPA technical report. May 1999. Planning Population & Development with a focus on Decentralisation and Quality of Care.

Both the aspects of 'product packaging' as understood by conventional marketers – the wrapping/ container and the combination of products/ services/ often, loans - are applicable to social marketing. One important difference, however, needs to be recognized. In business, packaging is a *'relational'* concept encompassing the physical packaging of the product together with the product related service, financing and other incentive add-ons. Rarely does such packaging involve dissimilar products. In social development, however, the packaging concept is essentially an *'enlarged'* one, including multiple areas of service. For instance, a conventional, integrated approach to population control will also call for education, preventive health, maternal and child care, and so on. Just the social product and its related services will rarely be sufficient in itself. Thus, in applying the concept of packaging to social marketing, a combination of both the relational and extended approaches appear to be essential. A word of caution though: in including various related issues in the main programme package it should not happen that the focus is lost. Organizations would 'want to have it all', but social marketers should not fall into the trap of trying to achieve all the objectives at once (Andreasen, 1995).

Competition.

In commercial marketing, competition is a factor taken well note of in deciding on a product. In social marketing, competition is a very large and important issue, essentially concerning those factors that obstruct behavioral change and adoption of a different lifestyle. Mckenzie-Mohr calls such competition 'barriers'. Such barriers can range from economic, social and religious beliefs to the lack of physical infrastructure. The most potent barrier towards a small family is the desire for one or more sons, essentially as old age insurance. Competition could also appear from the most unexpected quarters, for instance, the ingrained, selfish attitude of some of the community leaders. They might be benefiting from the availability of cheap labour from the family members of the poor! Indeed, marketing has to counteract inequal social structures wherein 'the relative advantage of some is maintained through the disadvantage of others' (Hartman et al. 1989). Such competition has also been documented closer home through the experience of the Ganaswastha Kendra Project in Bangladesh (Ray, 1986).

Subtle and indirect competition to the physical product can arise out of a popular conception that pills, IUDs, sterilization are all allopathic in nature, and therefore, fraught with serious side-effects. Therefore, there is often reluctance, if not open hostility to this programme from practitioners of other systems of treatment. *Knowledge of such competition is essential both for counteracting its adverse effects as well as for possibly including them in the partnership programme.* Obstructions to change often emerge out of poverty itself. In a situation of abject poverty, a family with one child is no better off than a family with more. So, the issue boils down to how forcefully a marketer can communicate the advantages of a changed lifestyle, thereby creating a demand for it. Some studies have highlighted the difficulty of disposal as a personal/social problem in the use of condoms in rural areas. If surveys indeed, show this to be true, the programme coordinator needs to find out locally acceptable solutions to this challenge. Somewhere, infant mortality is a potent competition; elsewhere, 'the pressure of numbers .. upon the parents.. is probably the most important single factor motivating adoption of family planning' (Kivlin et al., 1971). Administrators of social development programmers would be aware of many such examples, and since it is not practical to discuss all the possibilities, it is considered sufficient to state that, 'recommended behaviors always have a competition which must be understood and addressed' (www.social-marketing.org). *A listing of all the competition to the product – both the idea as well as the physical product – and the possible 'enablers' (an item that will be mentioned once again towards the end of this chapter) is expected to be invaluable.*

The initial steps taken through the psychographic survey would have thrown up the obvious obstacles/ competition in the path of acceptance of the social product. It may be worthwhile to spend a while longer on this aspect and detect more subtle competition through carefully organized focus groups. *Management experts favour the addressal of the easier ones first; essentially because that creates a conducive environment and impetuous for tackling the more difficult ones thereafter.* For instance, families that have already adopted progressive social behaviour like sending their child to school and/ or spacing their second child should be targeted first over those who strongly feel that an extra hand is economically more advantageous to their family. This is not to suggest that the latter be forgotten; just that they will require a long term and repeated approach.

Some social experiments have succeeded in disturbing an existing social balance and introducing a more equitable one simply by discussing and arriving at a mutually beneficial solution amongst the various segments, even with conflicts of interest. All that needed to be done – at the cost of appearing too simplistic -was to get the representatives of the different groups together, debate each other's support or objection to the recommended path, and then arrive at common objectives and thus at a compromise. Notwithstanding the difficulty, nay sometimes impossibility, such cooperation among partners and competitors is feasible as international attempts show (White, 1999). Reduction of competition is not only essential for the widest acceptance of the product(s) on offer, but also for the optimal sharing of resource, and consistency of goals and results.

Product quality, it bears repetition, is essential for programme goodwill and sustainability. A social marketer, in most cases, will not be in a position to influence the quality of physical products supplied nationally. Yet, he or she can, and should constantly monitor the feedback from users and take corrective action including the offering of alternatives. Most important, the quality of service – an aspect discussed earlier – and especially surgery, with due admiration to the sentiments of those who are taking such a bold step, must be caring, aseptic and competent. Post-operative care must be given as much importance as the operation itself. Mass campaigns, if organized, must not sacrifice quality for quantity. It may be recalled that marketing ideas have graduated from hardsell to quality and service, and social marketing should not go backwards.

Availability of caring service, like the availability of products can be well monitored. The usual way of doing this is through post-incident interviews, pre-paid response forms and indirectly, through increase or decrease in service acceptance trends. Programme feedback, as will be discussed later on, is worth paying attention to.

- Prescription:
  - Understand the competition.
  - Decide on the product(s) that is(are) to be offered depending on the positioning of the product, the organization's physical and financial resources, and the availability of trained manpower.
  - Ensure that health centers provide courteous service and all the nine items of care during pre and post interaction/ operation.
  - Establish a system of improving the product and the service depending on the feedback.

E. DECIDE ON THE PRICE/ RATE FOR THE PRODUCT, SERVICE

Price is what a consumer would be willing to pay, in terms of physical discomfort or financial or opportunity costs for availing a product/ service.

Monetary and non-monetary price, including opportunity costs, are indeed, important barriers to changes in behaviour. It is quite natural for a customer to calculate the price he or she will have to pay in terms of transportation to a medical center or to a special camp, for instance. Besides the loss of income, either regular or potential, or even the time and additional energy that would be required to complete non remunerative chores like house work, or the 'cost' of requesting a neighbour to look after the children and so on, are issues to be balanced with the expected benefits of the service being offered. Obviously, the marketing programme must not only aim at convincing the beneficiary that the gains in change are greater, but must also ensure that 'enablers' – physical, social, economic, cultural – are put in place. (This is further elaborated in the latter sections of the book).

Population stabilization and family welfare services are social costs normally borne by government, including the heavy costs that may be incurred if post insertion/ operative complications arise. Very often, the consumer has also to chip in if the required investigative facility or drug or consumable for an operation is not available. The requirement of blood is almost invariably to be arranged by the patient. *The solution lies not in disregarding the possibility but in providing reserve budgetary support for these contingencies or introducing medical insurance for family planning services.*

Partner organizations like the PSI, DKT, who promote what they call 'social marketing of contraceptives' (SMC) and service providers like Marie Stopes charge for their services because they feel it has certain advantages. 'Price can serve as a symbol and a surrogate for a product's quality. When target adopters have difficulty judging the quality of a social product, they often use price as a standard' (Roberto, 1989). Government supplies of condoms and pills are free. The parallel supply through the 'SMC' channel is priced. If a survey shows that beneficiaries link price with quality and would be willing to pay for an 'apparently' better product or service, then to a social marketer, it would make sense to push the priced product. Alternately, a differential push may be continued to cater to the needs of both the very poor and those who want something more and can pay for it. When two or more varieties of a product are available, a manufacturer has two options: to push the cheaper one, hoping to profit by volumes, or to push the costlier one, hoping to profit from limited sale, consequently limited sales expenditure and network. On the basis of simple economics, it would make sense to the seller to push the pill (Rs. 2 to 7 for a cycle of 30 days) over the condom (Rs. 0.5 to 6 for a pack of 3 or 4, i.e., over 3 to 4 days, presuming one-per-day use). From the point of view of the user, especially, the poorest, the first alternative seems more 'affordable' and easily understood. Local resources and preferences will, therefore, dictate the model to follow.

Locally acceptable, panchayat decided costs could perhaps be imposed for offering 'packaged health services' (see item on incentives) or ambulance/ transport services. There may also be a case for realizing additional consideration from well-to-do communities, living in distinctive locations i.e., industrial areas, government colonies etc., for specialized family planning services, including home service. Medical insurance is another option that needs serious consideration.

- Prescription:
  - Budget for supporting customers requiring medical help as a result of unforeseen

complications.

- Explore the possibility of introducing medical insurance for eligible couples.
- Explore the possibility of charging for family planning services.

F. DECIDE ON THE DISTRIBUTION NETWORK INCLUDING INVOLVEMENT OF THE OPINION LEADERS AND STAKE HOLDERS.

Reaching the identified product to the identified market, efficiently, is possible only through a well-planned, well-trained distribution network.

Very rarely do business organizations engage their own staff for undertaking all the field level selling functions. Surveys and advertisements are almost always farmed out to professionals; and products are pushed – sold, serviced, and sales-reported through a distributor-retail network. This is the commercial sector's way of entering a community through a set of vanguard members. This structure not only enables a great degree of flexibility and saving of resources, it permits the business organization to effectively test, anticipate and operate the important 'selling' function without getting directly involved in local sensibilities and politics. Capable distributors and retailers are encouraged while inefficient ones are simply dropped from the network. In contrast, most government and government-supported organizations plan and execute their allocated tasks, and then evaluate *their own* performance. Community involvement, whenever attempted, is taken as an exercise in mass mobilization: of the people, by the programmers.

Franchising is an innovative way of spreading the reach of service-oriented organizations, including fast food restaurants, testing and

diagnostic laboratories etc. Franchising ensures uniform cloning of standards and performance with respect to the parent. If a service organization is successfully delivering a product to one segment of the market and it has built up a reputation in the process, then nurturing another organization to deliver exact service to another segment may be feasible. The concept is being held aloft for pioneering social marketers to take note of.

Community involvement in social development programmes has not been possible except in some localized instances. In these places social movements have been spearheaded not by the programme staff but by the prominent members of the community *who already have had a hold* on it - either on account of birth (ex Rajas, descendants of a religious order or a village chief), or as leaders of a caste and/or political power (the Anand story), or long-term, selfless service (Baba Amte, Ramakrishna Mission, Satya Sai Trust, Missionaries of Charity, etc.), or financial or commercial strength (social support organizations of the house of Birlas, Tatas, etc.), or for some similar reason. A recent commentary showed that Kerala's success in the literacy and educational field was not due to the programmes carried out by the state government, but because of a tradition of community action spurred by certain groups. 'The initial spark for the spread of education began more than a hundred years ago with the Christian missionaries who set up the first modern open-to-all schools in the old state of Trevancore. This spurred the Nairs, led by Mannathau Padmanabhan to set up a vast number of community schools. Muslims and Ezhavas also led to the famous reading room movement and libraries came up in smallest villages' (Das, 2000).

Since mass mobilization, on account of divergent interests, is difficult to organize leave alone sustain, *the successful commercial pattern of retailer-distributorship appears to hold great promise and therefore, suggests application in the social sector.* The pattern can either be transplanted faithfully, i.e., the distribution network can be entrusted primarily to *sell* the physical product with a modicum of promotion (as in the social marketing of contraceptives), or it can be modified and enlarged to carry out *all* the marketing functions. Though the aforesaid decision should be best left to the social marketing organization, *the recommendation offered is for the latter model.* An acceptance of this recommendation would mean that *in addition* to the selection of retailers/ distributors (of condoms and pills) based on their financial strength and organizational capacity, the persons who wield great influence on the community – for whatever reasons – have also to be approached for becoming the honourary 'retailers/distributors' of social ideas. *The retailers/ distributors of social ideas – and we have earlier termed them as SHOPs - have to be the main 'movers and shakers' of community inertia.* The involvement of such 'injective' members of a community is considered to be the best way of entering and influencing it. Procedurally, having identified the SHOPs during the survey, the social marketer and his core team needs to interact with *each one* of them and try to involve them as partners in the programme – from the very beginning to the end. It is only through them that the programme can achieve the widest influence. Indeed, this seems to be the easiest way forward for government and semi-government functionaries (with their generally negative image), instead of having to carry out the marketing exercise alone, to enlist a powerful ally.

The practice of and attempt to distribute/ sell the simplest contraceptive *products* (condoms, and pills) may not only continue through appropriate commercial outlets (grocers, ration shops, hair cutting saloons, tea shops, 'panwallas', post offices, and the like), but this effort requires to be intensified and extended. Such of the products that cannot be sold/ distributed across the counter, like contraceptive pills for the first users and IUDs, the distribution/ retailing may continue to be with the professionals, both private and official. The programme coordinator needs to watch the stocking and movement of the products, outlet-wise so as to ensure the availability of the popular ones and also to recognize and encourage the particularly enterprising retailers. It would also be *useful to survey* the commercial establishments in the market in order to ascertain their attitude towards family planning and consequently, their interest in stocking condoms (including display), and promoting their use. Other organizations carrying out social marketing of contraceptives in the area should be encouraged and not considered as competition to be eliminated.

> In the Philippines, especially in the urban and semi-urban areas, under the 'Trust Express' programme for marketing contraceptives, condoms and pills have been delivered along with house delivery of groceries, eatables, licenses etc. ('Changing the Attitudes and Behaviors of Men Through Social Marketing', www.icomp.org)

An important constituent of a social marketing distribution network should be the *partners*, including the potential ones. Forming partnerships with public, private sector and government organizations working in the area is a very good way of concept development, sharing experience, achieving greater reach, ensuring credibility, and for supplementing financial resources including incentives and commissions. These organizations are most often more than happy to join the programme/ distribution network, and thereby improve their local, regional and sometimes national image. Partnership with private enterprise can open up alternate sources of funding, including the recently launched National Rural Development Fund (NRDF). Including the 'wider' medical fraternity in 'advocacy and counseling, for distributing supplies and equipment, and as depot holders' has been recommended by the NPP 2000 (C28- 31), and will be very welcome addition to any family planning drive. Partnership with Medical Associations, especially in imparting skills to the practitioners of the Indian system of medicine and homeopathy, is another area holding innovative potential and much promise. Partnership with the media houses will enable sharing of the promotional expenses besides availing of their expertise.

The Bangladesh Gana Swastha Kendra has imparted skill-training in IUD insertions to interested and intelligent village youths. They have even provided assistance at the time of tubectomy and vasectomy. To quote the GSK, 'An important indicator of the effectiveness of the training programme is that a paramedic (without any formal degree) can easily perform many jobs of a qualified doctor' (Ray, 1986). The hesitation to replicate this model in other places has been on account of complications that may develop. Yet, such complications may arise in the presence of practicing doctors too, the only difference being that regular doctors may be better qualified to handle such situations. Since similar responsibilities have not been sanctioned in India, one can try to seek partnership with the Indian or State Medical Associations with selected NGOs for such training and skill development.

Private medical practitioners, including those of the indigenous systems, are often reluctant to counsel their patients on family planning, for lack of time (non-remunerative). A Sri Lankan experience (Davis and Louis, 1975 cited by Harvey

1999) shows that they may be willing to do so if the work is reduced for them and limited only to the first advise, and the signing of a prescription. PSI, the NGO spearheading the social marketing of contraceptives programme involved the medical representatives in playing a major role in motivating the doctors (after understanding the characteristics of pills) and for supplying them with pre-printed prescriptions. The doctors were thus happy to do their bit for family planning without having to spend time on repeated counseling. On the basis of the pre-printed prescriptions, the users could then purchase the pills from any of the many advertised outlets. Once persons were registered in these outlets as users, PSI sent free information booklets to them (on the proper use, possible discomfort, benefits) in three languages. Six weeks after the first letter, in order to discourage early dropouts, a second letter was sent 'to remind her that she was well protected by a good method which she should continue'. An attractive plastic purse was also promised on return of two empty packets of pills representing a four months supply. Though the reference does not say so, it is presumed that the pills not being free, the possibility of their misuse just to get the purse was considered to be negligible.

The role of the existing machinery in providing the basic foundation for product distribution is not being minimized, yet not being specifically highlighted as being 'given'. Getting the best out of this structure is a management function; an important component of which is getting their involvement – an item discussed earlier. A standard social marketing 'distribution network' will thus look like:

SOCIAL MARKETING DISTRIBUTION NETWORK		
Distributors & Retailers	Selected on the commercial pattern.	Sells condoms, pills.
Honourary Distributors & Retailers (SHOPs)	Selected on the basis of community influence.	Sells the concept besides becoming programme partners.
Partners	Selected on the basis of community influence.	Supports the programme
Organizational staff	Will mostly be 'given'. However there will be scope of identifying and optimally positioning/entrusting.	For the entire programme

As has been mentioned in Chapter 3, easy *availability and choice of products* is an essential pre-requisite for changing behaviour into specific action and maintenance. Distribution of condoms through multiple outlets is one such way. Similarly, the introduction of oral pills and IUDs, preferrably at a nearby health camp, if not at the doorstep is another. Essential inputs for this would be mobility for the paramedical staff, a schedule for periodic home visits for health check-ups, including redress of IUD-use problems if any, and aseptic insertion. A concurrent activity would have to be the medically proper stocking of consumables, and the availability of trained medical personnel at health centers, particularly for carrying out any of the terminal methods. Taking a leaf from Wiebe's study, for any successful programme, the consumer/ beneficiary has to be made aware of at least the following:

- How and where he or she will have to go for the product/ service;
- The names of the health centers and the specified times (including the maximum number to be entertained on a day) for consultation/ operations;
- The days when trained staff will visit homes (if possible) for

IUD insertions;

- The days when trained staff will visit IUD users and those operated upon, whether in camps or at home (and this time, not if feasible but certainly) for post operative care/ assurance and management information collection;
- The names and location of the respective programme supervisors.

Marketing experts have advised that the programme coordinator, to the extent possible, should plan to 'make the exchange and its opportunities available in "places" that reach the audience and fit its lifestyles' (www.social-marketing.org).

In suggesting the roping in of SHOPs and commercial retailers into the family planning programme, what is not being trivialized is the immense effort that needs to go into the setting up of, and retaining this network. Indeed, this may turn out to be the toughest part of the social marketing exercise. As has been shown in Chapter 2, the SHOPs, who are after all, the leading figures of the community, and the retailers need to be motivated, trained and retrained not in the pattern of students and teachers in conventional teaching institutions, but as programme partners. The experience of the commercial sector that 'a born salesman- if that term refers to a gregarious, aggressive kind of individual- *may not* do really as well as his less extrovert colleague who has solid, specialized training' (Francis, 1978) is worth remembering.

The question that logically arises is why should the SHOPs and the retail commercial outlets take on this responsibility? There are two ways of approaching this issue. The standard one is that of bodies that are already carrying out the social marketing of contraceptives. The management of such organizations firmly believes that the commercial channel can be tapped only if there is an attractive commission. So, in tune with this experience, some incentive could be built in. Alternately, if budgetary provisions cannot be arranged, the *programme partners may be asked to help out directly or indirectly.* Such of the partners, for instance, whose products are already into the commercial distribution network may be persuaded to offer a higher margin on their products if tagged to the social product. *The non-standard approach suggests - if Maslow is to be believed – that their incentive and reward may be the social recognition they will gather in the process, including acknowledgement of their community leadership by the local administration.*

It has been discussed earlier that inducing behavioural change in favour of a small family is not easy since the *benefits are long-drawn and there is no scare of non-compliance.* The Sexually Transmitted Disease (STD) prevention programme, on the other hand, is something that deals with the immediate repercussions of irresponsible behaviour. Consequently, the communication messages on STD prevention can be more dramatic, if not scary. At the same time both the programmes recommend the use of condoms. *Hence, there seems to be sufficient justification for the family planning programme to link up intimately with the STD and HIV prevention set up, thereby extending the distribution network.*

◆ Prescription:

- Entrust field level motivation, supervision and feedback functions to SHOPs, rather than entirely to Government servants. Provide training to SHOPs together with programme staff and partners.
- Establish extensive outlets for multiple choice condoms and pills.
- Involve the authorized private and the official medical fraternity to provide reproductive health care and advice to all their patients, irrespective of whether they have come for such advice or for any other health related advice.

- Build in incentives for stocking and distributing condoms and pills.
- Plan for enabling those willing to use IUDs to get the service at their homes or at least at a local dispensary/ camp.
- Provide transportation facilities for persons wishing to go to health centers for tubectomy/ vasectomy. (The NPP 2000 has suggested ways of involving the youth and prominent persons in every locality for transportation and ambulance services).
- Form effective partnerships with all established organizations – government and non-government in a widespread, multiple choice distribution network. Gain sponsors from local public and private sector organizations – preferably in services and kind.
- Link up with the HIV/ STD prevention programme.
- Publicize the hierarchy of services available, the service timings and schedule, the names of the delivery personnel, and their supervisors.

G. DEVELOP A COMMUNICATION AND PROMOTION PROGRAMME

Having understood the mind of the target market, and having established a framework for reaching the products to them with the least inconvenience, the actual process of influencing the mind towards product acceptance begins with the designing of effective communication.

This is the stage wherein the attributes of the product are

woven, using the science of communication, with the characteristics of the segmented market into a framework to persuade the prospects into accepting the planned 'exchange'. The 'adoption of an idea, like the adoption of any product, requires a deep understanding of the needs, perceptions, preferences, reference groups, and behavioral patterns of the target audience', and effective communication enables us to 'maximize the ease of adopting the idea' (Kotler, 1975). Communication, recalling the insights gained in understanding and changing behaviour, has to be designed so as to *influence behaviour from the stage the customer is in to the stage of final acceptance and maintenance. But in order to be effective, it has to stand on the two portals built up earlier: the satisfaction of the physical requirements for bringing about change, and the workable alternatives to the external barriers to change.* While the last aspect will be further elucidated later on, in this section it is the first that is being developed.

A suggestion briefly touched upon in Chapter 2, i.e., 'creation' of demand needs to be flagged at this stage. According to Gregory Carpenter, an associate professor in the Kellogg Graduate School of Management, Northwestern University, USA, the evolving concept of marketing goes beyond simply giving customers what they want, but encompasses a gradual encouragement to learn new things, about fresh opportunities. 'Increasingly, strategies are being created on the assumption that, at least initially, buyers do not know what they want but instead, learn what they want'. Professor Carpenter asserts that *'It (marketing) is about being market driven and "market driving"'*. In other words, informing the market the possibilities of change and the benefits that are likely to be derived from such a move are totally in consonance with modern marketing. Social marketers, therefore, need worry no longer about ethical dimensions of demand creation. Indeed, psychographic survey, it has already been suggested, will enable programme planners to initiate demand creation while assessing lifestyle characteristics for the rest of the marketing exercise.

In order to design an effective communication package, the following issues have to be addressed:

- Who for?
- How?
  - The content
  - The vehicle
  - The tools

As explained in Chapter 2, the tools that will be utilized in delivering the package will be:

- Advertisement,
- Publicity, and
- Personal contact

Who for?

'Every programme element of the social marketing campaign should have precise objectives' (Sevakram and Waghmare, 1986). The first requirement of setting objectives is the targeting of beneficiaries and, therefore, what the communication package will hope to achieve. In planned social marketing, the beneficiary segments would have been already identified in the course of the preliminary survey. This would have further been honed during product and service positioning. While basically, one would like to offer a healthier and more fulfilling family, community and perhaps national life in exchange for a change in behavioral traits, 'programmes to influence action will be more effective if they were based on an understanding of the target audience's own perceptions of the proposed exchange' (www.social-marketing.org). What this implies is a clear understanding of the stage of behaviour of the identified target. If, for instance, the target is unaware of the possibilities, there is little sense in communicating details of the product or its availability. Likewise, it will be a waste of resource if basic information on the need for change is communicated when the target is really looking for ways of adoption. Although such surgically precise differentiation may not be possible, *in designing appropriate messages an awareness of the stage of the target is certainly called for.* As has been remarked earlier, it will be a waste of effort and resources if the message is designed for the literate while the target is not.

That apart, the designing of communication will have to take account of the product positioning as well as the product attributes. In the context of family planning certain sections of the population can be identified for targeting:

- Those who will have a direct impact on the Goals set for 2010 are 5 year olds today (assuming initiation to the reproductive group from the age of 15),
- Those who are 14 today (i.e., school going) will enter the target group next year.
- Those between 15 to 59 years (a classification adopted by the population stabilization programme) will increase from 519 million to 800 million by 2016.

It may be recalled that, this study has harped on the need to target the student community right from the primary stage. It bears repeating that motivating adults is very difficult and by the time results are achieved, many million offsprings would have come into this world. Motivating children, on the other hand, is easier and when they grow up, the benefits of a small family would have been deeply ingrained in their minds. The marketing mantra that 'action is undertaken whenever target audiences believe that the benefits they receive will be greater than the costs they incur' (social marketing institute web page) is specifically applicable to young minds as they have a prominent sense of social good and indeed, national pride. Similarly, for the various reasons discussed earlier, in social literature, and nationally, *women* as a group and especially the housewife are an important target for social communication.

While consumers are at the end of the line, one should not forget the *participants in the distribution network, the service providers and the partners.* Keeping in view the levels of knowledge of these sections, information and motivational packages need to be developed. Nor is it warranted that communication misses out *those who already have accepted the product* – an item that will be developed later on under the heading 'Post Purchase Cognitive Dissonance'.

◆ The prescription, therefore, is:

- Formulate communication packages specifically for
    - o School going children,
    - o Women,
    - o Members of the distribution chain,
    - o Health staff, and
    - o Partners.

How? – The Content.

The content of the message will depend on the objectives, the product positioning, the resources available, the socio-political environment, and the state of awareness of the target groups. It will also have to keep in mind their needs, attitudes, sensibilities, and apprehensions but at the same time and definitely highlight the benefits – as perceived by them and otherwise. The beneficiaries have primarily to be convinced that the concept/ programme is in their interest. They must be made to feel that this is exactly what they have been waiting for but did not know how to go about. Indeed, the designing of the message will depend on how deeply the marketer has understood 'behaviour' and the feedback from the survey. Since however, the marketing plan hopes to influence *personal and community behaviour* while taking into account the external influence, only the main issues that are *internal* to the thinking of the market are being discussed. The discussions thus begin with the following table which indicates in a nut-shell, the major interventions for influencing the 'internal environment', thereby encouraging compliance behaviour:

BEHAVIOURAL STAGE	INTERVENTION SUGGESTED
Unaware, uninformed	Inform, interact, follow-up.
Informed, unaware	Provide user information/ skills. Highlight disadvantages of present stage. Introduce benefits of change. Provide comparisons, Counter misinformation and competition
Aware, contemplating	Appreciate progress. Highlight incentives. Downplay yet introduce dis-incentives. Provide comparisons. Assist in developing a plan for starting. Provide social support. Show adherence to normative behaviour. Counter misinformation.
Recently changed. Practitioner.	Appreciate action. Provide recognition/ incentives Provide problem solving feed-back Devise self actualization measures. Involve in partnerships. Highlight disadvantages of slipping back.

Communication aimed at the student community must obviously be different from those aimed at the aged. The senior members of the society – and they have to be specifically targeted in view of the influence they wield within a family and the community - still value tradition and believe that 'old was gold' and the past was plentiful and cheap. The youngsters, in contrast, think they are being scientific by discarding tradition. They are more urban oriented and even westernized. They are emotional and often quick to excite with examples of injustice. Student related communication has, therefore, to be imaginatively drawn up, perhaps harping more on the idealistic bit. It has been mentioned earlier that messages aimed at the teenagers must appeal to their sense of fair play and social equality. It is also important tnat a high and mighty, all knowing, judgmental type of message must be avoided. It must be remembered that those teenage years 'are a time of exploration, rebellion and experimentation' ('Social Marketing: New Weapon in an Old Struggle').

In designing communication aimed at women, the predominant role that they are playing within the identified segment will be very relevant. If, for instance, they have to be addressed as housewives or mothers, their role as a member of the family needs to be kept in mind; if they have to be addressed as SHOPs, then it is their community role. Consumer insights following the launch and sale of women's personal products show that 'women value their family prestige a lot' and they do not want to do anything that mean 'letting their family down'. Messages stressing this finding are likely to carry. It is also relevant to recognize that most Indian families are still not 'nucleus' in the Western sense of the term. Therefore, depiction of a happy family centered around a woman and her children will be appropriate in most rural markets if the elderly parents of the eligible couples are also included. In case of products like contraceptives aimed at women from wider walks of life than a nuclear family, it is of course a challenge to design communication relevant for the groups concerned.

Suggestions on women oriented communication:

- Encouraging them to lead by example (even self admission of mistakes).
- Encouraging them to progressively increase their sphere of 'positive' influence: family to community.
- Encouraging them to design women related communication packages.
- Encouraging them to volunteer nursing service to adopters of family planning, whatever the illness.

The design of message for the educated must be more in the form of clarifications. Like the immunization booklets, simple question-answer booklets on all major aspects of contraceptive care as well as birth control measures are called for. In fact, such booklets on family planning are reportedly available at the national level and may have to be adapted to suit local conditions. Again, it is advisable to form partnerships with other organizations and bodies to procure and develop the appropriate message and information booklets. The content of messages need not differentiate between the literate and the illiterate, as in both cases, it is the state of minds that is sought to be influenced. What needs to be different, however, is the way these are to be carried. Obviously, communication aimed at the illiterate has to be audio or audio-visual or simply visual.

Except to the very poor parents whose immediate economic necessities force them to go for extra working hands, and therefore, more children, to most other parents, children's priorities are seen to be education and their well being. Thus a motivational package, harping on the 'Samajhdari' of a small family (enabling it to provide quality education and health to one or two children) on lines similar to the "Surf lady" promises to be persuasive. Ideas in the mind of target groups can be simulated by showing two pictures contrasting the present lifestyle to a new style if the behavioral change proposed is adopted. In effect, this is like encouraging some desirable goal that might supersede the desire to have more children, well-fed, well-educated children, children likely to become major income earners for the family and so on. *Messages need to 'go beyond slogans' and suggest a favourable change in lifestyle and emotional contentment.*

> 'It is often wrongly assumed that the question of birth control can be settled merely by stating the case for it. A better order of things in any realm of human endeavour, including a higher standard of living, presupposes a knowledge that such betterment can be attained by reasonable effort. To be aware of a station in life better than your own you must have either seen persons in better circumstances or are able to *imagine* what a fuller and more abundant life would be like' (Chandrasekhar, 1961). Mere understanding, however, does not lead to action. One may tend to justify and find reasons why others were more favourably placed.

Taking a cue from the immunization programme, for families who have crossed the stage of basic needs and are now searching for a societal role in life, the message, while harping on the need for a small family, should also establish a direct connection between a happy family with a social family to a proper citizen family. Targeting a person, a person as a member of a family, a community and a nation is, in such cases, important.

> SMALL FAMILY → HAPPY FAMILY → VALUABLE SOCIAL FAMILY VALUABLE CITIZEN FAMILY.

One word of caution: very often, unconsciously and in our enthusiasm, we carry out activities that may indirectly generate confusion in the mind of the target market. *Message content and participant action must always be complimentary.* It makes little sense to promote a small family and at the same time hold functions to publicize the birth of the nation's billionth baby. There is an issue of convenience too. Marketing is a voluntary, reversible effort. Stressing on permanent contraceptive methods across the board not only go against this idea, it also carries with it the suggestion, and thus the fear of an operation. Conventional contraceptive methods, on the other hand, being 'user friendly', the motivational exercises encouraging this will also be easier. Should the message be negative, positive or a mix of both? (The experience of successful programmes described in Chapter 4 suggests a combination approach).

> A controversial strategy for motivation is caste based. According to Ankeleswar Iyer, reported in the *Times of India* of the 3rd of June 2000, the idea is not to encourage casteism, but to take advantage of an existing social situation to introduce and maintain a social and development programme. Thus themes that satisfy caste characteristics will have greater acceptance among caste members. The potential of this approach is left to the social marketer.

Emotional issues have to be tackled with a kid glove. It is well known that Muslims, by and large, are not open to suggestions in family planning. It is also well known that Indonesia, a predominantly Muslim country has not accepted this view. Logic would, therefore, dictate that clergy from Indonesia be encouraged to interact with Muslim clergy in India in order to bring about a change in their mindset. The benefits that Indonesia has derived from this attitude are likely to be more telling than mere theory.

Another approach could be a survey of progressive Muslim gentry in India for the purpose of showing that they are all following a small family norm. Why would they be doing so, the communication message can harp, if a small family was not for their welfare, and specifically not against their religion? Though religion related communication programmes have to be handled very competently and perhaps at the national level, there is no escape from its relevance in the field where such religious segments form a distinct majority.

Demonstrations have contributed substantially to the success of the Green revolution. "If they can do it, why can't I" is a good motivator. "American advertisers are fast cottoning on to the fact that advertising after a sale is more effective than before in building brand loyalty." (Narayanan, 2000). Thus *messages that highlight the benefits that have accrued to programme acceptors will have a great impact on those at the 'contemplation' as well as the 'preparation' stage.* The corollary of this is the need to repeatedly assure the adopters that they have, indeed, taken the right decision.

> An important conjunct of selling is what commercial marketers call 'Post Purchase Cognitive Dissonance'. What this means is that buyers often carry with them a lurking doubt regarding any major purchase. Have they bought the best item? Could they have obtained a better product if they had only decided to investigate the market more thoroughly? This dissonance would naturally be stronger in the minds of those who agree to modify their personal behaviour in response to messages for change. The potential of such people reverting to the old behaviour is therefore, far greater than those who have simply purchased goods from the market. More serious

indeed, is the danger of such persons becoming programme dissuaders. Social marketers obviously need to recognize this danger and apply any one or more of the following correctives:

- Regularly send out advertisements aimed at programme acceptors, and their good sense.
- Ensure that the service or product providers invariably meet the acceptors and assure them that they have, indeed, taken the right step,
- Include the acceptors in all social programmes in recognition of their cooperation,
- Include all acceptors in the mailing list for future products and service, and
- Take prospects frequently to the adopters for mutual reinforcement of the desirability of the change.

The content of the message may have to be different for different forms of media. 'To explain the reasons why people select certain media, McQuail, Blumler and Brown (1972) developed a typology consisting of four categories: *diversion* (including escape from the routine and the burden of daily life); *personal relationships* (including substitute companionships); *personal identity* (including reality exploration and value reinforcement); and *surveillance* (informing ourselves about the world around us). The authors argue that people use media and consciously select media content to gratify one of these four needs' (Johnson, 2000). Selection of a particular media or its content is an exercise in establishing connectivity – with the identified market segments and more important, with its members depending on their stage of pre-contemplation/ contemplation/ etc as per the trans-theoretical model described in chapter 3. If messages have to be repeated or memory is to be 'prompted', then the print media, being comparatively inexpensive, is to be preferred. If thought provoking motivational packages have to be conveyed in order to stir the unaware into action, then plays, skits and serials on television may be effective, essentially because it approximates interpersonal interactions. Demonstrations appear convincing on television but so does success stories on print. Related issues will be discussed under the section 'How? - The vehicle.'

Finally, in designing the content of any message, the following basics must be kept in mind:

- The message is direct and unambiguous,
- It is relevant,
- It attracts attention of the literate/ illiterate as the case may be
- Therefore, it has a high recall factor,
- It does not criticize, and thereby alienate any section of the society,
- It is designed for the mental/ behavioral stage of the target,
- It generates a sense of belonging to the enlightened section of the community,
- It shows a way of doing an overall social/ religious good,
- It encourages contemplation and then a desire for action, and finally action,
- It encourages adopters to remain true and committed.

> The lack of funds for carrying out an advertisement programme is not the main hurdle that a CE or MO is likely to come across. It is the development of an effective programme that poses a hurdle. Assistance of NGOs, management institutions, or even private/ public sector organizations should be tapped in order to develop the right kind of

messages, for the right kind of beneficiaries, through the most appropriate mix of media.

'Selling a cause can also help in selling your brand'. A study by the Narsee Monjee Institute of Management Studies (NMIMS), Mumbai, showed that price and quality being equal, consumers were more likely to buy a brand associated with a social cause.

What are the mechanics of designing and conducting a message? In the very first instance the resource available will decide how the programme has to be conducted. *'It takes substantially more money to launch a campaign on some new issue than it does to keep an old one going'* ('Social Marketing: New Weapon in an Old Struggle'). However, certain areas need to be focused for optimal results. In addition, communication must be locally devised, guided if possible, by an advertising expert, pre-tested, applied and then evaluated. There could be variations of this. For instance, school and college students may be encouraged to draw, debate, or write essays on the subject in order to know how best to design a theme that is in harmony with the 'thinking level' of the target.

Taking a cue from studies in behavioural science that *it is easier to bring about incremental changes in attitudes and behavioural patterns than drastic and total ones,* communication packages should be designed for groups that have already accepted or are practicing some progressive measures — for instance, families that are already sending all children, including girls, to school. The theory behind this approach, it bears repeating, is that the receiver of a communication will find the contents of a communication (as designed by the communicator) jarring if totally alien to his or her belief/ experience but acceptable if it conforms to his or her inclinations or experience. The tools of 'commitment' and 'prompts' explained in Chapter 3 may be used whenever appropriate.

Communication will be considered effective if it has been able to provide the information required for making an intelligent and relevant choice among various alternatives, *followed by decisive action*. For this purpose, the message has to give a picture of the effect of choosing different alternatives, and preferably supplemented by verifiable examples. Continuous analysis will enable this chain of providing information and linking it to results and then back to supplement and reinforcing the information to be maintained. So, communication is not just dissemination of information. It is also adaptation to and 'management of feedback' (Wadia, 1999). It should also not be forgotten that communication aims at generating a response – be it a specific action or a query or suggestion. Such response calls for an appropriate, positive reaction in terms of product and service.

> Suggestion: Approach an institution like a factory or society. Seek two members who have identical income from the factory or society. Identify their assets – house, land, cattle, and family status – numbers, health, etc. If it is obvious that the one with the smaller family is better off in terms of health, children's education, acquired assets, etc., then seek permission to compare and publicize. If the difference is not noticeable, educate yourself as to why not. It will help in understanding the problem better.

> Suggestion: In order to overcome the inclination towards sons, search and publicize families who are well off on account of skilled and educated children rather than numbers. The message will, thus be towards a contented family with fewer children.

Communication experts frequently lament that 'pre-testing remains one of the least well developed areas of campaign planning'

('Social Marketing: New Weapon in an Old Age'). In deference to this, it is suggested that communication – plans and messages – *are tried out in manageable quantities before beginning any campaign.* Such trials need not be comprehensive but sufficient for assessing the impact on the receivers, and the involvement and functioning of the members of the delivery network including the staff and the SHOPs. The trial stage will also determine whether the message has passed undisturbed between the communicator and the recipient. Depending on the feedback, the programme can be launched in the final form. 'It is better (and cheaper) to avoid disasters than to measure them'.

- Prescription:
  - Identify/ engage, if possible a communication expert for guidance on the 'vehicle' and theme selection.
  - Involve members of the segmented market itself in devising imaginative yet practical themes under the guidance of the expert. Involve the beneficiary segments to evaluate and identify each other's best two or three outputs for trial.
  - Attempt to bring about incremental changes over drastic ones.
  - Introduce behavioural change in terms of the 'commitment' theory.
  - Create a brand image for your programme.
  - Devise communication programmes :
    - Based on survey feedback.
    - Stressing economic, social and emotional issues.
    - Pointing out the 'enablers' and suggesting ways out of the barriers.
    - Indicating what, where, how and when all the

services and products will be available.

- Provide communication support to the products identified in the strategy and positioned.
- Repeat, thus implanting the message.
- Use communication as memory 'prompts'.
- Demonstrate the behavioural patterns of respected personalities, suggesting the sense behind adoption.
- Justify behavioural change. Counter Post Purchase Cognitive Dissonance.
- Evoke emotional response through the use of 'live-shows'.
- Conduct a short trial for a period of three months and then survey and evaluate the impact and recall factor of the message(s).
- Begin the campaign only after the trial is successful or after learning from it.

How? -The Vehicle.

Studies show that '.. mass and personal communication interact and supplement each other. The rural sociologists studying diffusion of innovation discovered that different kinds of communication are more likely to be used at different points in the adoption process: for example, the mass media to bring about awareness, personal channels during the period of evaluation and decision, and both mass and personal communication when confirmation is desired' (Wadia, 1999). Other studies show that 'the process of personal influence itself is much more diffused and complicated'. The number of influencing points can be as varied as the number of established formal or informal channels of communication and influence in a society. In other words, an understanding of the role of opinion leaders as well as the formal and informal channels of influence is essential at the very beginning of any marketing activity. In a tribal society, for instance, the *'official' opinion leader* may be the village chief while the *'emergency' opinion leader* may be the medicine man. The 'official' channel comes into operation at normal times while the 'emergency' channel may come into operation at certain calamity situations.

Local or regional data will be available to indicate the inter se effectiveness of the print media (press), the radio, the cinema and the television in reaching the target population. There are studies to show that the co-relation between radio listening and health related innovations are highly significant (Kivlin et al., 1971). A feedback on the people's reading, listening and viewing habits would also be evident from the surveys. While this analysis can be the basis of proceeding further, a few findings are, nevertheless being discussed for a proper appreciation of a scenario that is not uniform throughout the country.

The first desirable step, it would seem, is to include the vernacular press in one's communication programme (Francis, 1978). Visions of the elderly, sitting on the doorsteps of houses or under a shady tree and reading the local edition are not uncommon in India. Specifically, the press can be motivated into a partnership for carrying serials on families that have adopted contraceptive use and their positive experience. (Indeed, the bad experience also can be a good feedback to the programme staff but one hesitates to suggest its publication. Restrictive communication may work more towards the overall objective).

In a study of the WHO and UNICEF in 1992, it was found that '60-80 per cent of the respondents interviewed had learnt about UIP from the health staff', relatives and neighbours while 38 per cent cited radio and television as the source (Singh and Bharadwaj, 2000). A later study on the role of television in bringing about social change, mentioned in Chapter 4 has, however, indicated a different picture. It seems that television is bound to continue its influence. In the process, it is expected to dilute the influence of elders on the young, and the influence of the community.

An American-Canadian study showed that 'direct mail was particularly effective for reaching the target audience' (Taylor et al., 1999). How far this will be applicable in India (which households and which part of India) needs to be determined. On the other hand, the fact that prominent multinational business houses are investing extensively on hoardings, billboards and walls indicates that this is a cheap and convenient vehicle under Indian conditions. Indeed, house walls are often offered for messages as it means better upkeep and maintenance, as well as additional income for the owner.

The defence forces know that one has to be still and, preferably in drab camouflaged clothing if one does *not* want to draw attention. *Taking a cue from this, if a message has to be noticed, it should be bright and it should be moving.* Hence, billboards on buses, trains, bus stations (movement is relative to the bus), and even on the shirts of sportsmen and traveling merchants are likely to be effective. 'Even the human body has become a walking billboard for Adidas and Calvin Klein. All types of clothing, including hats, t-shirts, sweatshirts and shoes are being used to promote messages' ('Social Marketing: New Weapon in an Old Struggle'). Local adaptations to such concepts can be thought of. The distribution of umbrellas containing family planning messages has been earlier suggested. In Bangladesh it may be recalled, shopping bags and sails on boats have reportedly been used effectively for spreading contraceptive brand name.

The UIP established links with the community by encouraging 'Sishu Rakshak Melas' (Child Protection Fairs). The National Literacy Mission adopted many different kinds of community involvement programmes – marches, events, plays/

dramas, competitions, sponsoring by prominent personalities and so on. Indeed, these events and experiments are all very well known to field level programme implementers and are, therefore, not being elucidated. The social sector scores a major point over the private sector in this method of communication and promotion.

In involving students and youth clubs in motivational drives, it is important to remember that 'using children to educate their elders is not compatible with the traditions of most Third World communities. It is for children to do the bidding of their elders, to defer to them at all times. So, to suddenly reverse roles and expect elders to sit at the feet of their children and learn from them, defies tradition' (White, 1999). *Instead, students should communicate to students, pre-school children and if at all to elders, through non-instructional modes like plays, theatres and so on.*

> Simple but innovative measures like imprinting a social message at the bottom of cups distributed during large gatherings have not been tried/reported whereas, the private sector, specifically Coca-Cola and Pepsi are regularly using this. Imprinting a message on a hand fan has subtle, mind influencing effect as the message keeps on flashing before one's eyes — something akin to what Coca-Coal in the early fifties was forbidden to do.

Programme adopters can also be considered to be vehicles for conveying messages to non-adopters. *Specific wall paintings for the houses of adopters, for instance, will not only raise their social standing, but will also draw the attention of those wishing to follow their example.* This aspect will be dilated during the discussion on incentives. The use of study tours in agricultural extension can be appropriately re-designed for demonstrating the benefits of a small family to SHOPs, prospects and clients. Indeed, representatives of the participative media should also be included.

The following table gives the basic features of the aforesaid 'vehicles':

VEHICLE	ADVANTAGES	DISADVANTAGES
Print: Newspapers/ Magazines	Low cost Vernacular circulation Multiple readership Archival possible Repetition possible Advertisements possible Publicity possible	For literates only Low circulation, except national ones Low targetting
Radio	Wide reach Selective reach possible (time-based) Programme flexibility Power dependant - timing - periodicity - duration - content Sponsorship possible	Investment needed - moderate at transmission end Private & Public use - low at receiving end
Television	Wide coverage Selective, time based reach High impact Programme flexibility - timing - periodicity - content - duration - Sponsorship possible	Investment needed- moderate receiver end - high at transmission end - moderate at receiving end
Others: Hoardings	Localized focus Can be repetitive/ act as prompts Inexpensive Good reach Can be mobile Income generating/ responsive	Non-target specific

Telephone	Great as follow-up Personal touch Inexpensive Target specific	Limited reach Limited to receiver convenience Limited to telephone owners
Mail	Great as an informant Great for follow up Inexpensive Target specific or wide	Limited to the literate
Live shows	Great impact Inexpensive Localized focus Can be repeated	Limited audience Participant dependant Small reach
Partners: - adopters/ - SHOPs/ - NGOs - Others	Great impact Inexpensive Resource generating potential	Needs motivation/ training Needs time Difficult to organize Prone to politicking

◆ Prescription on media selection:
- Select the most appropriate vehicle mix for reaching the message.
- Do not forget the 'living' – the adopter, social bodies etc., as communicators.
- Introduce study tours.

When? How often?

Most often physical and financial resources will dictate in what media mix and how often messages have to be conveyed. Quite obviously however, 'the more the exposure to various communication channels, both direct and indirect, the more the knowledge, approval and adoption ... (Kivlin et al., 1971). It has also to be recognized that 'despite the intense competition for their attention, consumers are willing to invest very little time to learn about new offerings' (Mittal and Sawhney, 2001). *In other words, there is a need to identify the periods when and who will be receptive and will have time to collaborate.* From a theoretical approach, agriculturists, including labour are likely to be available during lean seasons; industrial labour may also have slack periods/ seasons; and service holders on declared holidays. The elderly and the school children may not be able to participate during late nights; the women during meal times; the men during cultivation mornings and afternoons and so on. All motivational exercises must be designed at times *convenient to the beneficiaries and programme supporters.* The elderly, in general, have a lot of time to spare and may indeed, be willing partners at all times. Most challenging will be the involvement of the unemployed – offering them a purpose, and some token compensation in kind while in wait. A study by Weibe suggests that the acceptance of social messages will be higher if a person is already softened towards the idea following, say a natural calamity. Thus, a series of messages on the non-maintainability of a large family, following a drought period would be effective. Indeed, it will be ideal if an inkling of all this can be detected during survey.

How? - The Tools.

Having designed a basic communication and promotional plan, it is necessary to dilate on the 'tools' i.e., advertisement, publicity, and personal interaction. Each of these is effective in its context and it is up to the programme coordinator to match these tools with the market characteristics and the availability of resources. The following table gives, in brief, their strengths and areas of applicability:

TOOL	STRENGTHS	WEAKNESS	APPLICATION
Adverti sement	Mass effect	Expensive	For -informing, -inducing lifestyle changes based on psychographic survey
Personal contact	Intensive, Evaluative, Motivating, Good for feedback	Expensive, Needs training, Needs time, Subjective	For -imparting skill/ knowledge, -clearing doubts, -small samples,
Publicity	Intensive, Mass effect, Inexpensive, Improves organizational goodwill	May be confused with propaganda,	For -motivation through examples, -informing,

> 'We expected that the mass media would be sited more often as an information source for knowledge, and that persons such as neighbours, friends or relatives would be sited more often as an information source leading to adoption. This is essentially what we found. It also seems clear that the role of change agents is an important one (Kivlin et al., 1971).

Advertisement

Advertisement is mass communication at its best. Though often criticized as being very expensive, commercial marketing cannot do without it. In fact, marketing and advertisement has become synonymous. Advertisement is not cheap, yet it can get across to the largest numbers. *So, for practicing social marketers not flushed with funds, advertisement should be used sparingly – to inform, and that too over local, vernacular media. Publicity, if it can be organized properly, can be cheaper*. This is because the media pays for the space or broadcast time as a part of their news coverage. Though there is merit in making both advertising and publicity target specific, the very fact that advertisement is mass communication is also an advantage. 'Advertisement links business, policy makers and consumers and can stimulate product/ service development'. In effect, advertisement includes all players, including the potential ones.

Publicity

Publicity has to be handled very carefully and the pitfalls and the possibilities highlighted earlier in Chapter 2 need to be noted. Yet, even though social programme administrators are generally very shy of publicity, it can be very effective. The first step in organizing a planned publicity is to generate an active media response for the programme. For this, the perquisites are:

- Preparation of short information sheets showing status on a particular day prior to the commencement of the programme and the status periodically thereafter. It is worth remembering the possibility that 'if you don't interpret it for them (the media) they will have to do it themselves. Because they don't have the data interpretation skills, they will probably botch it' (Mintz and Steele, 1992).
- Locating and preparing short success stories, stories with 'human content' or big drives or melas and using these to feed reporters and also for attracting them to follow up on the stories. If media reporters can be persuaded to carry progress stories say once in two months, then a lot has been achieved.
- Getting photographs to support stories especially for the cable or TV network.
- Evaluating the response from the public in terms of queries, letters to the editor or supplementary coverage in regional/ national media.

Sponsored TV programmes are an important element of publicity. Since family based dramas attract a large audience, there is a case for the development of programmes on the population problem, highlighting the pros and cons of a small family. The result will be programme publicity by a neutral source, and therefore, likely to be more believable.

Publicity, as mentioned earlier, is certainly cheaper than advertisement; its expenses are generally limited to entertainment and travel.

- *Prescription:*
  - Succinctly document all success stories, behavioral patterns of SHOPs, relevant national developments and then introduce the same to the media.
  - Organize field visits for the media. Encourage them to report on success stories they witness.
  - Get partners to sponsor, including commercial sponsorship of family dramas on population control themes on TV.

Personal contact – selling, servicing, incentives, and atmospherics.

Personal contact is integral to social marketing for ideas are best put across during conversations. The initial survey is, in fact, the way suggested for initiating personal contact for 'selling the idea'. Subsequent and periodic contacts build relations. More important, it is only through the components of personal contact that a customer can be *nurtured into a partner*. Customers need to be understood and then interacted with so that they become 'clients' and not remain faceless customers. From a satisfied client, the objective of all progressive commercial marketers, and therefore, social marketers, is to turn them into programme supporters and advocates. The final stage to aim for is their conversion into programme partners.

PROSPECT → CUSTOMERS → CLIENTS — SUPPORTERS → PARTNERS

Personal contact, as has been stated earlier, can be individual based or conducted in focus groups. *Since most social marketers are likely to be facing constraints of time and resources, focus group is the method recommended*. Planning for and holding group meetings is an art by itself. Many learn from available literature and experience. Effectiveness of group meetings often depend on deciding the optimal size – not too thin as to have little community interest/ influence and not too large as to become a debating occasion. Large meetings serve only the purpose of information spread, not participation and involvement.

As for the product, the study has already pointed out that selling is a simple action where products (such as contraceptive devices) are taken to a potential customer and offered in exchange for cash. So, the opening of static outlets at convenient places or mobile counters in fairs and the like are all that is involved. At best, the vendor displays some banners and/ or uses a public hailer to draw attention.

> Innovations include keeping a track of all marriages in the market area, attending the marriage function; pre or post marriage counseling for the couple and 'selling' the use of contraceptives. Indeed, a present in the form of a useable item (e.g., a locally produced, ornate and colourful bag for the bride, for instance, containing a set of contraceptives and related information sheets) for every marriage may effectively act as a memory 'prompt'.

Selling is effective when all the previous marketing steps have been followed.

> Personal contact would be appropriate for applying the concept of 'commitment' described in Chapter 3. A prominent member of the target market may be requested to commit him or herself to a specific action that is in consonance with the programme goals. For instance, if the survey had indicated that, in a segment, the inconvenience of using a condom was a major problem, a *voluntary* commitment to try a method that the beneficiary feels is less of a problem, and to try that out for a month could be the first step. A programme promoter (could be staff or SHOPs) should approach the person well before the end of the term (having told the beneficiary at the commitment stage that they will do so in order to check if there were any problems) and congratulate the person on adhering to the commitment. With his or her consent, the achievement may be made known in the locality, thereby cementing publicly the achievement and the commitment. The same person can then be asked to motivate/ obtain simple commitments from others, followed by due public encouragement. In theory, a web-like effect can be developed, spreading from a nucleus to an ever-increasing boundary.

Servicing, the enduring aspect of product promotion, requires a long-term approach based on a regular feedback. Regular feedback from government sponsored programmers - in order that those who have accepted them do not get discouraged or worse, act as de-motivators - is extremely important. Generally, once the target has been covered, that is the end of the story. The experience of the private sector is a strong indicator that retaining a beneficiary is important, not only from the effort or experience point of view, but also to ensure that the beneficiary becomes a positive opinion leader. Service ensures conversion of a customer into a client into a partner and the whole exercise is cost effective in the long run - *'retaining customers is much less expensive than replacing them'* (Woodruff and Gardial, 1996). The need for avoiding Post Purchase Cognitive Dissonance has been touched upon earlier.

Incentives. It will always be 'difficult to attract poor villagers to any new activity which promises tangible rewards only in the distant future' (Ray, 1986). Ideally, 'any marketing programme should dramatize the benefits of the brand' (Jack Trout) but this is easier said than done in social programmes. One approach to incentives is free distribution or samples. These encourage the 'early adopters' and the 'early majority'. Incentive pricing encourages the distributive machinery with increased commissions. Non-priced incentives, in spite of its intangible nature, are slow acting but can encourage all.

In Chapter 2, a reference has been made to the recent phenomenon of stressing service and finance related marketing over marketing of products. For social sector programmes, service has always been important, but not financing. Yet, perhaps a cue can, indeed, be drawn from this new trend. It may be worthwhile to consider if some of the following facilities/ incentives can be made available, on an ID card basis, to the programme acceptors:

- Priority in bank loans. The example of organizations providing micro credit to the women, in Bangladesh (Mohammed Yunnus of Grameen Bank) and India (Ila Bhatt) is worth emulating. Their experience is that women loanees of small credit are not only sincere as regards implementation of their projects, but are also very prompt in repaying the loan. It is reasonable to expect that such women will act as positive opinion leaders.

- Reduced interest on loans.
- Easier repayment terms if reduction of interest without RBI intervention is not possible.
- Extra fertilizers/ seeds over normal quota.
- Stipend to children, in collaboration with partners, for attending school and even college.
- Priority seats in social functions. This is something that is entirely within the control of most programme administrators.
- Annual recognition in functions. Likewise.

> 'The Academy for Educational Development found that offering a chance at a lottery provided the cue that got many women in The Gambia to come to sessions to learn oral rehydration mixing skills' (Andreasen, 1995).

- Distinctive colour for houses adopting social programmes. In Indonesia, which has done remarkably well in family planning, adopters in villages are encouraged to display a red sign on their front door or porch. All prominent visitors are taken to these houses, thereby giving the family a special social standing.
- Nursing service. Encouraging volunteers, especially women to provide nursing service to adopters of family planning, whatever the illness,
- Seed money to open bank accounts.
- Commissions and incentives to teachers who, in addition to their basic task of imparting education and ensuring

attendance and marks above a certain minimum also actively support progressive social behaviour.

- Package deals against token payment. Even though better service against payment may be considered to be discriminatory by some, such service is quite routine in the commercial sector. Can similar service against payment be planned and cross-subsidized to the poor? What could perhaps be on offer is a monthly health checkup of the entire family in exchange for the adoption of a one-child norm and a recurring monthly deposit (or a lump-sum deposit following post harvest income). The quantum of deposit can vary with home visits. Obviously, this would be subject to the availability of medical resource and infrastructure.

> It has been mentioned in Chapter 2 that incentives can be used effectively to encourage compliant behaviour as well as for improving organizational goodwill. The 'Made for Each Other Contests' that were held regularly some time ago by a cigarette manufacturer is a case in point. Likewise, social marketing organizations, with or without partnership support, can organize locally relevant events for programme supporters, and in the process, satisfying both the aforesaid objectives.

Recalling that the involvement of SHOPs is on the pattern of distributors under commercial marketing, some form of incentives (akin to a dealer's commission) needs to be built into the system. Money may not always be appropriate as it is never a component of the social 'exchange' function. Instead, social recognition for SHOPs, and token, visible gifts would be appropriate. Even here, the appreciation and recognition of SHOPs by the official machinery should be handled carefully. 'If the recognition is for personal talent, qualities and achievements, it results in considerable enhancement of their prestige in their eyes of the people', but if it is for a cause in which the community as a whole has participated, then 'the recognition should be of the entire community along with the leader' (Krishan, 1965).

Atmospherics is an aspect of personal selling and has been touched upon in Chapter 2. In practical terms, atmospherics can be translated to mean imaginatively designed interiors of medical and family planning centres. Like in brand identity, colour schemes including uniforms for medical staff and even volunteers can be thought of. A comfortable seating space, convenient outlets for dispensing, drinking water and toilet facilities, and overall cleanliness are some obvious aspects of this. Since local conditions will determine all the possibilities, the suggestion is not being elaborated beyond the concept.

Quality of service is a component of atmospherics. The goals have already been suggested earlier.

◆ Prescription:

- Concentrate on providing personalized service.
- Tempt prospects with incentives; nurture new comers with incentives; convert adopters into partners through social recognition.
- Introduce a pleasant and encouraging atmosphere to all family planning infrastructure and activities.

H. IDENTIFY, DEVELOP AND SET IN PLACE THE 'ENABLERS'.

Enablers are those crucial activities that remove the obvious as well as subtle impediments in the path of change.

As discussed in Chapter 3, there are reasons internal and external to a person that influences his or her behaviour. Hopefully, all the reasons that support or discourage a behavioural change, as applicable to the market under consideration, would have been identified during the survey, including literature search. *At this point, it seems sufficient to highlight that such of the items that have not been covered in the foregoing discussions have to be specifically addressed by the social marketer*. For instance, it might turn out that the lack of facilities to look after the children of mothers wishing to attend motivational meetings or go for family planning services is an important reason for lack of response. One solution could be the formation of temporary crèches (funded and supported at the house of elders or through volunteers baby sitting). Other solutions, either tackling the problem itself or reducing the absence time, could be decided locally and in conjunction with the 'customers'.

The foregoing example was a reason external to a person. Similarly, there could, and indeed, would be factors internal to a person inhibiting a behavioural change. An identified and accepted reason why many parents go for more than one child is the desire for a son. Such a desire has been nurtured in Hindu families through their ancient religious texts and their interpretations. The underlying persuasion for a son is two-fold: the desire for the last rites to be performed by a son and therefore, enabling access to Heaven, and second, support during old age. While an acceptable alternative to the first barrier may not be readily available (though it is heard that to some families, similar rituals performed by reputed religious bodies like the Bharat Seva Sangh are perfectly acceptable), the second reason could perhaps be tackled, in a limited way, by involving pension and insurance programmes. Pointing out instances of equal, if not better care for parents by female children may help. A social marketer needs to address all such issues as best as he or she can even if it involves an extended series of nurturing motivation towards a change. Field experiments indeed show that this is perfectly feasible. Periodic interaction over just five months in Sidhi district of Madhya Pradesh, could remove a large measure of shame and hesitation in discussing sexual problems, contraceptive procedures and methods in public. (V.M Upadhyaya, 2000)

Experiencing is another enabler. This can take two forms: sampling or demonstration. Free sampling of a product, thereby avoiding costs and minimizing procurement inconvenience, the two main barriers to change, may very well shift a prospect from contemplation to action. This is indeed, the idea behind free distribution of condoms in most countries. However, free sampling cannot generally continue unless the possibilities of behaviour reversal are substantial, and, of course, the marketing budget can support it. Likewise, seeing a demonstration (in this case, the lifestyle of an adopter) may sway a group of prospects towards compliant behaviour.

An internal factor, briefly touched upon earlier but that needs further discussion, is buyer embarrassment: in this case, in seeking family planning services and products. Generally, no male or female member of a family would like to be seen asking for and buying a condom. Studies (Kotler and Roberto, 1989) show that in a supermarket stocking condoms,

- 83 per cent stopped to look,
- Of these 83 per cent, only 19 per cent picked up one to inspect,
- Of these 83 per cent, 72 per cent went around the shelf and returned, only when no one else was around,
- Of those who picked up one to inspect, either at the first instance or later, 88 per cent 'put some in the shopping cart (most of them placed

the pack underneath the other grocery items)', and more disturbing

- 70 per cent replaced the condoms at any convenient shelf before reaching the checkout counter.

So, ways of 'enabling' condom purchase has to be thought of, discussed, pre-tested and applied. Suggestions could range from packaging with innocuous monthly necessities like detergent packs and the like, to self-dispensing kiosks in prosperous urban areas, in appropriate secluded locations (factory corners, garage, bank ATMs, subways, etc.). Progressive partners may be willing to install these machines as their contribution to the programme. In the first suggestion, a nominal increase in the product price may be acceptable to the product manufacturer as a social contribution, and may not be grudged by the buyer who knows what he or she is getting. In rural areas, especially when fairs are held, distribution of condoms by 'outsiders' may reduce buyer embarrassment to some extent.

I. MONITORING & EVALUATION

Monitoring is the exercise that enables activity-wise performance assessment and correction. Evaluation is an 'end-period' evaluation of the broader programme objectives.

A social marketer needs to be totally absorbed in regular and periodic 'monitoring', leaving 'evaluation' at appropriate and fixed intervals to specific, independent teams or maybe, to outside agencies. Indeed, this approach is similar to that of the business sector: 'Commercial sector marketers rarely worry about final summative evaluations; instead they carry out focus group studies, small scale surveys, and the like along the way to permit up-to-date measures of programme effectiveness and rapid adjustments of strategy and tactics in response to market dynamics' (Andreasen, 1995).

Monitoring is in tune with the basic concept of social marketing: it is at the customer level that all activities start and end. How is the customer responding to the programme? What changes will benefit him or her? How can the programme content as well as the delivery mechanism provide greater satisfaction? Not just physical parameters, but the 'understanding on how customers define value becomes the guiding force for determining what to improve' (Woodruff and Gardial, 1996). In practical terms, monitoring indicates *how beneficiaries see success in their terms*. Is the customer satisfied? Customer fulfillment, it needs to be added, is important but its measurement is certainly not easy. At the same time, though contentment cannot be 'monitored just like physical assets' (Kennedy and Schneider, 2000) nevertheless, there can be 'indicators' like:

- Confirmed, or long-term usage,
- Voluntary feedback and service from satisfied beneficiaries,
- Good recall factors ranging from 3 to 6 months or more during surveys.

Programme monitoring enables mid-course corrections to be made wherever necessary. This is obviously better than finding, at the end of a hard campaign that some basic problems have been overlooked. Monitoring is also aimed at assessing the efficiency of the delivery mechanism. An important lesson learnt from agriculture extension is that farmers often gauge the importance of a programme from the sincerity of the extension workers as apparent from their interest in holding crop demonstrations. The extension workers in turn take their cue from the attention paid to these plots by the inspecting and supervisory staff (J.S Patel, Former Agricultural Commissioner, Government of India).

Though feedback on the programme content and implementation is first obtained from the stage of pre-testing of communication messages, the regular process starts from all the trainings and group interactions scheduled. In addition, feedback can also come from specific surveys and/or in a continuous manner from two other sources:

- Staff source:
  - Daily/ weekly/ monthly reporting
  - Attendance in medical institutions/ camps
- Market source:
  - Pre-paid, stamped letters in which responses have been already printed, leaving appropriate blanks for the beneficiary to fill up and post. In non-literate markets, this response has to be obtained through secondary sources like literate SHOPs or volunteers. Response to pre-paid letters is a clear indication of an inclination towards behavioural change.
  - Phone survey where circumstances permit. Indeed, in many cases, organizations are receiving public opinion through electronic mail.

Feedback has to be 'on line'. There is no point in designing a system wherein the cost of obtaining this information - within a time considered reasonable - exceeds any benefits derived from having it. Just as suggested for an objective oriented survey, if the evaluation methodology and parameters are by themselves not taken to be all important, then any method that enables an assessment of 'exactly what the initiative was originally expected to produce' ('Social Marketing: New Weapon in an Old Struggle') would be sufficient.

In the context of the population stabilization programme, *monitoring would translate into a set of trained staff to submit data on every step of the delivery process and also on beneficiary reaction and satisfaction*. At appropriate stages, beneficiary reaction received directly or from secondary sources should also be entered. It should not be difficult to design a programme by which the collected data and customer feedback is automatically transmitted to the next supervisory level for two specific actions:

- Programme and performance improvement – be it through augmented supply of products and/or service, and
- Programme, performance and trend analysis.

So, feedback is actually the additional material to fine-tune the entire exercise of social marketing. Indeed, for any continuous, long term programme – as most social programmers are apt to be - it is like re-tracing every series of steps just to ensure that the direction towards the ultimate goal has not been taken on incorrect premises and analysis. Evaluation, on the other hand, is an exercise 'at the end of a programme to answer very profound questions such as whether the programme had the impact it was supposed to have had, and if not, why not' (Andreasen, 1995).

◆ Prescription:

- Devise a simple, on-line mechanism for monitoring the programme as well as for gauging customer satisfaction.
- Decide on the period after which the programme should be evaluated.

Annexure 2.1 OBJECTIVE ORIENTED SURVEY

SAMPLE QUESTIONNAIRE

Objective to understand prospect attitude towards family planning and their experience

Are you adopting any family planning measures?

- Yes
- No

Why are you doing so?

- Because you already have — children?
- Because you want your child to have the best affordable

  Education

  Health

  Happiness

Other

- Because you want your wife to be healthy?
-

Why are you not adopting family control measures?

- Because you want a son
- Because you are afraid of medical complications?
- Because you want your children to earn for the family?
- Because you have been so advised (by whom?)
- Any other

(Questions directed specifically at the housewife)

Responsibility for a child-birth rests on:

- Father
- Mother
- Both

- God?

Are you aware that you can decide when or whether to have another child?

Yes/ No

Do you know that there is more than one method for avoiding pregnancy?

Yes/ No

What do you think are the advantages of the following methods:

Nirodh

Easily available

Easy to use

Difficult to dispose

Mala

Easily available

Difficult to remember daily

Objective : To find out who is the decision maker in the family.

Will you or your husband decide as to:

- What foodstuff to be purchased ?
- What will be cooked today ?
- Whether the daughter will go to school or look after the child?
- Whether the son will go to school or look after the child ?
- How many children to have ?
- Whether to go for an operation after the second child ?

Who else will you consult regarding:

- Household problems/ issues?
- Childbirth issues?
- Personal, physical problems?

Objective : To ascertain the stage of receptivity / change

Are you interested in having a small and healthy family?

Have you started taking steps in this regard?

What steps have you taken?

STEP	FOR HOW LONG?

What are the other steps you have planned?

STEP	TIME FRAME

Objective : To ascertain the best time for inter-personal communication

When are you most busy?

When do you get time to relax in a day?

Which periods of a year are you relaxed?

Do you go for holidays? If yes, where to?

Objective : To Sugest That Division of Finite Resources due to Additional Children over just two generations has resulted in loss of comparative well being.

Family Elder	Owner of following physical resources:
Grand Father/Mother	House: Area: Type (Mud/ Brick/ roof/etc): Homestead: Area: Area under cultivation: Number and type of trees: Agricultural Land: Area: Water source: Area under cultivation: Number and type of trees:

	Major Agricultural Implements:
	Bullock carts/ Tractors:
	Small industry:
Father/Mother	House: Area:
	Type (Mud/ Brick/ roof/etc):
	Homestead: Area:
	Area under cultivation:
	Number and type of trees:
	Agricultural Land: Area:
	Water source:
	Area under cultivation:
	umber and type of trees:
	Major Agricultural Implements:
	Bullock carts/ Tractors:
	Small industry:
Present owner	House: Area:
	Type (Mud/ Brick/ roof/etc):
	Homestead: Area:
	Area under cultivation:
	Number and type of trees:
	Agricultural Land: Area:
	Water source:
	Area under cultivation:
	Number and type of trees:
	Major Agricultural Implements:
	Bullock carts/ Tractors:
	Small industry:

Objective : To find out who the family influencers are

Who do you turn to when

- You need medical advice:
- You need financial help:
- You need spiritual solace:
- You need good company:

To find out the shops and their attributes

Who are the persons in your community that you admire, and why?

PERSON	ATTRIBUTE
1.	
2.	
.	
.	

Objective to find out the best three delivery systems

How do you rate the organizations doing social work?

Organization	Excellent	Good	Poor
Gobernment			
Health & Family Welfare			
Education			
Women& Child Development			
Etc			
NGOs			
1			
2			
3			

PUBLIC SECTOR

1

2

3

PRIVATE COMPANIES

1

2

3

Objective : To estimate the awareness of family planning services available so as to build on the konwn and develop image for the unknown

Which is the nearest service for:

Service	Facility	Service Available			
	Location	Doctors/Staff Lady Gent Friendly ?	Medicine Avail'ble/Not	Atmosphere?	Waiting Time
CC					
OP					
IUD					
Tub/ Vas					
Abortion					

Objective : To ascertain if family welfare services should be free or paid for

Are you satisfied (Yes/ No) with the service provided by:

- Government run health centers?
- NGO centers?
- Other?

What constitute better service?

- Staff availability?
- Friendliness?
- Intensive care versus quick disposal?
- Good patient recall?
- Others.

Would you be willing to pay for better service?

Service	Payment Amount		
	Per Visit or	Monthly or	Annualy
Staff availability round the clock?			
Friendliness?			
Intensive care versus quick disposal?			
Good patient recall?			
Others			

Objective : To ascertain the attitude of local level retailers towards family planning, stocking of condoms and pills, and Promotion.

Village	Shop Type	Owner	Attitude Towards (+ve/-ve)		
			FP	Stocking	Promotion

What kind of incentives will advance promotion?

Social recognition?

Commission?

Any other:

Objective to find out the most effective use of media based communication

Is there one radio in the house?	Yes	No
Are you saving money to buy a radio?		

Do you go to hear the radio in other's houses?*

If yes, then for how long every day?

What are the programmes you hear?

1.

2.

Is there a TV in the house? Yes No

Are you saving money to buy a TV?

Do you go to watch TV in other's houses?*

If yes, for how much time every day?

What are the programmes you watch?

1.

2.

Who watches what programmes on their home TV?

Member	Programme	Timing	No of hours
Grandmother			
Grandfather			
Father in law			
Mother in law			
Father			
Mother			
Eldest son			
Eldest daughter			

If the household subscribes to newspapers/magazines, who reads what page/item?

Member	Newspaper/ magazine	Page/ item
Grandmother		
Grandfather		

Father in law

Mother in law

Father

Mother

Eldest son

Eldest daughter

*Such visits often create strong relationships. Therefore, it can be used to communicate

Objective : To develop messages appropriate to illiterates.

Have you seen any advertisements recently? Where?

What did you see? What did you understand?

Did you understand the message from the picture?

Which message could you not understand?

Did you ask a friend to read out the script?

Do you listen to the radio?

Which programmes do you enjoy?

Do you recall any advertisements over the radio?

If yes, why did you find the message interesting?

Do you like advertisements with a song? In what language?

Epilogue

In studying social marketing and preparing a set of prescriptions, my first problem was how to identify and restrict myself to the key issues rather than attempt a 'mechanic's manual'. I have strived to establish the road-signs. The traveler can, thereafter, decide on the details, appropriate to the road conditions that he or she will have to encounter. I will be more than happy if the reader finds the subject useful and tries to put it into practice – irrespective of the social programme being pursued.

In recollecting my experience, the following sign posts - if I may call these such - appear prominent:

- For any social development programme, it is basic to know the life-style characteristics of the people with whom the marketer is involved. This cannot be done without segmentation and survey.
- A social marketing survey should be 'objective oriented' rather than academic.
- Survey time needs also to be utilized for 'leading' the surveyed towards the programme objective.
- Both during survey and thereafter, it is necessary to understand the basic survival needs of the segment in focus - as perceived by the people and not just by the planners - as well as their other hierarchy of needs.
- It is of paramount importance to understand why the prospects are not moving towards need fulfillment. The barriers to change have to be specifically addressed.
- It is the duty of social marketers to provide opportunities for need satisfaction.

- In communicating the avenues for need satisfaction, the best programme is that which offers the most tangible of benefits, and in a short time frame. Alternatively, a programme that dramatizes the ill effects of a situation, and yet offers a simple solution (e.g., immunization against polio) is the one to aim for. For all other situations, there is no short cut: communication, promotion, enabling a choice of action, post action service, training, and regular modification based on feedback, have all to be gone through, and over an inestimable period of time.
- It is as important to market the programme among the staff and the partners as it is to the end of line prospects.
- It is more vital to look after adopters than to seek new prospects.

Certain tools specifically highlighted for bringing about the desired behavoural change include:

- Image building. The social marketer needs build up an impression of quality service that the organisation is engaged in. For this, and in order to distinguish the specific programme from the rest, it might be advantageous to create a new brand.
- Knowledge of competition is essential both for counteracting its adverse effects as well as for possibly including competitors in a partnership.
- Continuous motivation and skill training for all programme staff, associates and partners is indispensable.
- The service to be aimed for is 'doorstep' or 'near doorstep' or 'mobile delivery'.
- Programme 'reach' can be increased by adopting the 'distribution' model or, if feasible, the 'franchise' model.

Other suggestions include:

- The encouragement of volunteers, especially women for offering 'emotional' service e.g., nursing, to *all* programme adopters.
- Though challenging, yet most desirable will be the roping in of the unemployed in the programme – offering them a purpose, and some token compensation in kind while in wait.
- The involvement of women, children and the youth in all intangible-and long-term-benefit programmes.
- Specific involvement of the retired military and paramilitary personnel.
- The search for and involvement of all adopters in all aspects of the programme, from the beginning to the end.
- The search for and involvement of partners in all aspects of the programme, from the beginning to the end.

- There is no point in addressing the toughest segments first. Instead, it is wiser to seek incremental change through groups already socially 'committed', in whatever way. I have called this 'the nucleus way'.
- There exists a great potential in harnessing collective opinion to supersede individual inclinations.

At no point of time should the fundamental concepts upon which the entire super structure of social marketing is based be forgotten:

That it is the customer who needs to be in the forefront, and not the marketer or the marketing organization, and

That in order to bring about a change in customer/ prospect behaviour, the marketer has to first understand the barriers against change by positioning himself or herself in the shoes of the prospect/ customer.

The book 'Introduction to Social Marketing' encourages innovations and adaptations. I will, therefore, be honoured if the guidelines are applied to specific situations, its scope expanded, its strengths and weaknesses studied and ways of learning from such experiences shared with me. I can be reached at gbm@nic.in

Bibliography

1. Mehta, C Subhash. *Indian Consumers: Studies and Cases for Marketing Decisions,* Tata McGraw Hill Publishing Company. New Delhi:1973.

2 Francis, GK. *Modern Marketing Management.* S Chand. 1978.

3 Kotler, Philip and Gary Armstrong. *Principles of Marketing.* Prentice Hall, India. 1994

4 Woodruff, R and S Gardial. *Know Your Customer.* Blackwell. 1996

5 Kotler, Philip. *Marketing for Nonprofit Organizations.* Prentice Hall. 1975

6 *Businessworld.* 26 June 2000.

7 Das, Gurcharan. 'The Truth about Kerala.' *Times of India.* 25/6/2000

8 Murthy, Nirmala ed. *Family planning Programme in the Organized Sector: Case Studies.* Sterling Publishers. 1983

9 Chandrasekhar, S. *Population and Planned Parenthood in India.* Macmillan, 1961

10 *National Population Policy 2000.* Government of India. Department of Family Welfare.

11 *Population Growth. Trends, Projections, Challenges and Opportunities.* Working Paper Series 2/2000-PC. Planning Commission. Government of India.

12 *Population and Human Development. Meeting Some Critical Needs in the New Century.* Report Reprint Series 1/2000-PC. Planning Commission. Government of India.

13 Francis, Geoffery K. *Modern Marketing Management.* S Chand and Co. New Delhi. 1978

14 Carol Bryant et al. 'Community-Based Prevention Marketing.' Fifth Annual Innovations in Social Marketing Conference, Montreal, Canada. 1999

15 Taylor, Melissa Kraus et al. From Marketing to Health: 'The Challenge of Applying Marketing Tools to regional Public Health Programmes.' Fifth Annual Innovations in Social Marketing Conference, Montreal, Canada. 1999.

16 Blamey, Russel and Trevor Sutton. 'A Socio-economic Decision-making Model for Understanding regulatory Compliance and Developing Social Marketing Programmes.' Fifth Annual Innovations in Social Marketing Conference, Montreal, Canada. 1999.

17 Weinberg, Charles B. and Robert Ritchie. 'Cooperation, Competition and Social Marketing.' Fifth Annual Innovations in Social Marketing Conference, Montreal, Canada. 1999

18 Greenlee, Timothy B. 'The Transtheoretical Model of Behavior Change: An Empirical Investigation.' Fifth Annual Innovations in Social Marketing Conference, Montreal, Canada. 1999

19 Kennedy, Janet McColl and Ursula Schneider. *Total Quality Management*. Vol II No 7. Taylor & Francis. 2000.

20 Online Tutorial on Social Marketing. Health Canada. 1999.

21 McKee, Neill. *Social Mobilization and Social Marketing in Developing Communities: Lessons for Communicators*. Southbound Publishers.

22 Social Marketing Institute web page: www.social-marketing.org

23 Singh, Mani Shekhar and Aditya Bhardwaj. *Communicating Immunization*. The Mass Media Strategies. *Economic and Political Weekly*. Feb 19-26. 2000.

24 'What is Social Marketing?' Centre for Social Marketing. University of Strathclyde web site: www.csm.strath.ac.uk/What

25 'Changing the Attitudes and Behaviours of Men Through Social Marketing: Philippine case.' www.icomp.org

26 Ray, Jayant Kumar. 'Organizing Villagers for Self-Reliance.' Orient Longman. 1986

27 Grifiths, Marcia. "Social Marketing: Achieving Changes in Nutrition Behaviour, from Household Practices to National Policies." UNU Press. www.unu.edu/unupress

28 Mintz, Jim and Michael Steele. 'Requirement for Marketing Health Information - the why and how of it.' *Health Promotion,* vol 31 Fall 1992. Health Canada.

29 Tanguay, Celine. 'Planning Health Promotion. The Marketing Communications Approach.' *Health Promotion.* Winter 1988/89. Canada.

30 Young, Eric. 'Social Marketing. Where It's come from; Where It's Going.' *Health Promotion.* Winter 1988/89. Canada

31 Henley, Nadine. 'Appealing to Positive Motivations and Emotions in Social Marketing: Example of a Positive Parenting Campaign.' *Social Marketing Quarterly* 1988.

32 Burnett, John J. *Promotional Management: A Strategic Approach.* St Paul West Publishing Co. 1988

33 'Social Marketing: New Weapon in an Old Struggle.' Health Canada website.

34 Johnson, Kirk. *Television and Social Change in Rural India.* Sage Publications. 2000

35 Sevakram and Vanashree Waghmare. *Extension Education Elixirs In Rural Development.* 1986. Metropolitan.

36 'The Ten Year Copper-T.' Paper presented by ARTH, Udaipur,

at the seminar on Reproductive Health On the Ground: Meeting Women's Needs in Southern Rajasthan. July 2000

37 Elster, Jon. *Nuts and Bolts for the Social Sciences.* Cambridge University Press. 1989

38 Littler, Dale. *Marketing and Product Development*. Heritage. 1985

39 Lazniac, Gene R et al. 'The Social Disorder of the Broadened Concept of Marketing.' *Readings in Marketing Management*. Himalaya Publishing House. 1987

40 Wadia, Angela. *Communication and Media*. Kanishka. 1999.

41 George, Shanti.. *Operation Flood: An Appraisal of Current Indian Dairy Policy*. Oxford University Press. 1985

42 Krishan, Ram. *Agriculture Demonstration and Extension Communication*. Asia Publishing House. 1965

43 Gerson de Cunha. 'Social marketing in development.' *Seminar* February 2001.

44 Kurien, Verghese. 'The Amul Saga.' *Seminar*. February 2001.

45 White, Shirley A. 'Participation: Walk the Talk.' *The Art of Facilitating Participation*. Shirley A White ed. Sage Publications. 1999.

46 White, Shirley A, ed. 'Confessions of an Outside Facilitator: Developing Educational materials in the Dominican Republic.' *The Art of Facilitating Participation*. Sage Publications. 1999.

47 Ascroft, Joseph and Ilias Hristodoulakis. 'Enabling Participatory Decision-making at the Grassroots.' *The Art of Facilitating Participation*. Shirley A. White ed. Sage Publications. 1999.

48 Harvey, Philip D. 'Let Every Child be Wanted.' *How Social Marketing Is Revolutionizing Contraceptive Use Around The World*. Auburn House. 1999

49 Andreasen, Alan R. *Marketing Social Change*. Jossey-Bass Publishers. 1995

50 Kotler and Armstrong, *Principles of Marketing*. Prentice–Hall India. 2001

51 McKenzie-Mohr, Doug and William Smith. 'Fostering Sustainable Behaviour.' *An Introduction to Community-Based Social Marketing*. New Society Publishers. 1999

52 Souvenir of Amul, brought out to celebrate 50 years of it existence. November 26th, 1996. Anand, Gujarat.

53 Lazniac, Gene R. et al. 'The Social Disorder of the Broadened Concept of Marketing.' *Readings in Marketing Management*. Himalaya Publishing House. 1987

54 Kotler, Philip and Eduardo L. Roberto. *Social Marketing. Strategies For Changing Public Behaviour*. The Free Press. 1989

55 Schutte, Hellmut. 'Asian culture and the global consumer.' *Business Standard*. 19/10/2001

56 'Connecting with Consumers: the Four Ds of Effective Positioning.' *Business Standard*. 19/10/2001

57 Swaminathan, M.S ed. *Wheat Revolution: A Dialogue*. Macmillan. 1993

58 Chopra, R.N. *Green Revolution in India*. Intellectual Publishing House. N Delhi. 1985

59 Kivlin, Joseph E et al. *Innovation in Rural India*. Bowling Green State University Press. Ohio. 1971

60 *Ninth Five Year Plan Document*. Volume II. 1997-2002. Planning Commission. Government of India.

61 Prasad, C et al. *First Line Transfer of Technology Projects*. Indian Council of Agricultural Research. 1987

62 Swaminathan, M.S. *National Demonstrations in Rice*. Indian Farming. 1966 (16-6).

63 Narayanan, Chitra. *The Times of India*. 28-11-2000

64 Mittal, V and M Sawhney. 'Managing Learning.' *Business Standard*. 2001

65 V.M Upadhyaya. 2000

66 Pastel, J.S. Government of India

67 Dutta, Kanika. *Business Standard*. 31-8-2001

68 Ciszewski

69 Nightingale

70 Bean, L.L

71 Blazing, Jennifer. 1999

72 Zoltner, Andris. 2001

73 Davis, J.J. 1995

74 Kotlak

75 Mc Quail, Bumler and Brown. 1972

76 Schramm, 1971

77 Nicholas, Ind.

78 Minkler and Wallerstein

79 Bracht. 1990

About India Research Press

India Research Press is a collectively run book publisher with support of Authors and Editors. Since our founding in 1999, we have tried to meet the needs of readers who are exploring, or are committed to the politics of change.

Our goal is to publish books that encourage critical thinking and constructive action on the key political, cultural, social, economic and ecological issues shaping life in the Indian Sub-continent and in the world. In this way, we hope to give expression to a wide diversity of democratic and social movements.

India Research Press publishes Original works-as well as-works under Rights with various University and Academic publishers throughout the world.

Since our conception, we have added two new imprints to our existing line of Academic publishing.The Group now has three seperate divisions & editors for its publishing programme and many new titles, scheduled in the coming months. The India Research Press also has New Overseas Distributors for the sale of its titles in the USA and the European continent. The group is proud to introduce its three divisions of publishing.

India Research Press **Academic Publishing Division.**

General Division – Mass Market including Fiction.

Swankit **General Division – Health, Non Fiction and Educational titles.**

The group is headed by Anuj Bahri Malhotra, its CEO & Commissioning Manager. He is assisted by an efficient and professional staff of Editors, Administrator, Office Assistants and Accountant. Born to a bookseller's family, running the most sought after bookshop [Bahri Sons] in the country, Anuj has a long 23 years experience in the Indian Book Industry.